Presented to:

_____

From:

_____

Date:

_____

Honor Books® is an imprint of
Cook Communications Ministries, Colorado Springs, Colorado 80918
Cook Communications, Paris, Ontario
Kingsway Communications, Ltd., Eastbourne, England

Daily Grace—Devotional Reflections to Nourish Your Soul
© 2005 by BORDON BOOKS

First printing, 2005
Printed in Canada
2 3 4 5 6 Printing/Year 09 08 07 06 05

Developed by Bordon Books
Manuscript written by Niral Russell Burnett, Rebecca Currington, Christy R. Phillippe, Robin S. Schmitt, and Mark E. Weising. Editing and project management by Kelli C. Portman in association with Snapdragon Editorial Group, Inc.
Designed by LJ Design

DAILY GRACE

DEVOTIONAL REFLECTIONS TO NOURISH YOUR SOUL

HONOR BOOKS

Inspiration and Motivation for the Seasons of Life

COOK COMMUNICATIONS MINISTRIES
Colorado Springs, Colorado • Paris, Ontario
KINGSWAY COMMUNICATIONS LTD
Eastbourne, England

Dear Reader:

Daily Grace: Devotional Reflections to Nourish Your Soul has been written and compiled with much love and care. As you read through these pages in the days, weeks, and months ahead, it is our prayer that the revelation of the riches of God's grace will abound in your heart and mind.

We've designed this book with you in mind, combining the wonderful truth of God's Word with devotional readings relevant to everyday life. A variety of writers were chosen—people from divergent backgrounds and seasons of life—to give each daily reading a fresh, unique perspective. And a "grace principle" has been included so you will have a bit of God's grace to carry with you throughout your day. For the weekend entries, we've taken excerpts from the works of classic and well-known writers and added a prayer to help you take hold of these remarkable insights and principles.

We pray that God will bless you as you read, fill your heart with grace and peace, and draw you closer to the God who gave His all to meet your every need.

The Publisher

THE LITTLE THINGS IN LIFE

Every day of my life was recorded in your book . . . before a single day had passed. How precious are your thoughts about me, O God!

PSALM 139:16–17 NLT

So many times it is the little things that drive us crazy. Big problems we can handle, but the minor inconveniences of day-to-day life can get under our skin! It's easy to get angry or frustrated when things go wrong: when we lose our car keys or hit every red light on the way to work. But sometimes, God uses the little things of our lives to place us right where He wants us to be.

GRACE FOR TODAY:

God is present even in the details of our lives.

After the tragedy on September 11, the head of security of the Twin Towers related amazing stories about those who should have been there that fateful day—but weren't. All of their stories had to do with the "little things" of life.

One man was late because it was his turn to bring the doughnuts. One woman's alarm clock didn't go off. One missed the bus. One spilled food on her clothes at the last minute and had to take time to change. Another's car wouldn't start. And one person couldn't get a taxi.

Perhaps the most amazing was the man who put on a new pair of shoes that morning and headed in to work, only to develop a blister on his foot on the way. Because he stopped at a drugstore to buy a Band-Aid for his foot, he is alive today.

God is concerned about every detail of your life—even the little things! So the next time you get stuck in traffic—or even get a blister on your toe—remember that God continues to look out for you. Be thankful every day for the gift of life you have been given and for the wonderful, loving God who cares for you and guides your steps throughout the day.

Mayday!

Samuel took a stone, and set it between Mizpeh and Shen, and called the
name of it Ebenezer, saying, Hitherto hath the Lord helped us.

1 Samuel 7:12 KJV

Have you ever faced a time in your life when total disaster seemed imminent;
times when the signs of distress are surrounding you, and there is nowhere to
go? We often hear stories of those who faced clear and present danger during wartime,
crying, "Mayday, Mayday, Mayday," over their radios aboard their doomed ships or
aircraft. But what of those whose job it is to be prepared for such an ominous call?
What of those who must take action even though the
one who has called cannot see them? These are the
unheralded heroes who may be out of harm's way at
one moment, but will enter it to answer the call of just
one soldier.

> **GRACE FOR TODAY:**
>
> Those who call
> upon the name
> of the Lord will
> be heard, and
> God has
> promised to
> rescue them.

The Lord our God is the one who answers our
"mayday" calls. When we call out for His help, He has
promised to hear us and be with us in our day of trouble. He will hide us in His presence, where no danger
can ever prosper against us. He is our Ebenezer, our
stone of help. He is our ever-dependable Savior, who
will not allow us to fall.

All of us face times in our lives when we are just
up against trouble, and it seems like there is no way
out. Our always faithful God is there, waiting for us to
ask Him for help. And once we do, our rescue is cer-
tain—though it will come bathed in His unfailing wisdom and counsel. Are you ready
to place yourself in His care?

A FOUNDATION FOR FAITH—GOD'S WORD

Forever, O Lord, Your word is settled in heaven.

PSALM 119:89 NKJV

T he basis for our relationship with the Lord is faith. Yet God does not demand blind faith from us; He generously provides us with sufficient evidence to support a thoughtful, rational decision to believe in Him and trust His promises. Some of this evidence he established at Creation, some of it He has demonstrated over time, and some of it He continues to reveal to us on a day–by–day basis.

One of the strongest, most tangible pieces of evidence God has given us is His Word, the Bible. The Scriptures are a collection of sixty–six books written over a span of more than fifteen hundred years by a diverse group of authors—among them a farmer, a tax collector, a doctor, a fisherman, the child of a slave, and a king—yet they join together seamlessly, firmly interlocking to reveal a remarkable story.

The Bible is unparalleled in its merits as a reliable historical document. Historians use several measures to determine whether an ancient text is trustworthy, including the age of the manuscript and the number of copies that exist. By these measures, the pedigree of the Holy Scriptures is outstanding. The Bible has more claim to truth than any college textbook on world history.

You can trust that what the Bible says is true. God has given us His Word, a document that He has caused to survive intact through the ages, which will always remain to testify to His existence, His goodness, and His faithfulness. The Scriptures stand as a rock–solid foundation for our faith and a conduit of God's daily grace.

GRACE FOR TODAY:

God has given us His supernatural Word to guide us on our journey of faith.

AMAZING GRACE

[Jesus said,] "God so loved the world that He gave His only begotten
Son, that whoever believes in Him should not perish but
have everlasting life."

JOHN 3:16 NKJV

During a conference on world religions held in Great Britain, some of the
greatest theologians in the world began a friendly debate as to what belief—if
any—in the Christian faith made it unique from the other religions of the world.

The debate soon grew heated as possibilities were considered and eliminated.
Could it be the Incarnation? No, there were other religions that had gods who took on
the form of a human. Could it be the Resurrection? No, there were some religions in
the world that held claim to accounts of a return from death.

Eventually C. S. Lewis entered the room to see what the commotion was about,
and when he heard the topic up for debate, he nonchalantly responded, "Oh, that's easy!
It's grace." After further discussion, the "experts" had to agree.

The idea that God freely offers salvation—no matter what good or bad deeds we
have done—is unique among all religions of the world. Buddhists in China, Muslims
in Saudi Arabia, Hindus in India—all are seeking a way to please God by the things
that they do, the sacrifices they make, the penances they perform. But God's love is
unconditional: Your performance doesn't matter! Jesus has already paid the price—and
because of His sacrifice, God's grace is available to you today. All you have to do is
accept it.

No wonder the famous hymn calls this sort of grace, "amazing"!

GRACE FOR TODAY:

Salvation cannot be earned. It is a freely given gift,
unearned and unmerited.

MOMENTS OF REFLECTION

There will be moments in your life when God extends His grace to you in surprising ways. Moments when He brings an event into your life that compels you to evaluate where you are going. Moments when He reveals something that causes you to reconsider your goals. And moments when you hear His voice and decide you want to make a real change.

Alfred Nobel, a man who had made millions of dollars during his lifetime from the manufacture of an invention he called "dynamite," encountered just such a moment one morning when he opened a newspaper and found his own obituary printed there. What disturbed him, as he read the lines, was not only the newspaper's mistake, but the way in which the author disparagingly implied that his success had come at the expense and to the detriment of others.

> GRACE FOR TODAY:
>
> God uses both our successes and our failures to keep us on the path He has planned for our lives.

Despite all his accomplishments, Alfred considered his success to be worthless if it meant that he would be remembered in such a negative way. Determining to do something about it, he put the bulk of his assets into a fund so that for generations to come the interest could be awarded to particular individuals whose work was deemed beneficial to society. This award is known today as the "Nobel Prize."

Such situations that God may bring into your life to cause personal reflection can often be painful, but it is important to remember that God uses them to gently lead you back on to the course that He wants for your life. So take some time today to reflect upon your own goals and ambitions, and thank God when things come your way that cause you to alter your point of view.

I have considered my ways and have turned my steps to your statutes.

PSALM 119:59

Salvation by Grace through Faith

By Gene Getz

P hilip P. Bliss, a well-known songwriter, understood the truth that we are saved by grace through faith. He wrote a poem and then set the words to music.

> Free from the law—O happy condition!
> Jesus hath bled, and there is remission;
> Cursed by the law and bruised by the fall,
> Grace hath redeemed us once for all.
>
> Children of God—O glorious calling!
> Surely His grace will keep us from falling;
> Passing from death to life at His call,
> Blessed salvation—once for all.
>
> Once for all—O sinner receive it!
> Once for all—O brother believe it!
> Cling to the cross, the burden will fall—
> Christ has redeemed us once for all!'

—〰—

HEAVENLY FATHER: THANK YOU FOR THE GIFT OF GRACE YOU'VE POURED OUT ON MY LIFE. I REACH OUT IN FAITH, BELIEVING THAT IT WILL COVER ALL MY FAILINGS, ALL MY IMPERFECTIONS, ALL MY SIN AND MAKE ME WORTHY TO ABIDE IN YOUR PRESENCE. AMEN.

Since we have been justified through faith, we have peace with God through our Lord Jesus Christ, through whom we have gained access by faith into this grace in which we now stand. And we rejoice in the hope of the glory of God.

ROMANS 5:1-2

I LOVE YOU, ANYWAY

God showed his love for us by sending his only Son into the world. . . .
We love because God first loved us.

1 JOHN 4:9, 19 GNB

U nconditional love may be the thing most sought after by every human heart.
One day a man finally decided to ask his boss for a much-deserved raise. That morning, before he left for work, he told his wife what he was about to do. All day long, the man was nervous and apprehensive, and he kept putting off what he knew he wanted to do. Finally, late in the afternoon, he summoned the courage to approach his employer. To his amazement—and delight—his boss agreed to the raise.

GRACE FOR TODAY:

William Arthur Ward has asked a very important question: "Does God love us because we are special—or are we special because God loves us?"

The man arrived home to a beautiful table, set with candles and the couple's best china. The man determined that someone at his office must have tipped off his wife! Finding her in the kitchen, he told her the good news, and after embracing, they sat down to a wonderful dinner. Next to his plate, the man found a beautiful card, which read: "Congratulations, darling! I knew you'd get the raise. I hope this dinner shows you how much I love you."

Later, as the man went back into the kitchen, he noticed a second card that had fallen to the floor. He picked it up and opened it. The card read: "Don't worry about not getting the raise, sweetheart. You deserve it, anyway! I hope this dinner shows you how much I love you."

What amazing acceptance and love! You may wish you had someone in your life who would be that encouraging of you—regardless of whether you succeed or fail. The good news is that you do. God loves you unconditionally—He loved you before you knew Him, and He will continue to love you throughout your life, success or failure, win or lose!

TRY, TRY, AGAIN

This is the confidence which we have . . . that, if we ask anything
according to His will, He hears us.

1 JOHN 5:14 NASB

Although Thomas Edison did not technically "invent" the light bulb—the idea had
been around for at least fifty years before he began tinkering with it—he did
develop a safe, practical, affordable, and long-lasting source of electric light, which no
one before him had been able to do. To accomplish this feat, however, Edison first had
to endure hundreds of failures before perfecting even his first light bulb.

Most people would have thrown in the towel at that point and admitted defeat, but
Edison had such confidence in his ideas that he viewed
failure not as a setback, but as merely a stepping-stone
toward a greater goal. In fact, when one young reporter
asked, "Mr. Edison, why do you keep trying to make
light by using electricity when you have failed so many
times?" Edison simply replied, "Young man, don't you
realize that I have not failed but successfully discovered
six thousand ways that don't work!"

When you truly follow the course that God has
laid out for your life, you can approach every task with
the utmost confidence that you will succeed. You can
trust that all the setbacks you endure are molding and
developing you into the type of spiritually mature person that He desires. Above all, you can rest assured
that as you encounter each frustrating problem in your life, He will extend His grace
to you and comfort you in your time of need, so that you will be energized and ready
to continue on in the tasks that He has prepared for you.

> **GRACE FOR TODAY:**
>
> God sees to it
> that every
> setback we
> endure helps
> us to become
> the people He
> created us
> to be.

THE FOUNTAIN OF YOUTH

On the inside, where God is making new life,
not a day goes by without his unfolding grace.

2 CORINTHIANS 4:16 MSG

"We're not getting older; we're getting better" sounds like a rationalization, an attempt to infuse hope into the reality of aging. But for the Christian this is a glorious truth. There really is a Fountain of Youth. His name is Jesus, and from Him flows the River of Life. Through faith in God's Son, we who are physically wasting away are day by day being spiritually renewed. To borrow language from the Broadway musical Camelot, a person in Christ "ages backward," or "youthens"!

The fact is every person is born old. That is, we inherit the old, sinful nature passed down to us from Adam and Eve. Through His death on the cross, Jesus allows us to "put off the old nature," as the Bible commands us. And by His resurrection, He allows us to "put on the new nature." Scripture portrays this transformation, called sanctification, as a gradual process, a work of the Holy Spirit made possible by God's grace.

We cooperate with this work by drinking from the Fountain of Youth daily and allowing God to mold us into the image of His Son. As you collaborate with the Holy Spirit in this endeavor, remember that putting off the old nature and putting on the new is an all-or-nothing proposition. Consider the contrast between the two: the old nature is weak, selfish, foolish, lustful, fearful, and unforgiving; the new nature is strong, loving, wise, pure, courageous, and full of grace. You cannot attain the positive qualities while clinging to the negative traits. You cannot be both old and new.

Your heavenly Father has a marvelous vision for you. Trust Him and let go completely of your old, sinful nature, embracing the new nature He offers. You will become the wonderful, godly person He created you to be.

GRACE FOR TODAY:

There really is a Fountain of Youth. His name is Jesus, and
through Him we have been given access to the River of Life.

Oscar the Grouch

When a man is gloomy, everything seems to go wrong;
when he is cheerful, everything seems right!

Proverbs 15:15 TLB

Oscar the Grouch of Sesame Street has come to be a beloved American icon, but even being the world's most famous grouch hasn't made his attitude any more pleasant!

Perhaps what's most interesting about the Grouch is not the fact that he manages to insult everyone he meets. Nor is it even the fact that he lives in a trash can! It's the story behind how Oscar the Grouch got his name.

In the early days of Sesame Street, Jim Henson and Sesame Street director Jon Stone would meet to confer about the show at a Manhattan restaurant, Oscar's Tavern. There they were consistently waited on by a man so rude and grouchy that going to Oscar's to eat almost became a sort of masochistic pleasure—most certainly a different form of lunchtime entertainment! And you guessed what the result of the waiter's attitude ultimately was: He was forever immortalized as Oscar the Grouch.

Attitude is important! As a Christian, you represent Jesus—in everything that you do. If you decide to be a "grouch" for a day, that is the witness for Christ you will display. God can help you control your feelings and your behavior. If you ask Him for help, He promises that His grace will be sufficient for you. Ask God to help you keep a positive attitude—you never know who might be watching!

Grace for Today:

Each day God is waiting, ready, and able to help us keep an attitude that rightly portrays the joy of our relationship with Him.

CHANGED THROUGH PRAYER

Prayer changes things. But have you ever wondered what "things" prayer changes? The answer might surprise you. For you see, when you pray, every "thing" about you changes. That includes your motives, your attitudes, your emotions, your perspective—and a whole lot more. Every aspect of who you are is adjusted, tuned up, and made better as you pray.

"Wait just a minute," you might be tempted to say. "I wasn't praying for myself; I was praying for my situation—and that hasn't changed AT ALL!"

It's true. Your situation may not change significantly as you pray. It isn't that God doesn't care about your situation. It's just that He cares a whole lot more about you. He wants you to grow in both faith and character. He wants you to become the person He created you to be. Though He doesn't cause your adverse circum-

stances, He often uses them to bring about change in you—His most precious creation.

King David, the great psalmist, cried out to God about his circumstances. He tells us that he laid on his bed and cried, felt that he was being pulled down to death, suffered loneliness and abuse. Throughout it all, God was there—right at his side—using the circumstances of David's life to make him a man whose heart mirrored his own. As David prayed, he was being changed moment by moment.

Take the time today and talk to the Lord. Tell Him your thoughts and concerns and listen for a response. You may be surprised by the "things" He wants to talk to you about, the issues He wants you to address, and the gentle, loving way He opens your eyes and your heart to help you become a better person.

All things you ask in prayer, believing, you will receive.

MATTHEW 21:22 NASB

TABLE OF STONE— HUMAN HEARTS

By Warren Wiersbe

When God gave the Law, He wrote it on tables of stone, and those tables were placed in the Ark of the Covenant. Even if the Israelites could read the two tables, this experience would not change their lives. The Law is an external thing, and people need an internal power if their lives are to be transformed. The legalist can admonish us with his "Do this!" or "Don't do that!" but he cannot give us the power to obey. If we do obey, often it is not from the heart—and we end up worse than before!

The ministry of grace changes the heart. The Spirit of God uses the Word of God and writes it on the heart. The Corinthians were wicked sinners when Paul came to them, but his ministry of the Gospel of God's grace completely changed their lives. (See 1 Corinthians 6:9-11.) Their experience of God's grace certainly meant more to them than the letters of commendation carried by the false teachers. The Corinthian believers were lovingly written on Paul's heart, and the Spirit of God had written the truth on their hearts, making them "living epistles of Christ."[2]

LORD GOD, THANK YOU FOR CHANGING MY HEART THROUGH YOUR MINISTRY OF GRACE—YOUR UNMERITED FAVOR. NO MATTER HOW HARD I TRIED, I COULD NEVER BE GOOD ENOUGH TO DESERVE TO BE IN YOUR PRESENCE. BUT YOU OVERRULED THE LAW AND RECEIVED ME BY AN ACT OF YOUR SOVEREIGN GRACE. TEACH ME TO WALK IN THE GIFT OF GRACE YOU'VE GIVEN ME, AND IN RETURN I WILL GIVE YOU ALL MY PRAISE. AMEN.

You were washed, you were sanctified, you were justified in the name of the Lord Jesus Christ and in the Spirit of our God.

1 CORINTHIANS 6:11 NRSV

THE DEE-DAH-DAY DANCE

This is the day the Lord has made; we will rejoice and be glad in it.

PSALM 118:24 NKJV

I n his book, *The Life You've Always Wanted,* John Ortberg tells the story of an evening bath he was giving his children a few years ago. He had three kids in the tub and was trying to get each of them cycled through the process of soaping, rinsing, and drying. It was the end of a long day, and John was hurrying his children along, when his daughter, Mallory, came up out of the water and began to perform what had come to be known in their family as the "Dee-Dah-Day Dance." As her father tried to dry her off, she kept putting her arms in the air, squirming out of his grasp, and dancing around.

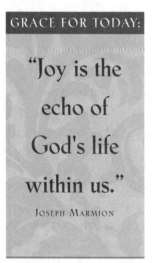

GRACE FOR TODAY:

"Joy is the echo of God's life within us."

JOSEPH MARMION

As John became more irritated, he snapped at her, "Mallory, hurry up!" His daughter turned to him and asked that question of all questions: "Why?"

He had no answer. At that moment, he had nowhere to go, nothing to do, no meetings to attend, no sermons to write. As he states, "I was just so used to hurrying, moving from one task to another, that here was life, here was joy, here was an invitation to the dance right in front of me—and I was missing it."

Many people think that the "good times" in life are the special times—like holidays or special occasions. But real life—and real joy—actually takes place between those events. As the proverb says, "Take time to smell the roses." Don't be in such a rush that you miss out on the joy around you. This is the day the Lord has made; rejoice and be glad—and do a "Dee-Dah-Day Dance"—in it!

SPROUTS IN THE WASTELAND

The desert and the parched land will be glad;
the wilderness will rejoice and blossom.

ISAIAH 35:1

There are areas in our hearts marked by devastation, wastelands that are the aftermath of highly painful experiences such as rejection, betrayal, emotional and physical abuse, infidelity, or death. We find ourselves wandering through these dry, barren places now and again, and although we work toward and pray for healing, at times it seems nothing will ever grow there again.

But our God specializes in resurrecting that which has died. The prophet Ezekiel learned this attribute of God through a powerful vision. The Lord took him to a valley full of dry, brittle bones and asked him if he thought they could live once more. Ezekiel answered, in effect, "Only You can answer that question, Lord." Whereupon God commanded him to prophesy that the bones would indeed live again, that the Lord himself would cover them with tendons and flesh and skin, then breathe new life into them. As Ezekiel obediently began to speak, the bones started to rattle, and before his eyes the bodies of those who had died were knit together by the One who had skillfully, fearfully, and wonderfully woven them in the womb. Soon Ezekiel beheld a vast multitude of people reborn, the valley of death filled with life!

> **GRACE FOR TODAY:**
>
> God has promised us hope and healing for all the barren places in our lives.

God promised Isaiah streams in the desert, blossoms in the wilderness. That hope is alive for us today. By calling forth His Son, Jesus Christ, from a cold dark tomb over two thousand years ago, God proved beyond doubt His ability to fulfill His promise.

Allow the Holy Spirit into the desolation; then watch carefully. Sprouts will appear in the wasteland. Day by day He will work a miracle of grace, transforming the barren places into the good soil Jesus spoke of, fertile ground in which God's Word can take root, grow, and produce a bountiful harvest.

NO EASY WAY OUT

He . . . who speaks the truth from his heart and has no slander on his
tongue . . . will never be shaken.

PSALM 15:2-3,5

I n one episode of the television series *The Wonder Years,* the main character, Kevin,
suddenly finds himself in possession of an answer key for all the tests his math
teacher, Mr. Collins, is going to give for the school year. Since he is tired of getting bad
grades in math, Kevin decides to use the key—and finds it surprisingly easy to get away
with. For a while, everything goes smoothly: his grades improve, his parents are happy,
the girl of his affections thinks he is smart—and all with no ill consequences. Cheating,
Kevin decides, isn't such a bad thing after all.

Unfortunately, Kevin's vastly improved grades soon come to his teacher's attention, who decides to put him in an advanced mathematics class. Once there, poor Kevin
is so hopelessly lost in a sea of equations that his classmates seem to be speaking a different language. Realizing that he is in completely over his head, he decides to approach
Mr. Collins and admit what he has done. But before he can even mutter his confession,
Mr. Collins takes off his glasses and with a wry smile says, "Had enough?"

Sometimes it seems like those people who "cut corners" to get ahead in life do so
without any ill consequences. However, like Kevin, these individuals eventually discover that their actions have cost a lot more than they bargained for. It is only a matter of time before dishonesty catches up with a person, but those who remain honest
in all their dealings can expect abundant grace and blessings from God. Even if it seems
that no one cares or even notices, remember that God is always watching and rewards
those with an honest heart.

GRACE FOR TODAY:

God showers His blessings on those who make
honesty and integrity guideposts for their lives.

WHERE IS GOD?

Heal me, O Lord, and I will be healed; save me and I will be saved, for you are the one I praise. They keep saying to me, "Where is the word of the Lord? Let it now be fulfilled!"

JEREMIAH 17:14-15

Where is God when you need Him? Certainly, many of us hesitate to ask such a question out of fear that we would anger God in some way. But it is not in the accusation of unfaithfulness that the sincere believer will utter these words. At times, it is in pure desperation. Perhaps the desperation comes from lying in a hospital bed another day. Or it could be a loved one who is in trouble that brings the desperate cry that wonders where to find the Word of the Lord. It could also be nagging financial problems that demand that God fulfill His Word, now.

Even when God is the center of our lives, even when we love Him more than the world, we may sometimes ask these desperate questions. The wonderful thing is that God is always there to answer. "I have not left you. I will never leave you," He says to us in the midst of our crisis. "Nothing can separate you from My love—nothing!"

No matter what storm is going on around you, reach out to God in faith. Praise Him for His faithfulness, for His grace, for being your ever-present help in time of trouble. As your praises rise, they will bring back to you the "Word of the Lord."

GRACE FOR TODAY:

The answers to our questions are wrapped up, ready to be unraveled by the praises of our hearts.

LIVING HOPE

"On Christ the solid Rock I stand, all other ground is sinking sand," goes the old hymn. How often have you built your dreams on sandy soil? How many times have you cast your hope upon quicksand? Too often, we do so on a daily basis.

First thing every morning, we wake and, unconsciously or not, our minds begin to search for hope, something to look forward to, a reason to get up and get going. If there is something interesting or exciting or positive happening in our lives, we latch on to that and climb out of bed, ready to face the day. Clinging to this hope, we whistle as we go about our day, doing what we can to make our wishes come true.

But many times our plans are frustrated, our hopes dashed. We wind up disappointed, impatient, and angry. Then we try to figure out why we struggle so much with these emotions. Is it any wonder?

The problem is, we keep grasping at "dying hopes," the transient, temporary promises that the world offers. We keep laying our foundation on sandy ground.

This dilemma troubles even earnest Christians who have made a steadfast commitment to anchor their lives on the Rock. Somehow we always keep adding on to our homes, building new rooms out over the sand. Then we notice that our roofline isn't quite as straight as it used to be; the house is falling out of plumb.

Praise God that each day He so graciously offers us a living hope, the hope of eternal life with Jesus Christ! It is the greatest of God's gifts to us; it is a sure hope, guaranteed; and like all the Lord's tender mercies, it is fresh and new every morning.

> **GRACE FOR TODAY:**
>
> **Jesus Christ is our living hope. When we build our lives on Him, we are building on solid rock!**

Because of [God's] great mercy he gave us new life by raising Jesus Christ from death. This fills us with a living hope.

1 PETER 1:3 GNB

DEATH—LIFE

By Warren W. Wiersbe

The Gospel gives life to those who believe because of the work of Jesus Christ on the cross. Paul was not suggesting that the Law was a mistake or that its ministry was unimportant. Far from it! Paul knew that the lost sinner must be slain by the Law and left help-lessly condemned before he can be saved by God's grace. John the Baptist came with a message of judgment, preparing the way for Jesus and His message of saving grace.

Preachers who major on rules and regulations keep their congregations under a dark cloud of guilt, and this guilt kills their joy, power, and effective wit-ness for Christ. Christians who are constantly measuring each other, com-paring "results," and competing with each other, soon discover that they are depending on the flesh and not the power of the Spirit. There never was a standard that could transform a person's life, and that includes the Ten Commandments. Only the grace of God, ministered by the Spirit of God, can transform lost sinners into living epistles that glorify Jesus Christ.

Paul's doctrine of the New Covenant was not something that he invented for the occasion. As a profound student of the Scriptures, Paul certainly had read Jeremiah 31:27–34, as well as Ezekiel 11:14–21. In the New Testament, Hebrews 8–10 is the key passage to study. The Old Covenant law, with its emphasis on external obedience, was preparation for the New Covenant mes-sage of grace and the emphasis on inter-nal transformation of the heart.[5]

—m—

PRECIOUS FATHER: I WAS HELPLESS TO SAVE MYSELF, BUT YOU REACHED BEYOND MY UNWORTHINESS AND MADE ME WORTHY BY YOUR GRACE. IF YOU HAD NOT, I WOULD HAVE BEEN LOST FOREVER, FOR I COULD NEVER HAVE KEPT THE RULES PERFECTLY. I THANK YOU FOR SAVING ME BY YOUR GRACE. AMEN.

[God] has made us competent as ministers of a new covenant—not of the letter but of the Spirit; for the letter kills, but the Spirit gives life.

2 CORINTHIANS 3:6

SEEKING GOD FIRST

Delight yourself also in the Lord, and He will give you the desires and
secret petitions of your heart.

PSALM 37:4 AMP

The great writer and theologian Henry Blackaby once had this to say about prayer: "Prayer does not give you spiritual power. Prayer aligns your life with God so He chooses to demonstrate His power through you. The purpose of prayer is not to convince God to change your circumstances but to prepare you to be involved in God's activity."

Many people become discouraged when their prayers are not answered, or when they are not answered in the way that they had hoped. But getting what you want isn't the purpose of prayer. The real heart of prayer lies in a relationship that you foster with the Creator of the universe, the one who knows your deepest desires—as well as what is best for you.

When Jesus gave His famous Sermon on the Mount, He addressed the matter of our priorities, especially in prayer. After He spoke to the people about money and material needs such as food and clothing, He shared one of the most important principles in Scripture: "Seek first [God's] kingdom and his right-eousness, and all these things will be given to you as well" (Matthew 6:33).

> GRACE FOR TODAY:
>
> "Prayer is not overcoming God's reluctance, it is laying hold of His highest willingness."
>
> R.C. TRENCH

Henry Blackaby would agree with Jesus on this point! When your prayers become less focused on your own needs, on changing your own circumstances, and they become more intent on your relationship with the Father and what He wants for your life, then you are praying the prayer that brings spiritual power. When you earnestly seek God's will for your life, then He will meet your needs and fulfill your deepest desires, the desires that He himself has planted in your heart. It's a win—win situation!

A GIFT WITHOUT REGRET

Each one must do just as he has purposed in his heart, not grudgingly or under compulsion, for God loves a cheerful giver.

2 CORINTHIANS 9:7 NASB

Each year, philanthropic organizations compile their lists of the various individuals and corporations who made the largest contributions to charity during that year. Often, the dollar figures given in these reports are staggering. For example, in 2003 alone, the chairman of one computer company donated more than $673 million; the chairman of a financial company donated more than $409 million; the chairman of a communications company donated more than $141 million; and the chairman of an Internet company donated just a little more than $80 million.

Now, without taking anything away from these incredibly generous individuals who gave these millions out of a genuine desire to help others, it is a bit easier to part with all this cash if you are the head of a profitable corporation with a net worth in the multi-billion-dollar range. It is much harder to part with when you have a net worth in the single-digit range and you're not sure there will be enough money to even get through the next week.

> GRACE FOR TODAY:
>
> God has given us the greatest gift of all—His precious Son, Jesus Christ.

The amazing thing is that God doesn't really care about how much money you give or even how often you give it. What He truly desires is that you trust in His grace and provision for your life, not in your own means. He wants you to give without regret, without worry, and without wondering if you will "get it back" somehow. For it is only when you let go and put your financial security in the Lord that He can truly bless you.

Your name will probably never appear in the paper because of your consistent, dedicated, or self-sacrificing giving. But be assured that no act of kindness or giving will go unnoticed by your Heavenly Father.

MEETING THE MASTER

"Death is swallowed up in victory. O death, where is your victory? O death, where is your sting?"

1 CORINTHIANS 15:54-55 NLT

A sick man once turned to his family doctor as he was leaving the examination room, and said, "Doctor, I am afraid to die. Tell me what lies on the other side."

Very quietly, the doctor replied, "I don't know."

"You don't know?" the man asked, distressed. "You, a Christian man, do not know what is on the other side?"

The doctor was holding on to the handle of the door, on the other side of which came the sound of scratching and whining. As the doctor finally opened the door, a dog sprang into the room and leaped on him with an eager show of joy and gladness.

Turning to the patient, the doctor said, "Did you notice my dog's reaction? He's never been in this room before. He didn't know what was inside. He knew nothing except that his master was here, and when the door opened, he sprang inside without fear. I know little of what is on the other side of death, but I do know one thing: I know that my Master is there, and that is enough. And when that door opens for me, I will pass through—not with fear, but with joy to see His face."

Christians have nothing to fear from death. You may not know exactly what Heaven will be like, but you can know who awaits you there! Jesus said, "In my Father's house are many rooms. . . . I am going there to prepare a place for you" (John 14:2). And when the time is right, you will pass through death to see your Master, face-to-face, on the other side.

GRACE FOR TODAY:

Our Savior has conquered death, stripped it of its power over us, and waits to welcome us to our new home.

It's Not about the Money

[Jesus said,] He will give you all you need . . . if you make the Kingdom of God your primary concern.

L<small>UKE</small> 12:31 NLT

S ilas Marner, in the novel by George Eliot, was a miserly fellow whose sole source of happiness consisted of counting out his gold each night before hiding it underneath his floorboards. Money was his security, his strength, and his only friend—for he was so fearful of losing it that he shunned his neighbors and turned them away when they came to his door.

When someone ultimately did steal his hoard, he was so distraught that he hardly knew how to carry on. Yet this problem resolved itself in an unusual way when a golden-haired orphan child appeared on his door, forcing Marner to step out of his house and seek the counsel and advice of those neighbors he had once shunned. As he grew to love the young child and accept the kindness of those around him, he found his desire to recover his lost coins growing less and less.

True wealth, as Marner discovered, was not found in money or possessions, but in loving others and sharing with them. As you go through your day, take a look at the things in which you place value. Is your idea of "wealth" the amount of money you can accumulate in your lifetime, or the number of relationships you can accumulate with others? Is it in the lasting joy you experience through living daily in God's grace, or the temporary joy you get when you count the cash you've got stored underneath the floorboards? As you analyze your values, ask God to show you His true definition of wealth—and happiness—in your life.

Grace for Today:

God opens our eyes to what is truly valuable in our lives.

FORGIVENESS: LOVE, THE SECOND TIME AROUND

To love the first time is not often a hard thing to do. But loving the second time is among the most challenging things we can do in our Christian walk. Such love can be the hardest kind of love to demonstrate. It is the love that tells us to love our enemies, even as they continue to cause us pain. It is the love that asks us to bless those who curse us. This love, the second time around, is summed up in the word forgiveness.

There may be some who have done such hor-rible things to you that to forgive them, much less love them, would be unthinkable. You might even feel that God is standing at a distance, watching your suffering and placing an additional burden on you—the burden to forgive. God is not cold and callous to your pain. He knows that you can take control of your pain and triumph over it only when you love the second time around. Can you do that? Jesus did. Even upon the cross, Jesus asked God to forgive those who were torturing and killing Him.

Make a decision to forgive—for your own sake. According to Luke 6:35, the promise of God to those who love their enemies is a "great re-ward." God knows that it is not easy, but to love the second time around is the path to your healing.

> **GRACE FOR TODAY:**
>
> **We are healed as we forgive others the way God has forgiven us.**

Jesus said, "Father, forgive these people,
because they don't know what they are doing."

LUKE 23:54 NLT

God's Grace Changes Us

By Gene Getz

"**A**s apostles of Christ, we could have been a burden to you," but, said Paul, that was not true. Rather, "we were gentle among you, like a mother caring for her little children" (1 Thessalonians 2:7).

What a contrast! Could this be the same man who several years earlier was "breathing out murderous threats against the Lord's disciples" (Acts 9:1), and now used a nursing mother to illustrate his style of ministry? What an example of God's grace! Paul was a changed man—a man of sensitivity and compassion.

It intrigues me that a man so tough, so rigid and unbending, reflected this kind of gentleness. No relationship better personifies gentleness than a mother who is nursing a baby. Yet Paul was not ashamed to identify with this analogy. This confirms the depth of change that had taken place in him.

This does not mean that Paul was unwilling to be frank, straightforward, and uncompromising. He never hesitated to confront wrongdoers—especially those whose motives were totally selfish (for example, see Titus 1:10-16). But Paul resorted to this methodology when he saw no hope, or when he saw Christians being deliberately led astray by false teachers. He believed that his initial approach should be a gentle one.

By the time Paul arrived in Thessalonica, he had learned a great deal about gentleness. And this Timothy observed in Paul's own ministry. With gentleness and tenderness he encouraged these Christians in their new life in Christ.[4]

FATHER GOD: CHANGE ME BY YOUR GRACE. MAKE OF ME THE PERSON YOU CREATED ME TO BE—A PERSON WHO IS PLEASING TO YOU AND OF SERVICE TO OTHERS. AMEN.

By the grace of God I am what I am,
and his grace to me was not without effect.

1 CORINTHIANS 15:10

LET YOUR LIGHT SHINE

[Jesus said,] "You are the light of the world."

MATTHEW 5:14 NRSV

Years ago a tornado destroyed a little church on the coast of England. The congregation was too poor to replace their building. One day, about six months later, a representative of the British Royal Admiralty called on the local minister. He was inquiring if the people of the church ever planned to rebuild. The pastor explained their unfortunate financial situation, and the caller, the British Admiralty representative, replied, "If you do not rebuild the church, we will. That spire is on all of our charts and maps. It is the landmark by which the ships of the seven seas steer their courses."

That particular church was known around that region for its building, but in most cases, churches are better known for the actions and attitudes of their members. In the Sermon on the Mount, Jesus said, "Let your light shine before men, that they may see your good deeds and praise your Father in heaven" (Matthew 5:16). As a Christian, you bear Christ's name, and you are His representative. And when you are seeking His will, following Him with your whole heart, and allowing others to see your light, you, too, can become a landmark, a beacon pointing the way back to God.

Hopefully, the church off the coast of England was rebuilt so that ships off shore could use its spire to steer their vessels safely back to harbor. But how much better it is when members of the Church also live out, in all areas of their lives, the example that Christ set for them, letting their lights shine, not just to sailors at sea, but to everyone they meet!

> **GRACE FOR TODAY:**
>
> God has shown His light on our path so that we may make our way to Him and share His light with others.

LOVE BEYOND MEASURE

God demonstrates his own love for us in this:
While we were still sinners, Christ died for us.

ROMANS 5:8

I n the English language, the word "love" is used to describe a vast array of emotions and affections. You can say that you "love" to take walks in the park, or that you "love" your spouse and children, or that you "love" your country—three very different concepts all contained in the same single English word.

However, when the writers of the New Testament speak of love, it is often a very different kind of love from any of these. This type of love, which in the original Greek is called agape, is a divine form of love that comes directly from God. Vastly different from mere human affection, agape is a type of love that God gives freely out of His grace and mercy to all who are willing to receive it, and for no other reason than because He desires to do so. agape is a love that He gives selflessly and without any expectation of receiving anything in return. And agape is a type of love that can be shared with others only if God has filled your heart with it first.

GRACE FOR TODAY:

God fills our hearts with His perfect love—agape love.

With all the types of conditional "love" that come and go among people today, it is difficult to comprehend a type of love that Paul in 1 Corinthians 13 describes as "patient, kind, not envious, not vain, not puffed up," but one that "believes all things, hopes all things, endures all things . . . and never fails." Yet this is exactly the kind of love with which God wants to fill you, to the point where you are overflowing with joy and want to share that same kind of love—true agape love—with everyone around you.

DEEP WATERS

He is the source of every mercy and the God who comforts us.

2 CORINTHIANS 1:3 NLT

Happiness is a shallow brook. Sadness seems to run deeper. Grief at times can be a current so dark you cannot see bottom. But peace is a mighty river, joy a fathomless ocean.

God's Word says, "The peace of God, which transcends all understanding, will guard your hearts" (Philippians 4:7) and "The joy of the Lord is your strength" (Nehemiah 8:10). These promises are true in moments of happiness, periods of sadness, or seasons of grief. These three depend on circumstances. Not so joy and peace.

Happiness often dries up, and sadness eventually wanders away. Grief may take months, even years, to run its course. But for the faithful, for those who trust in God and hold fast to Him, peace and joy remain. They are constant, steadfast, reliable—available every day.

How do you remember the beauty of the ocean when you are drowning in a muddy stream? How do you recall the soothing river when all you can hear is the raging flood? Can you experience peace when a family member is suffering? Can you really find joy when a loved one is dying?

Look for God's grace in the darkest moments of life. Listen for His whisper in the quiet, lonely times. Wait for His loving touch when the pain is too much for words. And keep trusting Him through it all. The Lord is faithful; He will deliver you from deep waters. Nothing can separate you from His love, and no circumstance can alter His peace and joy.

GRACE FOR TODAY:

For every stream of grief that flows into our lives there is a deeper river of peace that comes from the Holy Spirit.

JIM CYMBALA

PUMPING SPIRITUAL IRON

Discipline yourself for the purpose of godliness.

1 TIMOTHY 4:7 NASB

D iscipline is probably not an idea that you embrace with affection. It's never fun to realize that there are some unhealthy habits in your life that need to be changed, and even less fun to go through the hard (and often painful) process of correcting those behaviors. Yet discipline is a necessity in the life of every Christian, for it is the only way that you can put aside your old life and embrace the better one that God has for you.

Inigo de Loyola, the founder of the Jesuits, was a man who took spiritual discipline seriously. A former soldier who prided himself on his military discipline, Loyola realized that his personal life (which often consisted of gambling, brawling, and sword fighting) was in need of a change. While recuperating from an injury, he was given a copy of the Bible and came to know the grace of God and love of Christ. Yet when the old desires of his heart and unhealthy habits remained, Loyola decided to incorporate the discipline he had learned as a soldier into his spiritual life. Through discipline, he finally discovered the peace and satisfaction in life he desired.

Discipline is merely a form of training to strengthen your spiritual life. When you determine to set time aside each day to read the Bible and pray, you are practicing discipline. When you decide to do what you know in your heart is right rather than just taking the easy way out, you are practicing discipline. And when you admit your weaknesses to Christ and ask Him to fill you with His strength, He will extend His grace to you and help you lead a disciplined life.

GRACE FOR TODAY:

God strengthens our self-discipline with divine resolve, so that we can become the holy people He's called us to be.

ACCORDING TO PURPOSE

John Bunyan burned to tell the world that he had experienced God's grace. When he was in the militia, a stray bullet killed a comrade that had taken Bunyan's place on guard duty. Bunyan knew he was the one who should have died. The experience caused him to turn to God, but he continued to struggle in his efforts to turn from his old lifestyle.

Bunyan experienced God's grace again when he overheard the conversation of several poor women as they talked in a doorway as he passed by. The women spoke of new birth, the work of God in their hearts, and what words and promises had helped them resist temptation. The women spoke with such joy that Bunyan's heart softened, and he kept returning to learn from them. Eventually, he began to preach with powerful effectiveness.

God had another experience of His grace for Bunyan—the grace of persecution. He was imprisoned for most of twelve years while his beloved family was forced to rely on charity for their survival.

Those years of imprisonment were the darkest Bunyan had ever experienced. Yet it was there in his jail cell that he began his great work *Pilgrim's Progress*—an allegory of the Christian life that has encouraged and enlightened believers for nearly four centuries.

In jail, God answered Bunyan's desire to tell the world of God's grace in a far greater way than he could ever have imagined. Regardless of your situation, you can trust God to create something good in the midst of your difficulty.

> **GRACE FOR TODAY:**
>
> ## God's grace is still in full force; He is still for you, even when you don't feel it.
>
> RICK WARREN

We know that God causes all things to work together for good to those who love God, to those who are called according to his purpose.

ROMANS 8:28 NASB

OUR POWER SOURCE

By John C. Maxwell

A friend of mine was discussing the implications of Micah 6:8 with his seven-year-old grandson: "What does the Lord require of you but to do justice, and to love kindness, and to walk humbly with your God?" (NRSV). The little boy, who was memorizing this verse, said, "Grandpa, it's hard to be humble if you're really walking with God." That's great theology coming from a seven-year-old. When we begin to get a glimpse of the unlimited resources at our disposal—the power of God himself—then and only then will we sense the assurance that we are fully equipped to do whatever it is that God calls us to do.

We might feel like the little mouse who was crossing the bridge with an elephant. When they got to the other side, the mouse looked at his huge companion and said, "Boy, we really shook that bridge, didn't we?"

When we walk with God, that's often how we feel—like a mouse with the strength of an elephant. After crossing life's troubled waters, we can say with the mouse, "God, we really shook that bridge, didn't we?"

Hudson Taylor, the great missionary to China, said, "Many Christians estimate difficulty in the light of their own resources, and thus they attempt very little, and they always fail. All giants have been weak men who did great things for God because they reckoned on His power and His presence to be with them."

Like David, who said, "The battle is the Lord's" (1 Samuel 17:47), we also need to understand that Jesus is our source, and we can be directly connected to Him.[5]

HEAVENLY FATHER: YOUR GRACE HAS PROVIDED ALL THE RESOURCES I NEED TO LIVE A SUCCESSFUL, GODLY LIFE. WALK WITH ME THROUGH THIS DAY, I PRAY. TAKE MY WEAKNESSES AND MAKE THEM STRENGTHS FOR YOUR GLORY. AMEN.

I can do all things through [Christ] who strengthens me.

PHILIPPIANS 4:13 NRSV

WHAT'S THE PLAN?

In all your ways acknowledge him,
and he will make straight your paths.

PROVERBS 3:6 NRSV

I f you are like most people, you probably have made plans for your life. Whether it's figuring out how you are going to get a good job, ask that "certain someone" out for coffee, or just provide for your family, chances are you have a plan. It may even be a really good plan—a "sure thing" that is certain to guarantee you success. But is any plan ever a sure thing?

GRACE FOR TODAY:

God makes
His wisdom and
counsel available
to all those
who ask.

A general named Hannibal once came up with a plan he thought was a "sure thing." This plan consisted of sneaking his army, which included thirty-seven elephants, over the Alps to surprise his enemy, the Romans, on their home turf. The Romans, he believed, would be so bewildered at the sight of the elephants that they would flee in disarray.

Of course, getting over the Alps was nearly impossible, but Hannibal persisted and two weeks later arrived near Rome—with less than half his army intact. His plan worked well at first, until the Romans figured out how to scare the elephants and send them retreating back into Hannibal's front lines. Needless to say, Hannibal went home in defeat.

Many people think their plans are a "sure thing" only to find themselves getting trampled when those plans backfire. Fortunately, all you have to do to avoid such a disaster is include God in the planning process. When you trust in His grace, God will point out the problems in your plans, put you back on course, and provide what is best for your life. In the end, you will find yourself amazed at all the doors that will open and the places you will go that you never dreamed possible.

THE KEY TO FREEDOM

Bear with each other and forgive whatever grievances
you may have against one another.
Forgive as the Lord forgave you.

COLOSSIANS 3:13

I t was Alexander Pope who quoted the famous phrase, "To err is human, to forgive, divine," and no truer words have been spoken. As members of the human
race, we do a lot of erring and need the grace of God to forgive all those wrongs.
However, extending that same act of forgiveness to another person can often seem like
something only the "divine" can do, especially when
that person has hurt you deeply.

The interesting thing is that when God asks you to
forgive, it typically has less to do with the person who
wronged you than with your own personal well-being.
A 1998 Stanford University study of young adults
showed that forgiveness substantially reduced the
amount of anger they harbored—an emotion that has
been linked with increasing the risk of heart attack and
lowering the body's immune system. Other studies
indicate that those who forgive suffer less from disease
and medical symptoms.

If you struggle with forgiving others, ask God to
fill you with His grace. Acknowledge that you have
been hurt, but make a decision not to hold a grudge or seek retribution. Allow Christ
to fill you with His love so that you may offer that same unconditional forgiveness
toward the person who hurt you. It's the God—like thing to do.

> GRACE FOR TODAY:
>
> God asks us
> not only to
> forgive but also
> gives us the
> power and
> grace to
> forgive.

GOD'S OPEN ARMS

Blessed are those who are invited to the
wedding supper of the Lamb!

REVELATION 19:9

A little orphan girl from Russia is adopted by a couple from the United States, and soon the child is playing happily in the backyard with her new sister. She runs into and out of the house at will, and her new father laughs, scoops her up, and embraces her when she enters his domain. She eats at the table as if she belongs there—and she does. She scatters toys here and there as if she owns the place—and it's true. Her new parents have given her their home.

At the 2004 Summer Olympics, Ian Crocker cost swimmer Michael Phelps his chance to tie the record of seven gold medals. Ian performed poorly in his leg of a relay race, and the team came in third. In an amazing gesture of affirmation, Michael graciously offered Ian his spot in a subsequent race. Ian responded by swimming superbly, posting the second-best time ever for his leg of the relay, and helping the United States to set a new world record. Despite his failure, he remained a welcome, valued member of the team.

Every day, your Father in Heaven stands with open arms, inviting you—whatever your background, whatever your circumstances, whatever your mistakes—to become part of His family, to remain on His team.

GRACE FOR TODAY:

Grace . . . means that I, even I who deserve
the opposite, am invited to take my place at the table
in God's family.[6]

PHILIP YANCEY

A CLEAR REFLECTION

Be ye kind one to another, tenderhearted, forgiving one another, even as
God for Christ's sake hath forgiven you.

EPHESIANS 4:32 KJV

God's mercies are new every morning. And as children of God, we are remade
into our Father's image. We were created to reflect His very character and
nature, including an abundance of mercy. When others look at us—especially during
times of pressure, when others make mistakes that affect us—do they see a reflection
of our heavenly Father in our character and nature?

During Jesus' time on the earth He went about doing good. He did good because
He was God, yes. But He laid aside all His supernatural strengths and became human.
He relied on God's Holy Spirit in times of stress just as we do now. He reflected the
image of God as a human, because the time He spent with God as a human allowed
Him to experience God's love. That love then colored everything Jesus did. Jesus could
then say, "If you have seen Me, you have seen the Father."

How wonderful that when we experience God being merciful and tenderhearted
toward us, we experience a miraculous change. We become more loving and offer
grace and mercy to those around us. So the secret of a transformed heart of grace and
mercy is found in the time we spend in God's presence. Whatever we find there will
spill out of us all day long to bless our families and coworkers.

Spend some time with God today and start on the path to becoming a mirror in
which others see His face. When you spend time with God, you reflect the very character of God—His love, His mercy, and His grace—into the lives of others, even under
pressure.

GRACE FOR TODAY:

Our hearts are transformed as we spend time in
God's presence and feast on His grace and mercy.

PEACE FROM ON HIGH

Peace of mind is not something for which we can strive directly. It is a blessing that our gracious God bestows upon us when we are in a position to receive it. If we find ourselves growing frantic in stressful moments, we need to examine our relationship with the Lord. To experience the peace of Christ, the enduring peace of the soul, we must cultivate a close connection to God.

True peace is a work the Lord does within us. It is a fruit of the Holy Spirit, and fruit develops gradually, over time. A young tree sends its roots down into the soil, drawing moisture and nutrients from the ground as it grows tall, extends its branches, and unfurls its leaves to harness the energy of the sun. The tree must remain in proper relationship with earth and sky if it is to bear fruit. If the tree's roots do not stay in communion with the soil, fruit simply will not appear. If its leaves do not dwell in the sunlight, no produce will ever weigh down its branches.

Imagine sinking your roots deep into God's Word each morning, finding nourishment in the Living Water there. Imagine reaching heavenward in prayer each day, holding out your hands as you bask in the light of God's presence. Imagine the result when, having nurtured your relationship with your heavenly Father to the point that your soul is blossoming, you cry out, "O Lord, produce Your peace in me!"

You need not be a spiritual giant to know peace; even very young apple trees bear fruit. Just don't try to make fruit on your own. Foster a strong union with the Creator of all that is good, the One who breathed everything into being with just a word.

> **GRACE FOR TODAY:**
>
> The clearest evidence that God's grace is at work in our hearts is when we do not get into panics.[7]
>
> OSWALD CHAMBERS

[Jesus said,] "I give you peace, the kind of peace that only I can give."

JOHN 14:27 CEV

WE LIVE BY GRACE

By Warren W. Wiersbe

We must never forget that the Christian life is a living relationship with God through Jesus Christ. A man does not become a Christian merely by agreeing to a set of doctrines; he becomes a Christian by submitting to Christ and trusting Him. You cannot mix grace and works, because the one excludes the other. Salvation is the gift of God's grace, purchased for us by Jesus Christ on the cross. To turn from grace to law is to desert the God who saved us.

Keep in mind that God's grace involves something more than man's salvation. We not only are saved by grace, but we are to live by grace (1 Corinthians 15:10). We stand in grace; it is the foundation for the Christian life (Romans 5:1–2). Grace gives us the strength we need to be victorious soldiers (2 Timothy 2:1–4). Grace enables us to suffer without complaining, and even to use that suffering for God's glory (2 Corinthians 12:1–10). When a Christian turns away from living by God's grace, he must depend on his own power. This leads to failure and disappointment. This is what Paul means by "fallen from grace" (Galatians 5:4)—moving out of the sphere of grace into the sphere of law, ceasing to depend on God's resources and depending on our own resources.

Paul explains the relationship between the grace of God and practical Christian living. He shows that living by grace means liberty, not bondage (5:1–12); depending on the Spirit, not the flesh (5:13–26); living for others, not for self (6:1–10); and living for the glory of God, not for man's approval (6:11–18). It is either one series of actions or the other—law or grace—but it cannot be both.[8]

―⁂―

HEAVENLY FATHER: I CHOOSE TO LIVE THIS DAY BY YOUR GRACE—YOUR GOODNESS, YOUR SINLESSNESS, YOUR STRENGTH, YOUR TRUTH. AMEN.

If it is by grace, it is no longer on the basis of works, otherwise grace would no longer be grace.

ROMANS 11:6 NRSV

THE SECRET OF LOVE

Above all, love each other deeply,
because love covers over a multitude of sins.

1 PETER 4:8

The Reverend Billy Graham, "America's pastor," is one of the most respected and beloved evangelists of our time. He and his wife, Ruth Bell Graham—another beloved figure—have been married for more than fifty-four years. While their marriage might seem to be almost perfect to outsiders, they have had their share of disagreements and difficult times.

Reverend Graham recently appeared on *The Oprah Winfrey Show,* and when Oprah asked him the secret of love in his marriage, Billy Graham gave a surprising answer: "Ruth and I are happily incompatible," he said.

How unexpected! But how true. We would probably all get along better with those around us—spouses, friends, family members, coworkers—if we could adopt the attitude of happy incompatibility with their differences!

Be grateful for the people whom God has placed in your life, and remember to thank Him for your differences and disagreements too. Let Billy and Ruth Graham's "secret of love" be your "secret" as well, and you will build relationships that will last a lifetime.

> **GRACE FOR TODAY:**
>
> God takes our differences and makes them the secret of our success.

LONGING FOR HEAVEN

> "Eye has not seen, nor ear heard, nor have entered into the heart of man
> the things which God has prepared for those who love Him."
>
> 1 CORINTHIANS 2:9 NKJV

On November 24, 2002, the *Tulsa World* printed an article in which readers described what they thought Heaven would be like.

A five-year-old girl named Molly said, "I think Heaven has houses that are made out of candy!" But twenty-one-year-old Nicole wrote: "Heaven is a place where you can watch TV and never catch a glare. Your wildest dreams come true, and everyone is supportive of them. You never have to worry about visiting your mom in an old-folks home because she's just as bright and agile as she was at twenty-five."

Older readers had different ideas: "In Heaven, we will do activities beyond our comprehension. Ninety-year-olds will turn cartwheels with ten-year-olds," wrote seventy-eight-year-old Don. But perhaps Alzie Worthens, 85, summed it up best when she said, "I would prefer Heaven to hell, because I've heard the devil serves cold coffee, and I don't like cold coffee."

What do you think Heaven will be like? The Bible doesn't give us many details of our future heavenly home, but what you can be sure of is that it will far exceed your wildest expectations. Revelation 21:3-4 declares that in that place, "the dwelling of God is with men, and he will live with them. They will be his people, and God himself will be with them and be their God. He will wipe every tear from their eyes. There will be no more death or mourning or crying or pain, for the old order of things has passed away."

No more tears. No more pain. No more death! Heaven is the place every human heart longs for, the place where God will set all things right, and then dwell in the midst of His people—forever.

GRACE FOR TODAY:

If God hath
made this world
so fair, where
sin and death
abound, how
beautiful, beyond
compare, will
paradise be found.

ROBERT MONTGOMERY

THE ARMOR OF THE KING

Be strong with the Lord's mighty power.

EPHESIANS 6:10 NLT

G od gives us everything we need to stand firm as we face the daily struggles of life. Aware of our weaknesses, He knows how desperately we need Him. The extent to which the Lord prepares us for battle is a measure of His grace.

Consider the equipment He assigns us. This is not the issue of an ordinary foot soldier. It is the armor of God—the raiment of a mighty warrior, Christ the King. Wearing this armor, we are like a new recruit in the uniform of a four-star general. Grasping the weapon God has placed in our hand, we are like a lowly peasant holding the sword Excalibur.

We are girded with the belt of truth—God's eternal, unyielding truth. We wear the breastplate of righteousness—not ours but Christ's. Our feet are fitted with readiness, because we have heard the gospel of peace. We are crowned with the helmet of salvation—an impenetrable gift of God's grace. We hold the shield of faith—as trustworthy as the One we believe in. And we wield the sword of the Spirit—the very Word of God!

Ephesians instructs us to put on God's armor. We can't do this alone; the Lord must assist us. Jesus, who once washed His disciples' feet, takes on the role of a squire helping his knight to suit up. Then Christ begins to teach us, imparting to us by word and example the knowledge and skills we need to prevail.

Even after we are so excellently equipped and trained, however, God does not abandon us. He rides with us onto the battlefield, fighting beside us all the way. Most wonderfully, by the end of the war, through the process of sanctification He will have made us champions, worthy of the glorious armor we wear.

GRACE FOR TODAY:

God's armor protects us as we fight the good fight of faith.

Lasting Crowns

There is laid up for me the crown of righteousness, which the Lord, the righteous Judge, will give to me on that Day.

2 Timothy 4:8 NKJV

I n a world where time eventually steals away all our hard-won trophies, God in His awesome grace holds out to us rewards infinitely better, because they are eternal. The Lord offers us the opportunity to quit spending our energies in reaching for the temporary rewards of earth and set our sights on a much worthier, much nobler goal.

Longevity plays a key role in how we determine value in this life. That is why gold and real estate are worth so much. Gold does not corrode like other metals. And land, unlike an automobile or a building, does not degenerate over time. A piece of prime city property will be around long after the cars that grace its parking lots end up in the junkyard, and long after the skyscraper upon it falls prey to the demolition crew.

Shouldn't we use the same criteria when comparing worldly rewards with those that are eternal? Using sophisticated financial calculators, businesses are able to determine, in dollar terms, the present-day value of an investment, taking into account the expected useful life of an asset. Imagine the value that would be computed if infinity were plugged into the equation! It is beyond the capacity of our technology to calculate such a value. It's beyond the capacity of our imagination to conceive it.

The Bible says that if we seek God's kingdom first, everything else will be added as well. Make doing God's will and earning His reward the driving force in your life, and leave it to the Lord to decide how He will endow you with the things of this world. Our heavenly Father is gracious and wise, and He will choose for you those temporary blessings that will satisfy and sustain you on the road to everlasting glory.

Grace for Today:

God's rewards are infinitely better than the trophies of this world, because they are eternal.

THE PRINCE OF PEACE

Peace starts with God. This is why this world has trouble attaining it. Most can hardly define it. But as Christians, we have a direct connection to perfect peace—the Prince of Peace.

In this turbulent world, isn't it good to know that we have a refuge in times of trouble? When our nation is at war, when our schools are no longer the safe places they once were, when crime and godlessness crowd us on every side, the Prince of Peace rules our hearts. When we cannot trust what we read in our newspapers, when we are overwhelmed with bad news and sad news and conflicting reports, the Prince of Peace rules our hearts. When we are constantly bombarded by commercial images and battered by challenges to our faith, the Prince of Peace rules our hearts. When church leaders fail and scandals abound even in the most sacred places, The Prince of Peace rules our hearts.

God did not promise that we would live in a peaceful world. He did promise that we would live in peace in a chaotic world. Too often we expect God to calm the storms around us, but the truth is that He wants to calm the storms inside us. We are in this world, but we are not of it. We are people of peace in a crazy, mixed—up, angry world.

Are you searching for peace? Now you know where to find it. Open your heart to the Prince of Peace—His name is Jesus.

> **GRACE FOR TODAY:**
>
> God has given us a direct connection to perfect peace—relationship with Jesus Christ, the Prince of Peace.

His name will be called Wonderful Counselor, Mighty God,
Eternal Father, Prince of Peace.

ISAIAH 9:6 NASB

EXPRESSIONS OF WORRY

By John MacArthur Jr.

The word worry comes from the Old English term wyrgan, which means "to choke" or "strangle." That's appropriate since worry strangles the mind, which is the seat of our emotions. The word even fits the notion of a panic attack.

We're not much different from the people to whom Jesus spoke. They worried about what they were going to eat, drink, and wear. And if you want to legitimize your worry, what better way than to say, "Well, after all, I'm not worrying about extravagant things; I'm just worrying about the basics." But that is forbidden for the Christian.

As you read through the Scriptures, one thing you learn is that God wants His children preoccupied with Him, not with the mundane, passing things of this world. He says, "Set your mind on the things above, not on earthly things" (Colossians 3:2). To free us to do so, He says, "Don't worry about the basics. I'll take care of that." A basic principle of spiritual life is that we are not earth-bound people. Fully trusting our heavenly Father dispels anxiety. And the more we know about Him, the more we will trust Him.

I believe in wise planning, but if after doing all you are able to, you still are fearful of the future, the Lord says, "Don't worry." He promised to provide all your needs, and He will.[9]

—⁓—

HEAVENLY FATHER: I THANK AND PRAISE YOU FOR THE MIRACLE OF YOUR GRACE—GRACE ENOUGH TO PROVIDE EVERYTHING I NEED. I EXCHANGE MY WORRIES FOR YOUR PROVISION, MY ANXIETY FOR YOUR PEACE. AMEN.

You can be sure that God will take care of everything you need,
his generosity exceeding even yours in the
glory that pours from Jesus.

PHILIPPIANS 4:19 MSG

RIGHT WHEN YOU NEED IT

[Jesus said,] "Do not worry about tomorrow, for tomorrow will worry about itself. Each day has enough trouble of its own."

MATTHEW 6:34

The dramatic life of Corrie ten Boom is familiar to most Christians today. As a Christian young woman in Europe during World War II, she and her family helped to hide Jews from the Nazis—and were caught. She and her entire family were sent to concentration camps—and few besides Corrie survived.

GRACE FOR TODAY:

God gives us the antidote to worry—trust that He will be there to help us in every adverse situation.

As a young child, Corrie related, she had a conversation with her father that she clung to through the difficult times she later experienced. Corrie's father had told his young daughter about the early Christian disciples who had suffered greatly for their faith—but what her father told her brought fear to Corrie's heart. She told her father she didn't think she had the strength to suffer for Jesus.

In response to his daughter's fears, her father asked, "Corrie, when do you get your train ticket?"

Corrie quickly answered, "Right before I get on the train."

Her father explained, "Well, Corrie, that's when God's grace comes—right when we need it."

The worries you have for today are enough—you don't need to worry about your future too. No matter what you will face in your life, whenever you face it, God's grace will be there—right when you need it.

TOUGH TALK, TOUGH GRACE

Correct people's mistakes. Warn them. Cheer them up with words of hope. Be very patient as you do these things.

2 TIMOTHY 4:2 NIRV

A friend is heading down a path that you know will be disastrous. Maybe you've been down that same road before, known someone else who has, or just have a feeling that he or she is making some bad choices. You want to confront your friend, but should you? Will they understand you are trying to help? How can you know?

The author of Jude, the short letter in the New Testament that bears his name, had a similar dilemma. He wanted to write a letter to the believers concerning salvation, but "found it necessary to write to you exhorting you to contend earnestly for the faith which was once for all delivered to the saints" (Jude 1:3 NKJV). False teachers had crept into the congregation and had begun to lead believers astray. Jude felt the Holy Spirit compelling him to guide them back on track.

Jude obviously put a great deal of thought and prayer into addressing the topic before he began. In the same way, you should always pray before attempting to correct someone. While God may be compelling you to directly intervene, He may also just want you to intercede for that person in prayer. If you are going to intervene, you need to know that you are the correct person for the job. This knowledge requires discernment from God.

> GRACE FOR TODAY:
>
> God's discipline is always tempered by His grace.

When correction does occur, it should be tempered with grace. Jude related to his readers, reminding them of his love for them before getting to the rough stuff. Put yourself in your friend's place and share your personal experiences without "preaching" to him or her. It may not be easy, but in the long run, when the person realizes the error, he or she will appreciate the fact you stepped forward to point it out.

A FOUNDATION FOR FAITH—THE HOLY SPIRIT

God's Spirit touches our spirits and confirms who we really are. We know who he is, and we know who we are: Father and children.

ROMANS 8:16 MSG

God does not expect or require you to believe in Him based only on the words of the Bible, as reliable as they are. Becoming a Christian is not a matter of weighing the evidence for and against faith and drawing your own conclusion. It is not about calculating the odds of God's existence, putting your chips on the table, and waiting for the hereafter to discover whether you made the right bet. We become Christians when we encounter God through His Son, get to know Jesus personally and intimately, fall deeply in love with Him, and choose to commit our lives to Him. And all this happens through the ministry of the Holy Spirit.

At a miraculous point in time long ago, the almighty, invisible God came to earth and related to us as a fellow human being. For a few brief years we could see His face, hear His voice, touch His hands. Now that's no longer possible, yet soon after Jesus left this planet and ascended into Heaven, God gave His followers an unimaginable gift: He poured out the Holy Spirit into their hearts. At Pentecost the Holy Spirit became our new Immanuel—"God with Us." On that day God fulfilled His promise never to leave us or forsake us, and Jesus kept His Word to be with us until the end of time.

If all the Bibles in the world disappeared, if all the churches were gone, if all Christian books, CDs, radio stations, DVDs, and TV shows went away, every believer would retain the essential component of faith, the "one thing that's needed" according to Jesus—God's presence within. The Holy Spirit is our guarantee that God is real and we belong to Him. What an astonishing gift of grace!

GRACE FOR TODAY:

The Holy Spirit is our present—day Immanuel, our proof that God exists and we are His.

Joy Unspeakable

Whom having not seen, ye love; in whom, though now ye see him not,
yet believing, ye rejoice with joy unspeakable and full of glory.

1 Peter 1:8 KJV

S o many things in this world promise happiness, but few things ever deliver. There are some who believe that if they could get enough money, they could be happy. Others feel that if they could lose weight, or gain more friends, that happiness would be at their doorstep every day. Have you found that your Christian life has been redirected in a quest for happiness? If so, it is time to abandon your quest for happiness and try joy.

Joy is always at your disposal, and it is very much different from happiness. Happiness depends upon favorable situations. It waits until things are exactly the way they should be before it can be satisfied. This is why a young professional is not happy because he is not a millionaire. And millionaires are not happy because they are not billionaires. For the same reason, a person who wears a size eighteen is not happy because she does not wear a size ten. And the person who wears a size ten is not happy because she does not wear a size four. Happiness can find no satisfaction.

On the other hand, joy does not look upon situations in order to be satisfied. It draws from one source—God. With joy, a person can gain or lose great wealth and still find contentment and fulfillment in life. Such joy is what you see when a person is sick in the hospital, maintaining a positive, jovial attitude. Such persons may not know why they are joyful, but their hearts are full of glory, honoring God, despite the precarious situations they are in.

Joy does not need a reason. It is available to all who must live in this world of tribulation. It is available to you today, if you choose to walk in it.

Grace for Today:

God is the one and only source of joy in our lives.

SAY WHAT?

S everal years ago, Judge Claudia Jordan caused panic in her courtroom in Denver when she passed a note to her clerk that read: "Blind on the right side. May be falling. Please call someone." The clerk immediately rang for help, calling 911 and requesting that an ambulance be sent to the courthouse as quickly as possible.

When the judge was informed that paramedics were on the way, she quietly pointed to the sagging Venetian blinds on the right side of the room. "I was actually hoping for someone from maintenance," she said.

Everyone has experienced miscommunications of this sort in their lives. These sorts of things happen all the time, and at times they can be quite amusing! But whether you are talking to your spouse, your children, your friends, or your coworkers, clear communication is important in order to be able to effectively understand the needs, desires, hopes, and dreams of another person—and to be able to effectively share the Gospel.

The apostle Paul knew that good communication was important—especially when it came to believers sharing their faith with other people. Witnessing to others clearly, presenting the Gospel to them in ways that are meaningful and relevant to their lives, should be a priority for every follower of Christ. Begin to pray as Paul did—that your communication of the Gospel would be effective and bear much fruit for God's kingdom.

> **GRACE FOR TODAY:**
>
> If we ask, the Lord will faithfully give us the words to share our faith with others.

I pray that the sharing of your faith may become effective when you perceive all the good that we may do for Christ.

PHILEMON 1:6 NRSV

REPLACING WORRY WITH THE RIGHT FOCUS

By John MacArthur Jr.

God wants to free His children from being preoccupied with the mundane. Colossians 3:2 says as directly as possible, "Set your mind on the things above, not on earthly things." Therefore a materialistic Christian is a contradiction in terms.

The Greek word prótos ("first") means "first in a line of more than one option." Of all the priorities of life, seeking God's kingdom is number one. It is doing what you can to promote God's rule over His creation. That includes seeking Christ's rule to be manifest in your life through "righteousness, peace and joy in the Holy Spirit" (Romans 14:17). When the world sees those virtues in your life instead of worry, it's evidence that the kingdom of God is there.

What is your heart's preoccupation? Are you more concerned with the kingdom or with the things of this world? Don't be anxious for the goods of this world—or anything else for that matter. As Sherlock Holmes would say, don't just see but observe. And remember what Jesus told you to observe: abundant evidence all around you of God's lavish care for the needs of His beloved.[10]

—⁕—

DEAR FATHER: HELP ME TO TAKE MY EYES OFF THE THINGS OF THE WORLD AND PLACE THEM ON YOU AND THE VAST PROVISIONS YOU HAVE MADE FOR ME THROUGH YOUR GRACE. I BELIEVE THAT LIFE IN YOUR KINGDOM INCLUDES EVERYTHING I COULD POSSIBLY NEED IN THIS WORLD. I THANK YOU FOR GIVING ME MORE THAN ENOUGH. AMEN.

[Jesus said,] "Steep your life in God-reality, God-initiative, God-provisions. Don't worry about missing out. You'll find all your everyday human concerns will be met."

MATTHEW 6:33 MSG

ARE YOU A CHARLIE BROWN?

If anyone is in Christ, he is a new creature; the old things passed away; behold, new things have come."

2 CORINTHIANS 5:17 NASB

Have you taken a personality test lately? Not one of the technical psychological tests—but the dime–a–dozen types that are constantly being advertised on the covers of top–selling magazines or that circulate around on the Internet? Here are a few questions:

"Are You a Couch Potato or a Daredevil?"

"Cat Person or Dog Person—Which Are You?"

And, always a favorite: "Which Famous Leader Are You: Gandhi or Hitler?"

The most recent personality test circulating these days is the corniest yet: "Are You a Charlie Brown?" After answering ten deep and soul–searching questions—such as, "What types of movies do you prefer?" and "What is your favorite color?"—you can determine which cartoon character you are most like: Garfield, Snoopy, Dexter, Charlie Brown, and last but certainly not least, Sponge Bob Square Pants.

Why do people take such silly tests? Because they are fun, of course—but also because such tests show us a side of ourselves we might not know is there. They can, in many cases, give us a glimpse of who we are.

Fortunately, through Jesus, you can know who you really are—and you can rest secure in your identity in Christ: You are a new creature in Him, the apple of God's eye, bought with a price, and redeemed by the blood of Jesus. You are a beloved child of the King! That's better than being a Charlie Brown any day.

> **GRACE FOR TODAY:**
>
> **Because of Christ, we can be secure in our identity as God's children.**

The Appointed Time

Wait on the Lord: be of good courage, and he shall strengthen thine heart: wait, I say, on the Lord.

PSALM 27:14 KJV

A thletes from all over the world line up at the starting line, waiting for the crack of the pistol. It seems like forever as they wait to begin sprinting as fast as they can in order to attain a reward. If they begin the race before the appointed time, they'll be disqualified. This principle is also true in life.

Have you ever started a good thing at the wrong time? Many have done so, proving that waiting can be a hard thing to do, especially when dreams are involved. The hardest part about waiting is that it seems to require no action at a time when it appears that action is necessary. But this waiting period is part of God's timing. It is His opportunity to prepare the way for you. And He not only prepares the way but also prepares you for the way.

God does something special in the hearts of Christians who know how to wait. Such a Christian is at His disposal at the proper time. God uses these Christians because He knows that they are faithful to

GRACE FOR TODAY:

God's timing is always perfect—never late, never early, always just when we need it most.

wait for His command to move forward. Today, perhaps you have not yet heard the crack of the pistol, but you see the course you must run. Use faithfully the virtue of patience, and the race you run will be finished with the outcome you so greatly desire.

THE ONE TO TRUST

Nothing in all creation will ever be able to separate us from the love of God that is revealed in Christ Jesus our Lord.

ROMANS 8:39 NLT

A guy once called up his girlfriend to invite her on an important date. Something very special was about to happen, he assured her. She dressed carefully to look her best and waited nervously for the time of their date to arrive. The young man picked her up that evening in his antique jalopy, and as they drove along, he was quiet, obviously deep in thought.

Finally, the silence was broken—the young man enthusiastically told his girl that the big event was near. Anticipating a marriage proposal, she could scarcely contain her excitement.

At last, he declared: "The great moment has arrived!" He watched, overjoyed, as the car's odometer slowly passed the 100,000-mile mark. Almost delirious with excitement, he exclaimed: "Look! Everything is back to zero!"

The girl grimaced. "Back to zero is right," she said.

Life can be disappointing at times—especially when we place our hope, trust, and expectations in the wrong things. But no matter how other people or life's circumstances may have let you down, there is One whose promises hold true. He is completely faithful, and nothing can ever separate you from His love.

GRACE FOR TODAY:

God never disappoints, never lets us down.
His promises are always kept.

KEEP STILL . . . AND LISTEN

Draw close to God, and God will draw close to you.

JAMES 4:8 NLT

Having a quiet time with God each day is vital in the life of every Christian, for it is only through connecting with God on a daily basis that we can gradually strengthen our faith and build up our endurance to overcome temptations and trials. Like any friendship, it is only through repeated contact that we can grow to understand God's will for our lives and learn to trust in His purposes. And it is the only way you can appreciate the grace, mercy, and love of God.

However, finding time each day to be alone with God can be a struggle, and not knowing what to do once we get there can turn "quiet time" into "frustration time." Try reading just a few verses from the Bible each day. It's God's love letter to you. Then just talk to Him about what you've read. It isn't about understanding everything or speaking in eloquent, theological terms. It's about being with God, spending time with Him, enjoying His company.

If fact, it is quite all right to just be quiet in God's presence. After all, we do call it "quiet time." Open your spiritual ears and listen. He may not speak to you in so many words, but He will speak to the deepest recesses of your heart.

Whatever you do, don't put it off for another day. Take a few moments and tune in to God. Focus on Him. There is no sweeter communion on earth or in Heaven.

GRACE FOR TODAY:

The God of the universe not only loves us, His desire is to spend each day with us in sweet communion.

ALL YOU HAVE TO DO
IS ASK

We all have needs and desires—requests that if granted would greatly improve our ability to live happy, productive lives. But for some reason, we fail to ask. What a mistake! The Bible shows us that God is committed to answering us when we pray. And He wants us to have all those things that are needful to our health and well-being.

Perhaps it would be easier to pray if we could appreciate that our prayers are like sweet incense to God. He enjoys hearing our voices as we call upon Him to be an active part of our everyday lives. It brings joy to His heart that we actually trust Him to care for us by faith and put aside our worries. He likes it when we ask. And He likes to bring the answer. Isn't it great to know that our lives are secure, under the care of a God who answers?

The Word of God is packed with the answers to every prayer you can utter. There is no righteous desire that God cannot answer. But we have to go to God and ask in order to receive.

Perhaps now is the time to make a fresh commitment to go to God in prayer, without being afraid or ashamed to ask anything of Him. He is steadfast in His resolve to hear us and answer us. All we have to do is ask.

> **GRACE FOR TODAY:**
>
> God enjoys hearing our voices as we call upon Him to be an active part of our everyday lives.

[Jesus said,] "If you ask anything in My name, I will do it."

JOHN 14:14 NKJV

THE ALL-SUFFICIENT FATHER

By Luis Palau

No matter how great our earthly resources may be—friends, family, wealth, security, recognition—they are not an invincible fortress against the pressures of life. The external pressures over which we have little control—losing a job, financial disaster, personal tragedy, or serious family problems—can become too much for us.

Some of us suffer from inner despair: the unexplainable yet dreadful feeling of emptiness, loneliness, and fear that the Germans call Angst. We run from one adviser to another, seeking release from our inner turmoil.

Others suffer from the sheer boredom of daily routines. We rebel against doing the same unbearably mundane tasks over and over again. Suddenly we can't stand to go to the office, talk with friends on the phone, make another cup of coffee, or drive the kids to one more activity.

Today we see a growing number of people whose resources are insufficient to sustain them through the trials of life. But God can meet the deepest needs of our lives, even when we face external pressures, inner despair, or excruciatingly dull daily routines. In 2 Corinthians 1, Paul speaks of a God who is sufficient to meet all the pressures we face in life, One who is faithful to carry His children through them. Our all-sufficient Father can comfort and sustain us through life's pressures and enable us to live as victorious Christians!"

—⁂—

LORD GOD: I LAY MY PRESSURES AND RESPONSIBILITIES AT YOUR FEET AND REACH OUT FOR YOUR LOVE AND GRACE—GRACE THAT IS SUFFICIENT TO MEET MY EVERY NEED AND ENABLE ME TO LIVE A VICTORIOUS CHRISTIAN LIFE. AMEN.

Indeed, in our hearts we felt the sentence of death. But this happened that we might not rely on ourselves but on God, who raises the dead.

2 CORINTHIANS 1:9

A COOL SPIRIT

He who restrains his words has knowledge, and he who
has a cool spirit is a man of understanding.

PROVERBS 17:27 NASB

There are few things in life more difficult to do than restrain our words—especially when we feel strongly that we are right. How can we control ourselves
when the person or people bringing us conflict are certain to win if we do not speak
up? Of course, there are times when we are to raise our voices and be heard, but there
are times when our protest only makes matters worse.

Do you know of people in your life who seem to
always bring with them an argument over the simplest
things? Such people seem to be specifically assigned
just to bring grief and aggravation into your life. And at
times, it seems that the closer you try to walk with
God, the more they seem to target you as the one they
want to torment. By God's wisdom, you can either fight
back in your own strength or hold your peace.

When you hold your peace, it is peace that you
hold. Holding your peace means you have chosen to
disallow anyone from taking away God's gift of peace
to you. You retain something that others often do not. In doing this, you give yourself
room to hear from God, so that you will have the right words to say. God wants you
to have a cool spirit. This way, when life gets hot, you can take comfort in knowing that
His peace is always with you and His answer is soon to come.

THE SACRIFICE OF PRAISE

By him therefore let us offer the sacrifice of praise to God continually,
that is, the fruit of our lips giving thanks to his name.

HEBREWS 13:15 KJV

We live in a world that does not always make sense. Neither does it always seem to work in our favor. But when life gets tough, we can always begin to praise God in the midst of it all. To praise God can at times feel like the most ineffective and meaningless action we can take, especially when we are surrounded by challenges. So, why should we? Why should we sing a song to God when everything in life is fighting hard against us, and God seems absent?

God knows the end of every challenge we face, even before we have to face it. In His eyes, there is nothing but victory before you. His desire is never to bring you harm and destruction, but rather victory and peace. To praise God in the midst of your stormiest days shows that you are confident that God is in control. Your praise shines in the face of your spiritual adversary, declaring his impending doom. Such praise, which swells out of your heart and through your lips, professes that you will not let go of your faith, no matter what you face. Sincerity so great will never go unanswered.

While praising God during times of misunderstanding, trial, and even hardship may seem foolish, it is most often the way out of tribulation. Will you give Him your praise today? Will you tell God that you know who He is; how great He is; how exalted He is? If so, victory is yours, right now. You may see no immediate change at all in your situation, but one thing is clear—you will have changed. You will have shown God that your tears are wiped away and you trust Him with everything in you. Such is the sacrifice of praise.

GRACE FOR TODAY:

God is always helping us, especially when we are praising Him.

OUR REJOICING GOD

The Lord your God is in your midst, a victorious warrior.
He will exult over you with joy, He will be quiet in His love,
He will rejoice over you with shouts of joy.

ZEPHANIAH 3:17 NASB

Have you ever wondered how God feels? What His usual disposition is on a day like today? Is He sitting there grieved over the state of the world? Is He crying because of the sins that occur on the earth? Is He angry and cross as He views the evil and injustice that pollute His beautiful creation?

You may be surprised to know that God's primary characteristic is happiness! He is full of rejoicing and gladness. The image we so often see of an agonizing Christ upon the cross is not the depiction of Jesus today. He has proven himself to be victorious over the grave. He has completed His work of redemption on the cross. He has walked in obedience and facilitated God's gift of grace. Now He dwells in eternal dwellings, cheering us on as we go through life.

Certainly, it is not hard to praise a God who is happy and full of rejoicing! It is not a task to sing to a God who dances when you sing His song.

Does your concept of God need some changing? Toss away your religious images. Clear your mind. And then, ask God to give you a glimpse of Christ's glory as He sits at the right hand of His Father. He is rejoicing—over you! Seeing that will change your life forever.

GRACE FOR TODAY:

Our God is a happy God who rejoices over us.

MERCY, MERCY

Blessed are the merciful, for they will be shown mercy.

MATTHEW 5:7

During the Civil War, a young teenage boy enlisted to be a soldier in the Union army, but he was much too young to actually serve his country. So, when the first battle with the enemy began, he became very afraid and ran away. Because of his actions, he was caught, arrested, and accused of desertion. He was sentenced to death by a firing squad.

His parents were very saddened. They wrote a letter to President Abraham Lincoln, begging for mercy for their beloved son. Greatly touched by their heartfelt letter, President Lincoln investigated the facts of the case. When he discovered the truth, he gave the boy a full presidential pardon. Explaining his actions, President Lincoln wrote: "Over the years . . . I have observed that it does not do a boy much good to shoot him!" Obviously, President Lincoln understood the full meaning of mercy.

Later, when the war was almost over and the Union's victory was in sight, President Lincoln was asked how he would treat the Southerners after the war ended. He answered, "Like they had never been away." The interviewer protested, saying, "But Mr. President, aren't we supposed to destroy our enemies?" President Lincoln didn't miss a beat and responded, "Don't we destroy our enemies when we make them our friends?"

That merciful quality made President Lincoln one of the most popular leaders to ever grace the presidential office. He obviously had memorized the Beatitudes—especially the one that says, "Blessed are the merciful, for they will receive mercy."

How is your mercy level today? That whole command, "Do unto others as you would have them do unto you," definitely applies here. If you want mercy, you have to show mercy. Be merciful today.

GRACE FOR TODAY:

There is no quality in this world more God-like than mercy.[12]

JAMES W. MOORE

THE WAGES OF SIN

Rafiq Abdul Mortland clearly needed to choose another career. The work the thirty-eight-year-old man was doing was putting a lot of pressure on him—not to mention the fact that it was illegal! Mortland had committed a string of robberies in Hennepin County, Minnesota, and fortunately for him, he was eventually caught. After his capture, he received a sentence of eight to ten years in prison for having held up eight local businesses.

During his crime spree, Mortland received the nickname "The Rolaids Robber" after he repeatedly asked store clerks for antacid tablets, even while the robbery was still in progress. His explanation? Mortland needed the antacid because of the stress that came from committing these crimes!

Perhaps your crime spree is not as overt as Mortland's. It could be that your sins are small, almost unnoticed except in your own heart and mind. God says to stay away from sin because He knows that no matter how big or how small the offense, the eventual wages are death. That sounds dramatic, but if you're paying attention, you'll notice the tell-tale symptoms—restlessness, sleeplessness, dullness, and an inability to enjoy the blessings God has provided for you.

In light of the riches of God's grace, why would you want to live that way? Throw away the antacids and ask God to forgive you and sweep your house clean. Choose the path to life!

> **GRACE FOR TODAY:**
>
> **God is always ready to forgive our sins. The holy life He has called us to is a life of peace and blessing, hope and goodness.**

Trouble follows sinners everywhere, but righteous people will be rewarded with good things.

PROVERBS 13:21 GNB

THE SEAT OF MERCY

By Warren W. Wiersbe

The Judgment Seat of Christ is that future event when God's people will stand before their Savior as their works are judged and rewarded. (See Romans 14:8–10). Because of the gracious work of Christ on the cross, believers will not face their sins (Romans 8:1; John 5:24), but we will have to give an account of our works and service for the Lord.

The Judgment Seat of Christ will be a place of revelation; for the word appear means "be revealed." As we live and work here on earth, it is relatively easy for us to hide things and pretend; but the true character of our works will be exposed before the searching eyes of the Savior. He will reveal whether our works have been good or bad ("worthless"). The character of our service will be revealed (1 Corinthians 3:13) as well as the motives that impelled us (1 Corinthians 4:5).

It will also be a place of reckoning as we give an account of our ministries (Romans 14:10–12). If we have been faithful, it will be a place of reward and recognition (1 Corinthians 3:10–15; 4:1–6). For those of us who have been faithful, it will be a time of rejoicing as we glorify the Lord by giving our rewards back to Him in worship and in praise.[15]

—∿—

HEAVENLY FATHER: I THANK YOU THAT I WILL NOT BE JUDGED ON THE BASIS OF MY FAILINGS AND IMPERFECTIONS, BUT ONLY FOR THOSE THINGS THAT I HAVE DONE BY THE POWER OF YOUR GRACE. I LOOK FORWARD TO THE DAY WHEN I WILL STAND BEFORE YOU, CONFIDENT AND REJOICING. AMEN.

We will all stand before God's judgment seat. . . . So then, each of us will give an account of himself to God.

ROMANS 14:10–12

GROW IN GRACE

[Jesus said,] "And others fell on the good soil and yielded a crop,
some a hundredfold, some sixty, and some thirty."

MATTHEW 13:8 NASB

T he Christian life is like tending a vegetable garden. Consider the following: If you don't water a garden, it won't grow, and parts of it may even die. A garden has to be protected from the weeds that attempt to take root and rob the vegetables of water and light, and you have to get rid of the destructive insects (like caterpillars) while allowing the helpful insects (like bees) to thrive. If there is a major problem in a garden, you may have to seek help from expert gardeners and be willing to listen to their advice.

> **GRACE FOR TODAY:**
>
> God extends His grace to us through those who help us shore up our faith and live godly lives.

In the same way, if you don't nurture your Christian life with prayer, fellowship, and study in God's Word, you will not mature in Christ, and old habits, just like weeds, may even creep back into your life. You have to protect yourself from ungodly ideas that attempt to take hold and get them out by the roots. Furthermore, you must discern who among your friends are there to help you in your Christian walk while guarding against those who come your way who attempt to hinder it.

Most importantly, you have to realize there will be times when you need to call upon the grace of God to help you with certain struggles in your Christian walk. God is willing and able to bring mature Christians into your life to mentor and support you, but you have to be willing to let them in and allow them to help you. He wants you to bear good fruit for Him, and He will strengthen your walk if you open up and let Him pour His grace into your life.

DRAWING NEAR

Have I not commanded you? Be strong and of good courage;
do not be afraid, nor be dismayed, for the Lord your God is with you
wherever you go.

JOSHUA 1:9 NKJV

Has your growth in God come to a halt? Has sin crept into your life little by little? Does the fire that once existed in your heart seem to be quenched? If so, remember that God will not go away. He will not leave you to be alone at any time. You will always hold a special place in His heart. When Jesus became a reality in your life, God made some promises to you that He is dedicated to keeping, beginning with the commitment to be faithful to you. He so greatly wants to see you in His presence that He will remind you all the time to draw near to Him.

Imagine this: God sees you just where you are right now. Right where you sit at this very moment, God's watchful eye is upon you. His disposition is not to shake His head in disappointment as He gazes upon you. He is love. He is caring. He is full of mercy and grace. He only wants your fellowship again so that He can pour out His love and blessings on your life. He promised to never leave you. He is with you wherever you go.

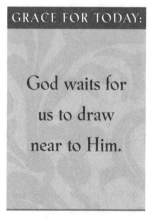

GRACE FOR TODAY:

God waits for us to draw near to Him.

Will you draw near to Him again in faith and love? To do so will bring joy to His heart, as well as yours. It will restore the youthful joy in having the faith of a little child. It will reward your life with unfettered fellowship with the Creator of the universe.

THE WAITING GAME

The Lord is not slow about his promise.

2 PETER 3:9 NRSV

In his book, *Sabbatical Journeys*, the late Henri Nouwen wrote about a family of trapeze artists—the Flying Roudellas. The trapeze artists described the special relationship between the flyer and the catcher when they are performing: The flyer is the one that lets go, and the catcher is the one that catches. As the flyer swings high above the crowd on the trapeze, the moment will inevitably come when he must let go. As he releases the bar and arcs through the air, he must remain as still as possible and wait for the catcher's strong hands to grab him in the air before he falls.

As one of the Flying Roudellas told Henri Nouwen, "The flyer must never try to catch the catcher. The flyer must wait in absolute trust. The catcher will catch him—but he must wait."

Waiting on God can be one of the hardest things a Christian can experience. Our busy society places great value on productivity—getting things done, and getting them done now. But waiting on God is a completely different matter! God's timetable is not our own. Joseph spent many years in prison before his dreams of leadership came to pass. The Israelites were in bondage for forty years before God delivered them. God uses times of waiting to prepare His people for greater things, but these waiting periods can be frustrating without trust in Him.

Are you playing the waiting game today? Do you feel as if you are dangling in the air, about to plunge to the ground, waiting for God to catch you before you fall? He is faithful, and He will fulfill all of His promises for your life—in His timing. Just as the flyer waits in absolute trust for the catcher, continue to trust in God that He has everything under control.

GRACE FOR TODAY:

God's promises are certain. They will never disappoint us, never let us fall.

SHOWING THE WAY

Jesus answered him, "I am the way, the truth, and the life."

JOHN 14:6 GNB

A well-known religious speaker was scheduled to speak at the town hall in an unfamiliar city. He decided to walk to the venue from his hotel room—but on the way, he got lost. When he saw a group of boys on the other side of the street, he approached them to ask for directions.

"Hey, kids," he said, "Can any of you tell me how to get to City Hall?"

"What are you going to do when you get there?" one of the boys asked in return.

Sensing an opportunity to invite the boys to the meeting, the speaker rather pompously informed them, "Why, I'm going to give a talk."

"About what?" came the expected response.

"I'm going to talk to the people of this town on how to get to Heaven. Would you care to come along?"

"Are you kidding?" the boy said, surprised. "You don't even know how to get to City Hall!"

It is easy at times for Christians to slip into a false sense of religious pride, but the truth is, without Jesus we are all lost, on the wrong path. But thank God that Jesus is the Way!

Have you found Jesus, the only Way to the Father? If so, say a prayer of thanks to God today that you are no longer lost, floundering in a world of sin and hopeless-ness. But then be prepared to show others the Way as well. When we humbly invite other people to join us on this journey—to accept Christ as their Lord and Savior—then we are following the great example of the apostle Paul: "As for praise, we have never asked for it from you or anyone else. We loved you so much that we gave you not only God's Good News but our own lives, too" (1 Thessalonians 2:6, 8 NLT).

GRACE FOR TODAY:

We are no longer lost, searching for our way to God.
Jesus has revealed it to us. He is the Way!

BEST OF FRIENDS

At the beginning of J.R.R. Tolkien's epic, *The Lord of the Rings,* Gandalf assigned a difficult task to his young, naïve, and ill-prepared little friend, Frodo. It was a task that would push and expand his little world and change his life forever after. It was a task that needed to be fulfilled, but was so difficult he couldn't guarantee Frodo that he would succeed. Yet he could offer this powerful bit of advice: " . . . you need [not] go alone, not if you know of anyone you can trust, and who would be willing to go by your side . . . but if you look for a companion, be careful in your choosing!"

Fellowship with other believers can make the difference between getting through a tough situation and letting the world get the best of you. Sharing your joys, sorrows, hopes, and frustrations with another in fellowship can strength-en you as an individual and help you determine the proper course to take. Fellowship can help you share the love of Christ with others. As you learn to lean on them, they will learn to lean on you. And through fellowship, you can experience the grace of God firsthand when you see others extend kindness and com-passion to you at just the right time of need.

Remember, even Paul took a friend like Barnabas or Silas along to share the burden of his ministry and have fellow-ship with him. Look for ways that you can build Christian friendships at your church, through a Bible study group you attend, or even at work. Ask God to bring friends into your life and take the time to seek out people who may want to have fellowship with you.

> **GRACE FOR TODAY:**
>
> God gives us friends in the faith—those who are with us when we need them most.

Bear one another's burdens,
and in this way you will fulfill the law of Christ.

GALATIANS 6:2 NRSV

LIVING FOR CHRIST

By Warren W. Wiersbe

Eternal life through faith in Jesus Christ, this is our experience of salvation. He also died that we might live for Him, and not live unto ourselves (2 Corinthians 5:15). This is our experience of service. It has well been said, "Christ died our death for us that we might live His life for Him." If a lost sinner has been to the Cross and been saved, how can he spend the rest of his life in self-ishness?

In 1858, Frances Ridley Havergal visited Germany with her father who was getting treatment for his afflicted eyes. While in a pastor's home, she saw a picture of the crucifixion on the wall, with the words under it: "I did this for thee. What hast thou done for Me?" Quickly she took a piece of paper and wrote a poem based on that motto; but she was not satisfied with it, so she threw the paper into the fireplace. The

paper came out unharmed! Later, her father encouraged her to publish it; and we sing it today to a tune composed by Philip P. Bliss:

> I gave My life for thee,
> My precious blood I shed,
> That thou might'st ransomed be,
> And quickened from the dead.
> I gave, I gave, My life for thee,
> What hast thou given for Me?

Christ died that we might live *through* Him and *for* Him, and that we might live *with* Him![14]

—⚬—

HEAVENLY FATHER: THANK YOU FOR YOUR GRACE THAT ALLOWS ME TO LIVE THROUGH YOUR SON, JESUS CHRIST. STRENGTHEN AND GUIDE ME AS I LEARN TO LIVE FOR HIM. AMEN.

In this the love of God was manifested toward us, that God has sent His only begotten Son into the world, that we might live through Him.

1 JOHN 4:9 NKJV

OUT OF CONTROL

[Cast] all your care upon him; for he careth for you.

1 PETER 5:7 KJV

Does your life seem out of control? Does it seem as though your most sincere efforts have fallen to the ground? If so, there is no need to worry. All you have to do is surrender. Yes, surrender. But to surrender does not mean to simply give up. It does not mean to accept defeat. It actually means very much the opposite. It means to give up control of your life to someone more powerful.

GRACE FOR TODAY:

When we are under attack, God fights our battles for us!

In life, surrender does not involve choice. Wars have been fought, only to see nations surrender to the will of those conquering them. They had no choice to whom they should surrender. But in Christ, we have a choice. We do not have to surrender to the will of a tempting adversary. We can surrender to the will of One who loves us—the One who will triumph against our adversary on our behalf. This is the hard reality the devil must face every day—He can never win against us because God is on our side.

When we give up control of our lives to God, He takes over where we have left off and fixes the things we once thought were unfixable. He takes the parts of our lives that are under attack and fights our battles in His own way.

Let this remind us that when life is out of control, it is we who should conform to His desire, rather than He conforming to ours. If we give up control, all we have to do is surrender to His mighty hand of grace.

GOD, PLEASE SHOW ME WHAT TO DO!

*If you want to know what God wants you to do—
ask him, and he will gladly tell you.*

JAMES 1:5 NLT

D avid didn't know what to say to his young children when they asked if their mommy was going to die.

David's wife, Stephanie, had begun to have seizures—at first they were mild and only occurred a few times a month. But over time, her symptoms began to worsen with rapidly growing speed. Although hundreds of friends, relatives, and church members held numerous prayer vigils for her, her weight dropped to ninety pounds, and her condition worsened. By 1996, the seizures were occurring at least daily, sometimes hourly.

David rarely left Stephanie's side, and he began to wonder if she would even make it to her thirtieth birthday. One night, in the wee hours of the morning, David had reached his limit. The situation looked hopeless, and he was exhausted. David paced the family's backyard, lit only by the moon and the stars above, and then he fell on his knees. "God!" he cried out. "I can't take this anymore. Please show me what to do!"

It was a desperate prayer, prayed by a desperate man. But that moment, a sense of calm filled David's heart, and immediately the name of a doctor entered his mind. The next morning David gave the man a call. The doctor looked at Stephanie that very day and diagnosed a rare chemical deficiency—one that the other doctors had overlooked.

Within a week, Stephanie's seizures had disappeared. Her eyes sparkled, and her mind was clear. David's prayer to God was sincere: "Thank You, God, for giving me back my wife!"

God still answers prayer today, and He loves it when His children come to Him with their needs. When you don't know what to do, when you need His wisdom the most, just ask—He offers it freely!

> **GRACE FOR TODAY:**
>
> God promises us that He hears our prayers—and He answers them!

GUARANTEED GROWTH

The God who started this great work in you [will] keep at it and bring it
to a flourishing finish on the very day Christ Jesus appears.

PHILIPPIANS 1:6 MSG

Maturing physically is often frustrating for kids. Young children are eager to be taller, stronger, faster. They struggle to do things that are beyond their ability, as if they yearn to be more highly developed but just aren't there yet. Progress seems so gradual, it's almost immeasurable. Sometimes they despair of ever growing up.

Their parents reassure them that the process takes time. They remind their impatient youngsters that it can't be forced and encourage them to cooperate with nature by practicing the habits that foster growth—eating well, exercising regularly, getting sufficient sleep. "Have a little faith," parents say. "Growth will come."

Maturing spiritually can be just as frustrating for Christians. It's discouraging when you know where God wants you to be, you have a great desire to be more holy and good, you even practice the spiritual disciplines, but nothing seems to be happening. The whole process is confusing. You realize that holiness begins and ends with God's grace and that your part is merely to cooperate with the Holy Spirit's work. Yet like a child trying to assist in the kitchen, you are often not sure when you're being helpful and when you're just getting in the way. It's tempting to give up.

What a blessing it is to remember that no matter how disheartened you become about your walk with the Lord, no matter how certain you are that you'll never make it, God will never give up on you. He is nothing if not loyal to His children and His promises, and He has sworn to uphold you throughout your journey, until one day you stand before Him completely sanctified. (See Jude 1:24–25.) Imagine your joy in that moment when God smiles and says, "Look at you, all grown up!"

GRACE FOR TODAY:

Our heavenly Father never gives up on us—EVER!

WITH ALL DUE RESPECT

[Be] full of sympathy toward each other, loving one another with tender
hearts and humble minds.

1 PETER 3:8 NLT

H onor and respect are often communicated differently in other cultures than the
way they are in the United States. In some Australian Aboriginal tribes, for
example, members will purposefully use special "avoidance languages" when speaking
to in-laws to avoid certain topics in the presence of their respected elders. In the
Chinese culture, members will avoid direct eye contact when speaking with someone
in order to demonstrate respect. And in some cultures in India, speakers show respect
for those in authority over them by addressing them in the third person.

Yet in the busy lives of most Americans, respect is something that often gets overlooked or pushed aside. People use "avoidance language" to avoid having to take the
time to speak with someone or do something for that person. They avoid eye contact
to indicate disinterest and to show their unwillingness to have a lengthy conversation.
Instead of taking the time to help others with their problems, many will just say "I'm
not the right person to help you with that" and refer them on to someone else.

In the Christian "culture," honor is of the utmost importance. The Bible specifically
commands believers to honor their fathers and their mothers (Exodus 20:12), respect their
spouses (Ephesians 5:33), and give the proper respect to everyone in their lives (1 Peter
2:17). Even more important, honoring others is the greatest way to demonstrate Christ's
command to "love your neighbor as yourself" (Matthew 22:39 NLT).

When you go out of your way to tell people how much you appreciate them, defer
to their wishes, or just take the time to sit down and listen to them, you honor them
and demonstrate your love for them. And that is a tremendous way of portraying God's
grace to them.

GRACE FOR TODAY:

God has honored us by sending His Son to help us
become all that He created us to be.

75

ADMIRAL ONBOARD

Life is not a cruise on a pleasure ship, void of all responsibility. God has put you in charge of your boat, made you the captain. He requires you to use your wits and abilities on this voyage. However, God doesn't merely cast off the lines and wave as you set out to sea; He graciously sends His Son Jesus along to travel with you on your journey. Now as you face the wide, uncertain ocean, you can draw comfort from the knowledge that your Admiral is on deck.

Before you signed on with this navy, you thought being under Jesus' authority would be threatening, constricting, demeaning. Now you find it reassuring. You don't have to sail alone through life, threatened by shark-infested waters, stormy skies, and enemy ships. You must remain at the helm, your hands on the wheel, but now you have an officer onboard who can guide you and encourage you, empower you and protect you. Jesus is ultimately responsible to see that you arrive in safe harbors, and He has the divine wisdom and ability to make it happen. He has dominion not only over you but over all creation. Under His leadership, you can rest secure, enjoying the ride, glorying in the adventure, even as you are tested daily and challenged to grow in your seamanship.

As you traverse the open waters, Jesus trains you, mentors you. God's purpose for this journey is not merely to get you into port but to change you along the way. By the time you reach your destination, you have become much more than a seasoned captain; your poise and demeanor are such that were it not for the insignia on your uniform, no one could tell you apart from the Admiral himself.

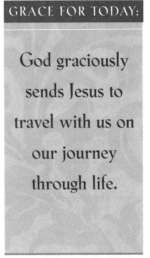

GRACE FOR TODAY:

God graciously sends Jesus to travel with us on our journey through life.

[Jesus] stood up and told the wind to be silent, the sea to quiet down: "Silence!" The sea became smooth as glass.

MATTHEW 8:26 MSG

IT IS DIVINE

By John MacArthur Jr.

To put it simply, peace is an attribute of God. If I asked you to list the attributes of God, these are the ones that would probably come most readily to mind: His love, grace, mercy, justice, holiness, wisdom, truth, omnipotence, immutability, and immortality. But do you ever think of God as being characterized by peace? In fact, He is peace. Whatever it is that He gives us, He has and He is. There is no lack of perfect peace in His being. God is never stressed. He never fears. God is never at cross-purposes with himself. He never has problems making up His mind.

God lives in perfect calm and contentment. Why? Because He's in charge of everything and can operate everything perfectly according to His own will. Since He is omniscient, He is never surprised. There are no threats to His omnipotence. There is no possible sin that can stain His holiness. Even His wrath is clear, controlled, and confident.

There is no regret in His mind, for He has never done, said, or thought anything that He would change in any way.

God enjoys perfect harmony within Himself. Our Bibles call Him "the Lord of peace," but in the Greek text a definite article appears before the word translated "peace," meaning He literally is "the Lord of the peace." This is real peace—the divine kind—not the kind the world has. Paul's prayer is that we might experience that kind of peace. Its source is God and God alone.[5]

—⁓—

HEAVENLY FATHER: I NEED YOUR PEACE IN MY LIFE. I NEED YOUR CALM, YOUR SERENITY, YOUR CONTENTMENT. I WANT TO EXPERIENCE PERFECT HARMONY. I ASK YOU TO POUR OUT YOUR GRACE ON ME, LORD—YOUR GRACE AND YOUR PEACE. AMEN.

May the Lord of peace himself give you peace at all times and in every way.

2 THESSALONIANS 3:16

JESUS, OUR SUBSTITUTE

[Jesus] was pierced for our transgressions, he was crushed for our iniquities . . . by his wounds we are healed.

ISAIAH 53:5

In the movie *The Last Emperor*, the young child who was anointed as the last emper-
or of China lived a life of luxury with a thousand servants at his command. "What
happens when you do wrong?" his brother asked, to which the boy emperor proudly
replied, "When I do wrong, someone else is punished."

To demonstrate this unique power he held, the boy
intentionally broke a jar, and one of his servants took
the beating that the boy himself deserved.

What an amazing illustration this is of what Jesus
Christ has done for us. However, in what happened on
the cross, the pattern was actually reversed: When His
servants sinned, the King took their punishment. All
the sins of the entire world were laid on our Savior at
that time, and when He died, with His last breath, He
breathed the words: "It is finished." The debt had been
paid, and God's justice was satisfied.

The good news for you is that because of what
Jesus did, the punishment for your sins has already
been paid. Because of Jesus' sacrifice, you can be completely forgiven! John, the Beloved Apostle, knew Jesus
well when He was on the earth, and this disciple
penned these comforting words about what our Savior
has done for us: "If we confess our sins, he is faithful and just and will forgive us our
sins and purify us from all unrighteousness" (1 John 1:9).

GRACE FOR TODAY:

Through Jesus'
sacrifice on the
cross, the debt
for our sin has
been paid, and
God's justice has
been completely
satisfied.

A SHIMMERING OASIS

Those who hope in the Lord will renew their strength.

ISAIAH 40:31

Hope invigorates and keeps us going. But only as long as we have placed our hope in the real thing. False hope will eventually be revealed, and when that happens, it can crush the spirit. A man crawling through a desert will perk up when he sees an oasis ahead. Suddenly he finds a fresh burst of energy and rushes to his new-found source of hope. If it turns out to be a mirage, he will fall to the ground, forlorn and weary; if he finds water, his eyes will brighten, and his strength will return.

GRACE FOR TODAY:

God is a spring of living water able to satisfy all our needs.

This world offers innumerable things in which to place your hope. God shows you ahead of time, in His Word, which hopes are empty and false. He does this because of His grace, knowing that if you place your hope in anything other than Him, sooner or later you will be terribly disappointed. Trusting in the Lord is the only sure hope there is, and it leads to renewed strength every time. That's because God is real and able to satisfy your needs.

The hope of water will sustain a man in the desert for only so long; at some point he must drink of water itself. The Bible describes God as a spring of living water (Jeremiah 17:13) and says that those who rely on Him are blessed and move from strength to strength (Psalm 84:5-7).

God is worthy of your trust. He is a shimmering oasis—not one that wavers, distorted by heat waves rising from the sand, nothing more than a hallucination, but one that gleams on the horizon, the brightest, surest hope of all.

POWER IN PRAYER

Devote yourselves to prayer, being watchful and thankful.

COLOSSIANS 4:2

In Luke 11:1, Jesus' disciples made a simple request: "Lord, teach us to pray." They knew the importance of prayer and had listened when Jesus spoke about going to God in prayer with an attitude of humility and faith. However, like many people today, the disciples still questioned whether they were praying the right way and for the right things. They wanted Christ to give them an example of how to pray.

As an act of grace, Jesus gave the disciples the "Lord's Prayer," which is an incredible teaching tool for just what should go into prayer. Beginning with the address, "Our Father who is in Heaven," Jesus instructed his disciples to respect God the Father and offer Him worship and praise. He told them to focus on God's will rather than their own and acknowledge they were there on earth to serve Him. Only then did He include teaching on how to ask God for their daily needs and for forgiveness in their lives, with the reminder that they should likewise forgive those who have wronged them. Finally, Jesus instructed His disciples to ask for strength to resist temptation.

As you can see, prayer can accomplish a great many things. It is the means for expressing praise to God and telling Him that you submit to His authority. Through prayer, you can ask God for the things you need and know that He has heard you. Through repentance in prayer, you can admit when you have stumbled and ask Him to extend His grace and forgiveness to you. And it is through prayer that you establish a relationship with God and receive His blessings as He helps you mature in your Christian walk each day.

GRACE FOR TODAY:

God is so anxious to answer our prayers that He has given us a beautiful prayer to use as a guide when taking our requests to Him.

THE ILLUSTRIOUS PATIENCE OF GOD

God passed in front of him and called out, "God, God, a God of mercy
and grace, endlessly patient—so much love, so deeply true."

EXODUS 34:6 MSG

If anyone has the right to sound His own trumpet, it is God. When the Lord
revealed himself to Moses, He hid him high in a cleft on Mount Sinai and passed
before him with great formality, proclaiming His holy name and heralding His wonderful attributes. Perhaps no one else can announce someone as distinguished as the
Almighty. Perhaps only God can truly introduce himself properly, with all the fanfare,
honor, and glory He deserves.

The biblical writers echoed these attributes of God over and over, attesting to His
patience and love in the Psalms and elsewhere. They quoted God's description of himself not only because He uttered it but because again and again throughout history, He
proved it to be completely accurate. God's patience is renowned. He is famous for
being slow to anger and quick to forgive. And all who turn to Jesus Christ are the
grateful recipients of God's mercy and grace.

The Lord's celebrated patience means that you do not have to panic when you sin,
or sadly bear the guilt of your error, or desperately try to work your way back into
His favor. As He proclaimed before Moses, God is also noted for His faithfulness, and
He has promised in His Word that if you will only go to Him and confess your sins,
He will forgive you and wash them completely away (1 John 1:9).

God wants you to follow His example and be slow to anger (James 1:19–20) and
to forgive others as He has forgiven you (Colossians 3:13). In this way you can extend
the grace you have received from Him to everyone around you. If you are faithful in
this respect, when you enter Heaven one day, you too will be honored for your patience
and forbearance.

GRACE FOR TODAY:

All who turn to Jesus Christ are the grateful recipients of
God's mercy and grace—demonstrated by His patience.

FORGIVE—ON THE SPOT

They hammered the nails into His hands, binding Him to the cross. Then, His feet were also nailed to the instrument of His death. They did this, after beating Him mercilessly and humiliating Him in public view. The crowds mocked Him, and His disciples hid their faces from Him. Yet, even during such suffering, He was able to forgive—on the spot.

Jesus understood that without Him, mankind is capable of the vilest, most wretched acts possible. The sin of mankind caused a separation from God without any road back to God. And the cross He took was the road to their redemption. It is also the road to yours.

We have all done things in life that were wrong. All of us have sinned. Isn't it good to know that even while we were sinners, our loving Christ died for us in order to bring us to God? He showed us favor that we did not at all deserve, just so that we can have perfect fellowship with Him. Forgiveness does not get greater than this.

As you go through your days, remember to be quick to forgive. When life gets dramatic and eventful (and you can rest assured that it will sometimes), remember the passion. Remember the sufferings of Christ. And just as He did, you should also forgive on the spot. It just may be the very thing that will shine a godly light through you so great that it will save a lost soul, just as it did yours.

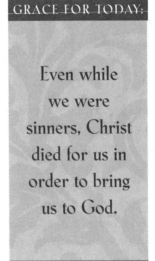

GRACE FOR TODAY:

Even while we were sinners, Christ died for us in order to bring us to God.

[Jesus said,] "Whenever you stand praying, if you have anything against anyone, forgive him, that your Father in heaven may also forgive you your trespasses."

MARK 11:25 NKJV

STOP! THIEF!

By Warren W. Wiersbe

"**P**aul's doctrine of grace is dangerous!" cried the Judaizers. "It replaces law with license. Why, if we do away with our rules and abandon our high standards, the churches will fall apart."

First-century Judaizers are not the only ones afraid to depend on God's grace. Legalists in our churches today warn that we dare not teach people about the liberty we have in Christ lest it result in religious anarchy. These people do not understand Paul's teaching about grace, and it is to correct such misunderstanding that Paul wrote the final section of his letter (Galatians 5–6).

Paul turns now from argument to application, from the doctrinal to the practical. The Christian who lives by faith is not going to become a rebel. Quite the contrary, he is going to experience the inner discipline of God that is far better that the outer discipline of man-made rules. No man could become a rebel who depends on God's grace, yields to God's Spirit, lives for others, and seeks to glorify God. The surrendered Christian who depends on the power of the Spirit is not denying the law of God or rebelling against it. Rather, that law is being fulfilled in him through the Spirit (Romans 8:1–4).[16]

—m—

FATHER IN HEAVEN: I'VE MADE A MESS OF KEEPING YOUR RULES. NO MATTER HOW HARD I TRY, I JUST CAN'T DO IT WITHOUT YOUR HELP. THEREFORE, LORD, I THROW MYSELF ON YOUR MERCY. POUR OUT YOUR LOVE AND GRACE ON MY LIFE AND HELP ME TO LIVE A LIFE THAT'S PLEASING TO YOU. AMEN.

We through the Spirit eagerly wait for the hope of righteousness by faith. For in Christ Jesus neither circumcision nor uncircumcision avails anything, but faith working through love.

GALATIANS 5:5–6 NKJV

THE JOY OF REALLY LIVING

Our mouths were filled with laughter, our tongues with songs of joy. The Lord has done great things for [us].

PSALM 126:2-3

I n the streams and ponds of North America, two similar–looking animals with very dissimilar work ethics often reside side–by–side. One animal, the beaver, studiously works throughout the day toppling trees to create large river dams. The other animal, the river otter, delights in making a game of everything. Otters catch what they need to survive, but also make time to chase after pebbles, slide down slopes, and tweak the tails of their more industrious neighbors.

GRACE FOR TODAY:

True joy in life is found in knowing that you are living under God's grace and He will provide for your needs.

Both animals live about the same length of time, but you have to believe that otters enjoy life just a bit more. Otters seem perfectly content if they have enough food and are happy to live in little mud holes along the river. Even in old age they never miss the opportunity to toss a stone in the water and catch it before it hits bottom.

Are you a busy beaver, always working to get ahead? Do you think that will bring enjoyment? According to a 2000 study, Americans today are twice as wealthy as they were in 1957, but the number of people who claim they are "very happy" has actually declined. In fact, as people work harder to accumulate more wealth, the only thing that seems to increase is their expectations—not their happiness.

True joy in life is not found in work or accomplishments, but in knowing that you are living under God's grace and that He will provide for your needs. So relax and take the time to see a movie with a friend, play ball with your kids, or just read a good book. Ask God to help you appreciate the blessings that He, in His grace, has given to you, and share that joy with others you connect with throughout the day.

FREEDOM OF CHOICE

Those who live to please the Spirit will harvest
everlasting life from the Spirit.

GALATIANS 6:8 NLT

I t's a reflection of God's gracious nature that He always gives you the freedom to
choose—the privilege to elect entirely on your own whether to accept His Word
as true, whether to embrace the good news of the Gospel, whether to accept Jesus
Christ as Lord and Savior. From the beginning of His relationship with you, He allows
you to decide.

If you decide to become a Christian, God continues to permit you freedom of
choice. As a believer, you have many opportunities to pick between alternatives, some
of which reflect God's desire for you, and some of
which do not. Every day, God gives you important
decisions to make. You choose whether to please your
old, sinful nature or God's Spirit (Galatians 6:8). You
decide whether to serve God or money (Luke 16:13).
You select which to seek first, God's kingdom or life's
necessities (Matthew 6:25-33). You determine whether
to fix your eyes on temporary or eternal things (2
Corinthians 4:18). You resolve whether to trust God's
wisdom or your own understanding (Proverbs 3:5).
You decide whether to worry or focus on the positive
(Philippians 4:4-9). You choose whether to seek glory
for yourself or for God (John 8:54).

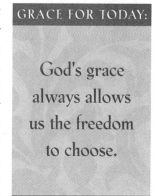

GRACE FOR TODAY:

God's grace
always allows
us the freedom
to choose.

God not only gives you all these choices, but through the Holy Spirit, the Bible, the
church, Christian ministries, and other believers, the Lord helps you to make the right
decisions and to follow through with them. In all these ways He offers wisdom, encouragement, and power to take the correct steps in your spiritual journey. The right choice
always brings great reward; however, the choice remains yours. What a blessing it is to
God and you to know that you are walking with Him under your own free will!

SWEET REPOSE

God gives rest to his loved ones.

PSALM 127:2 NLT

T he Bible says that some of God's grace, like sunshine and rain, touches all people (Matthew 5:45). Sleep falls into this category. Whether you are a Christian or not, sleep is a blessing from the Lord. Sleep is peaceful, warm, and cozy, a time for dreaming, a time for refreshment and renewal. If you're a believer, however, your repose is especially sweet, because you see sleep as a picture of salvation, and you rest secure in the knowledge that God, who never slumbers, is always watching over you (Psalm 4:8; 121:3-4).

In today's hectic world, the minutes before you drift off to sleep may be the only time you have for deep reflection. It's a good time to meditate on God's character, on His deeds, on His promises. It's a good time for honest, heartfelt fellowship with Him, as you are never more yourself, never more open and childlike, than in your last waking moments.

In Heaven, you may or may not need to sleep (there is never any darkness there), but here on earth it is a mark of God's grace. It's a reflection of the temporary nature of life, an illustration of dependence on the Lord, and a promise of future resurrection. The day comes to an end, and darkness descends; you commit your spirit into your heavenly Father's hands and trust Him to sustain you through the night; and then God raises you at dawn's early light, just as He did Christ on that first glorious Easter, just as He will raise you one fine morning.

God gives rest to those He loves—saints and sinners alike. He earnestly desires to adopt all people into His family through faith in Christ, so they can enjoy all the blessings of sleep. God's children truly rest in peace.

GRACE FOR TODAY:

God gives His children rest, both now and throughout eternity.

MUSIC TO THE SOUL

Speak to one another with the words of psalms, hymns, and sacred songs.

EPHESIANS 5:19 GNB

Music has been described as beautiful noise, but for anyone who has been deeply stirred by the sound, it's nothing less than a gift of grace. Combined with words and truths from Scripture, music can touch the heart with God's healing, lift the spirit with His promises, exalt the soul with His love. The fruit of a godly composer's creativity opens up for us a space for greater intimacy with our Creator.

The words and truths of the Bible are powerful in and of themselves, yet they seem to take on a new dimension when masterfully interwoven with music, becoming even more living and active, if that were possible. Think of the great hymns and classical compositions of the past, splendid and potent reminders of God's holiness, majesty, and amazing grace. How sweet the sound! Even a king could not remain seated when the magnificent strains of the "Hallelujah Chorus" first blessed an audience.

Contemporary Christian songs, like Rich Mullins' "Awesome God" and Mercy Me's "I Can Only Imagine," minister to believers today in many ways, helping them to focus on God's attributes and promises, filling their minds and hearts with truth, encouraging them to persevere in their faith.

A young mother stretched to the limit by the demands of caring for two little children, one a newborn, was distraught to learn that she was pregnant again. The prospect of another child seemed overwhelming. She felt moved to tune her car radio to a local Christian radio station. And in a subtle yet dramatic way, the music ministered to her, replacing her stress and uncertainty with peace and trust. Today she thanks God for her beloved daughter, and for using spiritual songs to carry her through a difficult time.

Inspired music is truly an echo of Heaven, a serenade from God.

GRACE FOR TODAY:

God blesses us through the ministry of godly music.

DEEP LAUGHTER

The hallmark of the Christian life is laughter and joy. Yes, there is a time for weeping and mourning, and believers are called to grieve with those who are hurting. This fallen world is racked with pain. But the miracle of faith is that by God's grace, His people can journey through life with eyes wide open, compassionate toward others who suffer and endure their own sorrows, yet knowing an abiding sense of joy and peace.

God blesses us with laughter at an early age. It's a very human trait: all children laugh, but despite the laughlike sounds some animals make, none of them really do. Our ability to laugh reflects the divine image we bear. And laughter is good for us, physically and emotionally. It provides a healthy way to relieve stress and produces a wholesome sense of well-being. Those who are wise cherish the gift of laughter, carry it from youth into adult-

hood, and nurture it throughout their lives, remembering Jesus' promise that the kingdom of Heaven belongs to the childlike.

How do you cling to the precious gift of laughter as you grow older and increasingly more aware of life's tragedies? Remember that laughter is a blessing with deep roots. Dig down a little, and you'll discover joy. Dig deeper, and you'll find faith. Farther down you'll reach God's promises. At the deepest level you'll encounter God himself. The sound of laughter in your life need never fade away, because it is ultimately rooted in the love and faithfulness of God, who never changes.

The Bible describes a person of noble character as someone who can laugh at tomorrow (Proverbs 31:25). All believers in Christ share that privilege, because their future in Heaven is secure, and it will be filled with shouts of joy, singing, and laughter.

> GRACE FOR TODAY:
>
> Laughter in your life need never fade because it is rooted in the love and faithfulness of God.

A merry heart makes a cheerful countenance.

PROVERBS 15:13 NKJV

LIVING A VICTORIOUS CHRISTIAN LIFE

By Luis Palau

When I became a believer I learned about forgiveness and never really doubted that God had forgiven me. But I didn't understand much about how a Christian progressed in maturity and holiness. I longed to get past the continual struggles and find victory in my life.

I wasn't alone in my desire for greater victory. The other young men I spent time with wanted victory too. And we needed it! We had many weaknesses. We made sarcastic remarks, despised certain denominations, and had our temptations with women—just to name a few. So whenever a big-name preacher came to our church for revival services, we would take him out for coffee and ask him how we could have victory in our lives. We never told him too much about our reason for wanting greater victory; we just hinted that we had some little weaknesses in our lives.

Over and over we were told to read the Bible, pray every day, and work for Christ. If we did those things, our advisers promised, we would be happy, holy Christians.

Not one of those great men of God ever said, "Listen, the secret is not reading, praying, and working. The secret is that Christ lives in you. All of the wisdom, power, and resources of Jesus Christ are available to you because He lives in you."

The secret of victory is not what we do for Christ but what He does through us! When we abide in Christ, and our relationship with Him is the most important part of our lives, He will bring us into authentic victory.[17]

—⚡—

HEAVENLY FATHER: THANK YOU FOR YOUR PROMISE TO LIVE WITHIN ME, MAKING ALL YOUR STRENGTH AND RESOURCES AVAILABLE TO HELP ME LIVE A HOLY LIFE. I CHOOSE THIS DAY TO INVITE YOU IN. THANK YOU FOR DOING FOR ME WHAT I COULDN'T DO FOR MYSELF. AMEN.

The mystery in a nutshell is just this: Christ is in you, therefore you can look forward to sharing in God's glory.

COLOSSIANS 1:27 MSG

GADGETS AND GIZMOS

Every good and perfect gift comes down from the Father.

JAMES 1:17 CEV

W hen God finished creation, everything was in place: matter, energy, light, sound, fire, water, air, gravity, electricity, nuclear power, the laws of physics, the mathematical relationships, and life itself—most importantly, humankind. People, God's crowning achievement, were crafted in His image, endowed with intelligence, creativity, and dexterity. Creation was perfect and rife with potential. The Lord made the understatement of all time when He surveyed it and said, "Very good."

> **GRACE FOR TODAY:**
>
> **Among His other gifts, God has endowed us with human ingenuity and creativity.**

Despite the Fall, creation is still awfully good. By God's grace, today we enjoy many technologies that facilitate and enrich our lives. Thanks to the Lord's forethought at Creation, we now have heating, air-conditioning, refrigeration, cell phones, fax machines, computers, the Internet, global positioning systems, digital TV, satellite radio, CDs, DVDs, automobiles, trains, ships, aircraft, even space shuttles.

We give God the glory for the wonder and beauty of nature, but we tend to credit humanity for science, industry, and technology, as if all that were mankind's idea, not part of the Lord's original plan. Surely, however, God intended for people to advance in their understanding of the world and apply that understanding in practical ways. Isn't it feasible that if Adam and Eve had never sinned and had been allowed to continue tending the Garden of Eden forever, one of them would sooner or later have invented the wheel, and eventually they would have built themselves a tractor?

The Bible says there will be a magnificent city in Heaven, and although people will not build it, they will be given authority to help manage it. There is no doubt that innovation and technology are attributable to the infinite mind of God; He planted the seeds for our every modern convenience in the soil of Creation. God deserves the credit and the glory for all the wonders of the world.

HARD KNOCKS

The Lord corrects those he loves, as parents correct
a child of whom they are proud.

PROVERBS 3:12 GNB

W hen lectures and warnings fail, parents sometimes decide to step back and
let a child experience the natural consequences of his or her misdeeds.
They don't do this to be cruel, but rather to allow the school of life to teach their child
a valuable lesson. So if a youngster insists on jumping into a puddle of water, his mom
and dad may resist the urge to immediately fetch him another pair of shoes. When he
gets tired of running around with wet feet, they reason,
he'll put two and two together and decide that playing in
water puddles isn't such a good idea.

This "tough love" approach to discipline is a good
illustration of how the Lord chastises His children
whenever they go astray. Through the Bible, God has
given us all the information we need to live righteously. He has clearly explained the difference between good
and bad behavior, and He has spelled out the results of
each, warning us that we will reap what we sow. Now
He stands back and gives us the freedom to make our
own choices, and sometimes—much as it grieves
Him—He resists extending His hand of protection over us when we choose foolishly.

GRACE FOR TODAY:

God embraces
us with His
mercy the
moment we
return to Him.

As the parable of the prodigal son demonstrates, the school of life can be very
harsh. If God were to turn His back on us completely, the consequences of our sins
would overwhelm us. But like any loving parent, God graciously mitigates the natural
results of our rebellion and allows us to suffer them only as long as necessary. When
we come running home, He doesn't reprimand us more. Instead He embraces us and
gives us good gifts—just as Mom and Dad welcome their contrite son at the door with
hugs, dry socks, and hot cocoa.

POTATOES CAN BE HEAVY!

[Jesus said,] "If you forgive men when they sin against you,
your heavenly Father will also forgive you."

MATTHEW 6:14

A teacher once decided to try an interesting experiment with her class of ninth-grade students. She told each of them to bring a clear plastic bag and a sack of potatoes to class. Then, for every person they were refusing to forgive in their life's experience, they were to choose a potato, write on it the name of the person and the date, and then place it into the plastic bag. Some of the students' bags turned out to be quite heavy.

The teacher then told them to carry this bag around with them everywhere they went for one week, putting it on the seat next to them on the school bus, on their nightstands when they went to bed, lugging it along with their other packages through the mall.

The hassle of lugging the potatoes around with them made it clear to the students what a weight they carried when they refused to forgive—how they had to pay attention to it all the time in order to not forget and leave it out in an embarrassing place.

Naturally, the condition of the potatoes deteriorated to a nasty, smelly slime—a great metaphor for the price paid for hanging on to past grudges and hurt feelings.

Are you needlessly lugging around a proverbial sack of potatoes? Is there someone you need to forgive today? You may often think of forgiveness as a gift to the other person, but don't forget, it's a gift to yourself too!

GRACE FOR TODAY:

God enables us to forgive others by first extending
His forgiveness to us.

JUST A MINUTE

We pray that you'll have the strength to stick it out over the long haul—
not the grim strength of gritting your teeth but
the glory-strength God gives.

COLOSSIANS 1:11 MSG

With a sigh, Clara looked over at the clock on her nightstand. It was 7:00 A.M., and her thirteen-month-old was wide awake. Although she would have much preferred to just stay in bed a bit longer, she opened her tired eyes and "embraced" the new day.

"Okay now, sit still," she said a few minutes later as she attempted to dress the little boy. He was squirming around and making it difficult to get any clothes on him. No sooner would she put his arm in the sleeve of his shirt than he would have it out again. He took his socks off four times in a row, then rolled up his toes to make it difficult to get his shoes on. When Clara finished adjusting the hat on his head, he tossed it across the room.

Needless to say, Clara was blessed with an incredible amount of patience. Although she was in a stressful situation that made her feel frustrated and angry, she had the ability to remain calm and not succumb to those feelings. In the same way, patience allows you to take a step back from any stressful situation and think before you act on your frustrations.

While it may seem impossible at times to display patience in every situation, it is important to remember that God is always patient with you. In the same way that He chooses to extend grace to you, you can choose to be patient with those who may require a little bit more of your time and effort. Acquiring patience may be a slow and tiresome process, but it is one that will allow you to reflect God's grace onto others and demonstrate His love and care.

GRACE FOR TODAY:

We are able to extend grace to others because God
first extended it to us.

GODSPEED

Has anyone ever wished you Godspeed?

In this fast-paced world, it would be nice if the Lord helped you move more quickly. But that's not what Godspeed means. The term is derived from the Middle English phrase "God spede you," which means "God prosper you."[18] It's a prayer for God's blessing of success. If no one's ever prayed it for you, you might try praying it for yourself. God would approve; He wants you to be hugely successful.

However, the Lord wants you to thrive according to His terms of prosperity. This won't seem very exciting if you're caught up in the world's view of success. But think for a moment about God's terms! His thoughts are much higher than ours (Isaiah 55:9), and His will is good, pleasing, and perfect (Romans 12:2). God takes an overarching view of prosperity, wanting to bless His children not just for a lifetime but for all eternity, not just with earthly treasures but with all the riches of Heaven.

God has so many ways in which to bless His faithful ones, ways that transcend possessions, fortune, and fame, such as good health, strong relationships, spiritual growth, opportunities to serve Him. If you commit to the Lord all of your activities and allow God to decide how to bless you, He will prosper you in ways that are ultimately in your best interest. This commitment takes faith on your part, but God is worthy of your trust.

God wants you to commit to Him whatever you do, but He also commands that whatever you do be done for His glory (1 Corinthians 10:31). You may be required to examine your motivations and reorder your priorities, but if you are willing to live according to God's terms, He will speed you beyond your wildest dreams.

> **GRACE FOR TODAY:**
>
> **God blesses us— always in ways that are in our best interest.**

**Ask the Lord to bless your plans,
and you will be successful in carrying them out.**

PROVERBS 16:3 GNB

Free for All

By John Wesley

The grace or love of God, whence cometh our salvation, is free in all, and free for all. It is free in all to whom it is given. It does not depend on any power or merit in man; no, not in any degree, neither in whole, nor in part. It does not in anywise depend either on the good works or righteousness of the receiver; not on anything he has done, or anything he is.

Receiving God's love and grace does not depend on a person's endeavors. It does not depend on his good temper, or good desires, or good purposes and intentions; for all these flow from the free grace of God; they are the streams only, not the fountain. They are the fruits of free grace, and not the root. They are not the cause, but the effects of it.

Whatever good is in man, or is done by man, God is the author and doer of it. Thus is His grace free in all, that is, no way depending on any power or merit in man, but on God alone, who freely gave us His own Son, and with Him freely giveth us all things.[19]

―⚬―

FATHER GOD: THANK YOU FOR SAVING ME WHEN I COULD NOT SAVE MYSELF. I KNOW THAT I DON'T DESERVE YOUR LOVE AND GRACE, BUT YOU HAVE GIVEN IT TO ME DESPITE MY UNWORTHINESS. I WILL CALL UPON THAT GRACE EVERY DAY AS I WALK OUT MY SALVATION. AMEN.

God is able to make all grace abound to you, so that in all things at all times, having all that you need, you will abound in every good work.

2 CORINTHIANS 9:8

AS HAPPY AS YOU CHOOSE TO BE

Fix your thoughts on what is true and good and right. . . . Think about all you can praise God for and be glad about.

PHILIPPIANS 4:8 TLB

Two men fell on hard times, having lost their jobs and used up almost all of their savings accounts. But try as they might, they still couldn't find work. When they heard that a museum was willing to pay fifty dollars each for live rattlesnakes, in desperation they decided to try to catch some snakes and earn some money.

Outfitted with a net and a basket, they hiked to a remote area known for its large snake population. After looking for a while, they didn't see any snakes. But then, just as they tried to cross a steep ledge, the rocks gave way, and they tumbled down the slippery bank— right into a deep pit crawling with rattlesnakes!

One of the men yelled out in horror and dismay, but the other, quickly sizing up the situation, shouted excitedly to his friend: "Hey, Jimmy! Lookit—we're rich!"

Some people have the gift to see the good in just about anything! But much of having a good attitude has to do with your perspective on life. Your greatest power lies in your power to choose. As Abraham Lincoln once wisely said, "Most people are about as happy as they make up their minds to be."

You can choose to focus on the difficulties that life will inevitably bring, or you can set your mind to think on good things. The choice is up to you!

> **GRACE FOR TODAY:**
>
> God has graciously given us the ability to see the good in just about anything—if we are willing to see it.

SILVER LININGS

The Scriptures say, "God commanded light to shine in the dark."
Now God is shining in our hearts.

2 CORINTHIANS 4:6 CEV

The blessed life that God offers is not a life void of difficulty and heartache. This fact is so obvious in today's world that to believe otherwise, you would have to put on rose-colored glasses and bury your head in the sand! God never promised some kind of blissful fantasy life, but rather to walk with you through an often painful reality. He won't deliver you from all of life's storms, but He will endure them with you. What's more, He will bring good out of every dark situation, gracing every black cloud with a gleaming silver edge.

GRACE FOR TODAY:

How does the Lord accomplish this miracle? At times in the Old Testament, God's glory was visible for all to see, like sunlight bursting through an overcast sky. Later God poured His glory into human form, and it blazed forth from Jesus' face at the Transfiguration. Now the Holy Spirit lives in the heart of every believer, and God's glory radiates from His people. If you are a child of God through faith in Jesus Christ, look about as you stand buffeted by the winds. God's silver lining is you!

God's Spirit gives you godliness in every situation.

God's Spirit within gives you comfort, wisdom, courage, and strength to weather life's storms. And like a silversmith, the Holy Spirit uses harsh conditions to refine and perfect you (Psalm 66:10). At the same time, He enables you to be a blessing to others caught up in the tempests of this world. The Bible says that God's Spirit is the source of all love, joy, peace, patience, kindness, goodness, faithfulness, gentleness, and self-control (Galatians 5:22–23). Dwelling within your heart, He will empower you to be loving and good despite any evil circumstances that surround you.

THE PROBLEM WITH WAITING

Delight yourself also in the Lord,
and He shall give you the desires of your heart.

PSALM 37:4 NKJV

D o you normally enjoy a traffic jam? Is it at all amusing to wait for an eleva-
tor? Do you wake up in the morning, looking forward to your visit to the
subway station? How much fun is it to watch the clothes in your dryer finish their
course? Most of us do not enjoy these things, and the reason is because all of these
events require waiting—a forced pause, valuable time wasted while we do nothing.

You may feel the same way about waiting for God. The Bible tells us that His timing is not ours—it's higher, better, more productive. But it sure doesn't feel that way. It
can leave us fidgeting, fretting, and pacing. Still, unlike the traffic jams, subway rides,
elevators, and laundry, waiting on God is never a waste of time.

So instead of sitting there, wringing your hands and wondering when God will
decide to move on Your behalf, take time to thank Him. Give Him praise for His faithfulness, His promises, His grace, His love, His intervention on your behalf. Thank
Him for the opportunity He's given you to prepare for His answer, to make your heart
ready for the changes His answer will bring to your life.

It's true—waiting can be tough. But waiting for God can be a blessing in disguise.
It can be the catalyst you need to receive His best answer in His best way in His perfect timing.

GRACE FOR TODAY:

God sends His perfect answers at the perfect time.

GOD'S IN CONTROL

By John MacArthur Jr.

God's grace saves us, helps us cope with our anxieties, equips us for service, and enables us to grow spiritually and to be rich in God. Like God's peace, it is always available, and there is no limit to it. And again, like God's peace, the conditions for receiving it are trusting God, forsaking sin, enduring the refining process, doing good, and living by the Word. As we are what we ought to be, God infuses us with His peace and grace. And that peace and grace has a wonderful way of crowding out anxiety.

A few days after presenting this very message to my congregation at Grace Church, I had an unprecedented opportunity to apply it to my life: I was notified that my wife and youngest daughter were in a serious auto accident, and that my wife, Patricia, would probably die. Everything seemed like a blur to me, the details frustratingly sketchy. I was afraid she was already dead.

During my hour-long drive to the hospital, I had a lot of time to reflect on the severity of the situation. Yet I experienced a deep and settled peace simply because I knew God had not failed me—His grace was at work in my family's lives, and He was in complete control. I am happy to report that God spared both their lives, and that Patricia has recovered beautifully. If you too rely on God's grace, He will see you through the most difficult trials.[20]

—◦◦◦—

FATHER: I THANK YOU FOR THE GRACE THAT IS AT WORK IN MY LIFE. AND I THANK YOU FOR THE PEACE THAT COMES AS A RESULT. I KNOW THAT YOU WILL NEVER FAIL ME. AMEN.

The grace of our Lord was poured out on me abundantly, along with the faith and love that are in Christ Jesus.

1 TIMOTHY 1:14

WHAT WILL YOU SAY TO HIM?

If ye abide in me, and my words abide in you, ye shall ask what ye will, and it shall be done unto you.

JOHN 15:7 KJV

We live in a world that can be overwhelming, to say the least. We have wars on nearly every continent. Poverty and famine are an epidemic. Diseases are mercilessly taking lives by the millions. Even middle–class families are suffering the tragedy of teenage suicides, drug use, and natural disasters. What can we do to handle the calamities that exist all around us?

The answer could be sitting on our bookshelves. God not only gives us peace in the midst of storms and tragedies. He also gives us the power of His Word and the power of prayer. This means we not only find a refuge from all the trials of life, but we also have a sword that we can use to defend ourselves against spiritual attack. We have the ability to impact the situations that exist in this world through God's power—if we believe that the Bible is true.

If the Bible is true (and it is), then there is nothing impossible to us. Whatever we ask the Father, in the name of Jesus, can be done if we ask in faith. We have power and authority over all of the evil that pervades this earth. Through prayer and the Word of God, very real issues can be affected by God's power and strength. The next time you go to pray, remember that you are operating under an open heaven. You are using power that is far greater than your own ability. You are connecting to God, and He wants to answer you. What will you say to Him?

> GRACE FOR TODAY:
>
> The next time you pray, remember that you are operating under an open Heaven.

Chasing the Wind

God exists and rewards those who seek him.

Hebrews 11:6 GNB

In the book of Ecclesiastes, King Solomon wrestled with meaninglessness, lamenting that life seemed as futile as chasing the wind. And Solomon believed in God! The Lord had spoken to him personally in a dream, and Solomon wrote countless proverbs about God. Even if you're a believer, living seems purposeless when you take your eyes off the Lord and fix them on the world. God's grace is that when you earnestly seek Him—whether as a nonbeliever or as a recommitted believer—He will bless your life with significance and meaning.

As Solomon poured out all his thoughts and feelings in Ecclesiastes, the Lord helped him discover the antidote to life's meaninglessness: "Fear God and keep his commandments" (12:13). This revelation must have seemed obvious to such a wise man as Solomon, and you can almost imagine him slapping his head and saying, "Of course!" But to understand this cure, it's important to observe that it is rooted in faith.

> GRACE FOR TODAY:
>
> **God will bless your life with meaning when you earnestly seek Him.**

To revere and obey God, you must first acknowledge that He is real and put your trust in Him. Solomon had already taken this step. You may need to take this step, or like him you may need to realign your sights. When you believe in and focus on an awesome, loving God, revering and obeying Him becomes an end in itself, and life is rich with purpose.

God wants you to know that He lives, and He wants you to know that you will find Him if you seek Him wholeheartedly (Jeremiah 29:13). Now, the Bible says that God is a Spirit, and His Spirit is often described as a wind. So here's an easy way to remember the key to finding or rediscovering meaning in life: When you feel as if you're chasing the wind, begin chasing the Wind.

GRACEFUL HUMILITY

Humble yourselves before the Lord, and he will lift you up.

JAMES 4:10

W hen Galileo Galilei first peered through his telescope and gazed upon the planet Saturn, he confidently declared that it consisted of one "star" surrounded by two moons. When later observations indicated that these moons had disappeared, Galileo had to retract his statement and admit that his theory was incorrect. "I do not know what to say in a case so surprising, so unlooked for, and so novel," he wrote.

Like most great scientists, Galileo possessed the courage to introduce new ideas that often challenged people's perception of the world. Yet a greater ability that he possessed was the humility to admit when those ideas were wrong. Such humility on his part allowed others to pick up where he had left off and eventually discover that these "moons" were in fact rings orbiting the planet.

In the same way, humility is required in the life of every Christian, for it is only by admitting your faults that you can "uncover" the truth of God's grace and receive His provision in your life. When you humble yourself and admit you have done something wrong, or submit to another's will, or forgive those who have wronged you, you demonstrate the love of Christ in your life and reflect His grace.

So be courageous and acknowledge when you are wrong. Practice being gracious when you receive correction and guidance from others. Look for ways to serve others and let them take the glory and praise. Be quick to forgive others and don't hold a grudge against them. Practicing humility is not easy, but you will find that God's grace is there to help you do it.

GRACE FOR TODAY:

When we walk in humility, we are reflecting
God's image.

THE LESSON OF EWOK

God does not judge by outward appearances.

GALATIANS 2:6 GNB

A family was so excited to go white-water rafting for the first time. When one of the guides, Joe, stepped forward to give instructions, they instantly knew that this was the guide they wanted: He was good-looking, strong, and clean-cut. Unfortunately, Joe was not to be their guide. That honor fell to Ewok, the guide they immediately disliked.

Ewok had long hair that hung down his back, cut in sort of a Mohawk style. There were only a few inches of his rather round body that weren't covered in tattoos. The family's first impression was disappointment: Clearly, Ewok was not the guide that would be best for their family.

But as the day progressed, their impressions slowly began to change. Joe turned out to be somewhat of a "jerk"—continually splashing the people in his raft with the river water and then laughing about it. But Ewok's appearance belied the gentleness and expertise underneath. He turned out to be the most experienced guide on the river that day. He was a true gentleman, helping the kids with their lifejackets and making sure their day was a pleasant family memory to be shared for years to come.

Appearances can be deceiving. Many times Christians prejudge people based on appearance and their own past experiences. God does not judge by outward appearances—aren't you glad? Thank God He doesn't judge the way we sometimes do!

GRACE FOR TODAY:

God doesn't look on the outward appearance. He looks to see what is in our hearts.

LISTEN WITH YOUR HEART

A study conducted by the Detroit Public Schools several years ago revealed that most people spend approximately 45 percent of their day listening to others. However, similar studies indicate that people typically only comprehend and retain about 25 percent of what they hear. While some of this difficulty can be attributed to outside factors (such as room noise), the truth is that most people just don't listen well.

It takes a great deal of effort to successfully listen to others. When you choose to listen, you consciously suppress your own desire to express your feelings in favor of letting others speak. You demonstrate respect by allowing them to share their experiences without interrupting with your own observations or advice. And when you listen intently, you communicate that you value their opinions and

care about what they have to say.

During Jesus' time on earth, He didn't go around rattling off a string of sermons, but He interacted with people and listened to their questions and needs. Sometimes He asked additional questions to get at the heart of what they were seeking. Other times, He told them parables to communicate a particular point more clearly. Even if they didn't like what they heard, they always knew Jesus had listened and understood.

As you go through your day, remember that He still listens to you, and try to extend that same grace to the other people with whom you interact. And when you spend time with God in prayer, be sure to be open when He wants you to listen to Him so that you can receive His grace in your life.

> GRACE FOR TODAY:
>
> God is always ready to hear us when we speak to Him—all day, every day; all night, every night.

My heart has heard [the Lord] say, "Come and talk with me." And my heart responds, "Lord, I am coming."

PSALM 27:8 NLT

THE GOD OF ALL COMFORT

By Luis Palau

Several years ago a submarine, with all its crew, sank off the Atlantic coast of North America. Once the vessel was located, frogmen went down to assess the damage and the possibility of salvaging the wreck.

As divers neared the hull of the vessel, they were surprised to hear a message being pounded in Morse code. Someone actually was alive in the submarine! The divers listened carefully. The message was a frantic question beat against the walls of the aquatic tomb: "Is there hope? Is there hope?"

You and I may pose the same question when a problem or tragedy strikes us. Who, after all, is totally free from the crushing pain of losing a loved one, the burden of ill health, the fear of financial difficulties, the anguish of a fragmented home, or any of a hundred other problems?

When such problems beset us, we may feel trapped and submerged by the weight of our circumstances. We wonder, Is there any hope of overcoming this problem? Can anyone really comfort us in our pain? We embark on a desperate search for comfort—but usually wind up unfulfilled.

The apostle Paul says God himself declares that He is the Father of compassion and the God of all comfort. In fact, Paul uses a derivative of the word comfort ten times in these verses. So when we face external pressures—as all of us do from time to time—we can be assured that we have a Heavenly Father who is the Father of compassion and comfort."

—m—

LORD GOD: I NEED YOUR COMFORT RIGHT HERE, RIGHT NOW. TOUCH ME WITH YOUR COMPASSIONATE HAND AND LIFT ME OUT OF MY PAIN AND SUFFERING. I PLACE MY HOPE IN YOUR GOODNESS AND GRACE. AMEN.

Praise be to the God and Father of our Lord Jesus Christ, the Father of compassion and the God of all comfort, who comforts us in all our troubles, so that we can comfort those in any trouble with the comfort we ourselves have received from God.

2 CORINTHIANS 1:3–4

CAT UP A TREE

[The Lord's] plans endure forever; his purposes last eternally.

PSALM 33:11 GNB

*T*he Book of Heroic Failures tells the story of the 1978 strike of British firefighters, in which the army was forced to fill the gap for the missing firemen. One afternoon the replacement firefighters got a call to rescue a cat that was high up in a tree. The soldiers rushed to the scene, put up a ladder, brought down the cat, and handed it safely back to its owner. The woman was so grateful that she invited the firemen in for tea. After a wonderful time, they said goodbye, got back into their truck, and backed away—right over the cat.

The question could be asked of this "rescue" mission: Was it really a success?

The successes we experience in this life—no matter how well deserved or difficult to achieve—are still just that: a part of this life, temporary and prone to disappear at a moment's notice. But true success—success that will last throughout eternity—is based on fulfilling God's will for our lives and living in obedience to Him.

The things we do for the Lord will last for eternity, while the things we do for ourselves, to promote ourselves and to gain the world's success here and now, will eventually fade and wither like the grass. Living life God's way is so much more gratifying, and let's face it: When we live this way, we'll be living much more safely, all four paws securely "grounded" in the Lord!

> GRACE FOR TODAY:
>
> God gives us true success—the kind that will last for eternity—when we find His will for our lives.

EXPERIENCING GRACE

Your troubles have come in order to prove that your faith is real.
It is worth more than gold.

1 PETER 1:7 NIRV

After beating the record for the fastest mile run by an American on U.S. soil, winning his first international race, and scoring victories at the U.S. trials' championship, Alan Webb thought he was ready to take on his first Olympic race. He was focused, determined, and willing to train hard. When the day of the race arrived, he was confident he had all the elements for success.

But when the race got underway, the twenty–one–year–old Webb realized he lacked one important element—experience. Other runners stepped on him, nudged him with their elbows, and knocked him around like a pinball. Unaccustomed to such a physical race, Webb floundered along as the other racers forced him into an outside lane and passed him by. By the time it was over, Webb knew that his lack of experience had cost him any chance he had for winning a medal at the Olympics.

It may be hard to view trials as a gift of grace from God when they come your way. However, sometimes these trials are the only way for you to gain the experience you need to handle a bigger problem down the road. Failure sometimes seems like a step backward, but you always learn more from mistakes than victories. The knowledge you gain from setbacks today can pay great dividends in knowing how to handle similar (and often more important) events in the future.

The good news is that you won't have to go through these times alone, for God always puts people with experience into your life to guide and mentor you. All you have to do is be willing to accept God's grace and listen to their advice.

> **GRACE FOR TODAY:**
> Our trials and tribulations are never wasted. God uses them to build strength and character in our lives.

THREE SIMPLE WORDS

Yea, I have loved thee with an everlasting love: therefore with
lovingkindness have I drawn thee.

JEREMIAH 31:3 KJV

J esus is the best thing that can happen to a person. He saves you from a life of sin.
He takes you out of the darkness and loneliness of your situation and offers himself as a faithful companion and a help in time of need. And He places His Holy Spirit
in you to give you purpose, insight, comfort, encouragement, love, peace, joy—the list
covers any and every human need you might encounter. In a sense, the Holy Spirit is
God's way of saying "I love you."

That's a wonderful thought, isn't it? The Bible reminds us that there are many who
have not yet heard God utter those three simple words to them. They aren't aware of
God's love and grace. They haven't experienced the indescribable glory of being
released from their sins, forgiven and restored. They don't yet know that Jesus is the
best thing that could happen to them.

That's where you come in. Share those three simple words with someone today.
Someone who doesn't yet know Him. Someone who doesn't know that God's love and
grace are there for the claiming. Someone who doesn't know that Jesus is the best thing
that could ever happen to them.

Ask God to show you who He wants to love through you. Whatever He says to
you, do it. Wherever He sends you, go. Don't stop until you've passed along those
three simple words to at least one other person. It's a small investment that pays eternal dividends.

GRACE FOR TODAY:

God loves us more than we can possibly imagine—and
He always will.

WE ARE NOT ALONE

The earth is the Lord's, and the fulness thereof.

PSALM 24:1 KJV

H ave you ever stood by the edge of a lake before sunrise and looked at the stars? Everything is quiet. The only light that shines is the light of the moon that cov—ers the water. The very stars that Adam and Eve saw are still there, shining just for you. It seems as though the darkest part of night brings out the brightness of God's cre—ation. In fact, if you stare long enough, you can see even more stars across the early morning sky. The beauty of such a moment can be described a thousand different ways. It is a sight that once beheld, the watcher can only conclude that God alone can show this splendor to mankind. Such an awesome beauty could never have come by chance.

One thing that we learn from such a quiet time is that we are not alone. God made His creation beautiful just for us. The same God who put the moon and stars in place is the God who promised to be with us, always. He is the one who loved us with an everlasting love by sending His Son to die on the cross for us.

The next time you feel alone, remember that the God who created the universe is the God who promised to live inside your heart. You are never alone. His watchful and loving gaze will never depart from you. And His presence and power will never cease to be active in every aspect of your life.

GRACE FOR TODAY:

The same God who put the moon and stars in place is the God who promises to be with us—always.

I LOVE TO BE IN CHURCH

Rich Mullins was a beloved artist and songwriter in the world of Christian music, and before he was tragically killed in a jeep accident on September 19, 1997, he had written many beautiful praise songs that had touched the hearts of numerous people. Eric Hauck, a close friend of Rich, recalled being with him in a worship service just a few days before he died. Some friends just wanted to gather together and praise God, and everyone had brought instruments to play together. The music sounded awful—even the leaders were singing out of tune.

Rich later went up to the microphone and said, "I love to be in church. I love to listen to people sing and play from their heart. In my profession, we worry about being in tune and sounding good, but this music tonight is the most pleasing to God, because it is so real, and it comes from the hearts of the children of God." That was the last time Eric ever saw Rich Mullins cry.

Today Rich Mullins is worshipping God in Heaven, but while he was on the earth, he loved to be in church and worship with his fellow Christians. One of his band members once said, "For Rich, even an hour in a bad church was better than not going at all."

God desires that His children be in fellowship with each other. We need other believers around us to encourage our faith—and to help us worship God with our whole hearts. Don't "give up meeting together" with other believers—it will bless you more than you can imagine.

GRACE FOR TODAY:

God has given us the gift of each other.

Let us not give up meeting together . . . but let us encourage one another.

HEBREWS 10:25

THE GOD WHO RAISES THE DEAD

By Luis Palau

Despair seems to have several different forms. The most common type occurs when a person is beset by "external" troubles—such as financial difficulties or poor health. People who experience this particular form of despair usually are convinced that if only their external circumstances were better, they'd feel fine.

On the other hand, some people experience inner despair even though their external circumstances are ideal. They have all the money they want, all the friends they need, all the education they can stand—but an inexplicable emptiness still haunts them. This type of despair may well be the worst; its source is not definable, and it's suffered alone.

We often consider Paul to be the dynamic, unquenchable apostle, but he too suffered from inner despair. Paul's despair, however, was not due to "external" failures or the emptiness that accompanies the quest for personal gain.

Rather, his resulted from difficult circumstances he faced in the fulfillment of his ministry. Yet Paul found comfort and victory in the God who raises the dead—a comfort we can find too!

Perhaps you've gone through an experience similar to Paul's. Believe it or not, that could be the most exciting moment of your life—a moment of real victory, when Christ can step into the situation that is troubling you. He can take over the haunting inner despair of your heart that you share with no one. He can cleanse you and transform you. He can fill you with His Spirit and give you peace.[22]

—∿—

HEAVENLY FATHER: I WANT TO EXCHANGE MY DESPAIR FOR YOUR COMFORT. I REACH OUT TO YOU NOW, EXPECTING THIS TO BE THE MOST EXCITING MOMENT OF MY LIFE. AMEN.

In our hearts we felt the sentence of death. But this happened that we might not rely on ourselves but on God, who raises the dead.

2 CORINTHIANS 1:9

THE WAYS OF WORSHIP

I will praise you, O Lord, with all my heart. . . . I will give you thanks.

PSALM 9:1; 35:18

When you stop to consider all the things that God has done for you, you can't help but want to worship and praise Him for His incredible mercy and grace. Worship is a natural reaction to the feelings of joy and happiness you experience when you follow God and walk in His ways. Through worship, you are not only able to express your gratitude to God, but also to indicate that you believe He is worthy to receive your utmost honor and devotion.

The Israelites of the Old Testament understood just how much God had done for them when He led them out of captivity in Egypt and raised them up as His chosen people. They expressed their worship to God in a variety of ways, such as through the lifting of their hands in praise (Hebrew yadah) or the bowing of their heads in humble submission to Him (barouch). Their worship was often loud and boisterous as they shouted out the praise of His glory (shabach), picked up their instruments and glorified Him in song (zamar), or just danced and celebrated in His presence (halell). They also lifted their praise to God in time of need and regardless of the circumstances (towdah).

Always take time to look back over your day and consider the many blessings God has given to you. Whether you prefer to worship in a loud and celebratory manner or a more quiet and introspective way, be sure to tell God just how much His gift of grace means to you in your life. No matter what situations come your way, there is always something that you can be thankful for and express to God in worship.

LORD, GIVE ME PATIENCE—RIGHT NOW!

A patient man has great understanding.

PROVERBS 14:29

Gladys and Rhonda walked along the sidewalk after church, heading toward home, thinking about meals planned for later that afternoon and casually discussing the morning service.

"That was a great sermon on patience," remarked Rhonda.

Gladys replied, "Yeah, but he went five minutes too long."

Have you ever felt this way about cultivating patience in your life? Most people probably have at one time or another. Our society races along at a frenetic pace, and responsibilities and obligations stack up, often creating frustration and impatience—especially when the light turns red just as you approach or the older lady in front of you in line at the bank has forgotten how to fill out her deposit slip. Perhaps you have recently prayed the infamous prayer: "Lord, give me patience—

GRACE FOR TODAY:

God has promised that the results of patience will be well worth the struggle to achieve it.

right now!" But patience isn't developed in our lives overnight. We can only acquire it through circumstances that test it—and many times these circumstances are unpleasant, to say the least! Even those we love—children, spouses, coworkers, bosses, friends, neighbors, fellow church members—often try our patience, and we wonder how long it will be before God is convinced we've learned our lesson.

Fortunately, God has promised that the results of patience are well worth the struggle to achieve it: "A patient man [or woman] has great understanding" (Proverbs 14:29). Do you need more understanding? Then you probably need more patience. Ask God to give it to you. He will—in His perfect time.

SERVICE WITH A SMILE

Each one should use whatever gift he has received to serve others, faithfully administering God's grace in its various forms.

1 PETER 4:10

I n a diary entry made just before her seventeenth birthday, Florence Nightingale
wrote, "God spoke to me and called me to His service." She had no idea what that
service would be but accepted the call and waited for God to give her further instructions. Seven years later, she felt compelled to serve in the London hospitals nursing the
sick.

Unfortunately, in her day nursing was considered one of the lowest jobs a person
could have. Most nurses were disabled army veterans with no formal training.
Hospital conditions were so appalling that most patients did better when they were not
in them. However, Florence was determined to serve God in nursing and committed
herself to improving medical conditions in London. Her innovations, including a system of call bells and dumb-waiters to help nurses avoid exhaustion, laid the foundation
of the modern hospitals of our time.

Florence trusted God enough to answer His call and serve Him, and this single
act of obedience saved the lives of hundreds of people. In the same way, when you
commit to serving God and helping others, He will use your abilities to glorify His
name—and bless you with His grace in the process.

No matter what talents or skills you possess, offer them to God and ask Him to
show you ways to serve. Look for opportunities to serve in church as an usher, teacher,
or mentor to someone. Be the first to offer a helping hand when you notice a friend in
need. Though it may not seem like much, your simple willingness to serve will
demonstrate God's grace to others and bring them into His kingdom.

GRACE FOR TODAY:

God will use your abilities to glorify His name—and
bless you with His grace in the process.

CAN YOU LOVE ENOUGH?

God hath not given us the spirit of fear; but of power,
and of love, and of a sound mind.

2 TIMOTHY 1:7 KJV

There was once a young mom who took her daughter to the local zoo. As she stopped at a concession stand to get some snacks, her little girl wandered off. After spending frantic minutes searching for her, she saw that her little girl had squeezed through the barricades to get a closer look at the bears. Without hesitating to look around or call for help, the young, 120-pound mother ran past the barricades and snatched her daughter out of harm's way. We've all seen it before. A mother's love is a powerful force.

God's love is also powerful—so powerful, in fact, that it caused God to send His only begotten Son to give His life for our sins. So powerful that God fought to redeem us—His tarnished creation—even before we were aware of our condition. So powerful that it has flamed hot throughout the ages and will burn just as brightly for all of eternity. So powerful that it pursues us without hesitation, ready to snatch us out of harm's way.

When you've been loved like that, you never forget. It transforms you from the inside out. It causes you to do things you would never have considered doing before. It inspires you to give your all for others without question, without hesitation.

Are you looking for that kind of powerful love? All you have to do is ask for it, and it's yours. His name is Jesus, and He's been waiting for you all your life.

GRACE FOR TODAY:

God's love is so powerful that it transcends space and
time and meets us right at the point of our need.

THE TALE OF THE TOWER CLOCK

There is an old tale of a village that bought a fancy tower clock. Some time after it was installed, a visitor to the town discovered that all the people were sleeping during the day and working at night. When he questioned them about this behavior, they answered, "We have the most unique town in America. After we got our new clock, we began to notice that the sun kept rising earlier and earlier every morning. Finally the daytime hours were dark, and the night hours were light. We are petitioning the President for special recognition as the only town in America with such a situation!"

As it turned out, of course, the new clock had been running slower and slower—because sparrows were roosting inside of it. The people had allowed themselves to be controlled by this man-made device.

The tyranny of the clock can rob us of our enjoyment of life. Daily hassles can so easily become the norm—"Hurry up, or we'll be late!" "I've only got five minutes to get to my meeting!" Such pressures are normal, but when they begin to take over your life, it's time to slow down.

In the midst of the busyness of life, hear Jesus' words to you: "Come with me by yourselves to a quiet place and get some rest." The yoke of Jesus is easy, and His burden is light. So take a little break: Take your eye off the clock and unload your worries on Jesus. "Leave all your worries with him, because he cares for you" (1 Peter 5:7 GNB).

> GRACE FOR TODAY:
>
> **In the midst of our busy lives, God beckons us to come and rest.**

[Jesus said to His disciples,] "Come with me by yourselves to a quiet place and get some rest."

MARK 6:31

WHAT IS GRACE?

By Warren W. Wiersbe

What is grace? It is God's provision for our every need when we need it. It has well been said that God in His grace gives us what we do not deserve, and in His mercy He does not give us what we do deserve. Someone has made an acrostic of the word grace: God's Riches Available at Christ's Expense. "And of His [Christ's] fullness have all we received, and grace for grace" (John 1:16 NKJV).

There is never a shortage of grace. God is sufficient for our spiritual ministries (2 Corinthians 3:4–6) and our material needs (9:8) as well as our physical needs (12:9). If God's grace is sufficient to save us, surely it is sufficient to keep us and strengthen us in our times of suffering.

In the Christian life, we get many of our blessings through transformation, not substitution. When Paul prayed three times for the removal of His pain, he was asking God for a substitution: "Give me health instead of sickness, deliverance instead of pain and weakness."

Sometimes God does meet the need by substitution; but other times He meets the need by transformation. He does not remove the affliction, but He gives us His grace so that the affliction works for us and not against us.

Paul claimed God's promise and drew upon the grace that was offered to him, which turned seeming tragedy into triumph. God did not change the situation by removing the affliction; He changed it by adding a new ingredient: grace. Our God is "the God of all grace" (1 Peter 5:10), and His throne is a "throne of grace" (Hebrews 4:16). The Word of God is "the word of His grace" (Acts 20:32), and the promise is that "He giveth more grace" (James 4:6). No matter how we look at it, God is adequate for every need that we have.[23]

—∽—

PRECIOUS FATHER, TRANSFORM ME BY YOUR GRACE THAT I MIGHT WORSHIP YOU MORE FULLY. AMEN.

When I am weak, then I am strong.

2 CORINTHIANS 12:10

CURSING THE RAIN

We rejoice in our sufferings,
knowing that suffering produces endurance.

ROMANS 5:3 RSV

When you were a child, did you ever sit at the window on a rainy day reciting the old rhyme, "Rain, rain, go away. Come again another day"? In our blessed and privileged lives, we often wish away the rain, while across the world many are desperate for a simple downpour as they agonize under the sun. We, too, should bless the rain.

GRACE FOR TODAY:

God turns our rainy days into showers of blessing.

And there are other reasons we should be more appreciative of rainy days. The next time you go for a walk on a warm summer day or go for a hike through a forest, behold God's creation. Take notice of the beautiful blossoming flowers in spring, the golden oranges and reds of autumn, and the bounty of fruit in its season. Take note of the carefree wildlife that enjoys all God has provided for them. None of this grandeur would be possible without those gloomy, rainy days. And where would we be without the rainbow. Rain is one of God's most precious gifts.

The same is true of rainy days in our hearts. They are often necessary in order to produce the lush greenery of spiritual growth or the colorful splendor of good character. Without the rainy days, we would agonize in the bright sun of our own self-centered pursuits. The rain that falls in our souls so often amounts to showers of blessing.

Have you been cursing the rain? Maybe it's time for you to take another look. It's possible that you have been missing one of God's most remarkable gifts.

THIS I KNOW

We ourselves know and believe the love which God has for us.

1 JOHN 4:16 GNB

An infant knows she is loved when she feels her mother's tender embrace, sees her father's adoring eyes, and hears their soothing, nonsensical words. A toddler knows he is loved when one of his parents gets on the floor with him and rolls a ball back and forth. A five-year-old knows she is loved when her mother buys her pretty barrettes for her hair. A ten-year-old knows he is loved when his father takes time to help him fix his bicycle. And deep down, a teenager knows she is loved when her parents set limits on her comings and goings, and discipline her when she exceeds them.

When such tangible expressions of affection are offered each day, a child will hear real meaning at night when Mom and Dad whisper, "I love you."

God shows love to His children in a myriad of ways. Each day He causes the sun to rise, giving us light and heat and, through the food chain, life-giving energy. Every day the Lord, who made the earth and everything in it, sustains His creation, keeping every atom in place according to His will. God sustains us as well, keeping our molecules intact and providing us with all the necessities of life. He comforts us with His presence, inspires us with His promises, guides us by His Spirit, and showers us with blessing after blessing to satisfy our needs and desires.

Long ago God allowed His Son to die on the cross so His children could live. Afterward, in John 3:16, God whispered to the whole world, "I love you."

From a young age many of us have sung, "Jesus loves me, this I know, for the Bible tells me so." Children know that words by themselves are meaningless, while words fused with actions mean everything.

> **GRACE FOR TODAY:**
> God's actions prove His words of love.

FLY FISHING WITH GOD

Take your everyday, ordinary life—your sleeping, eating, going-to-work,
and walking-around life—and place it before God as an offering.

ROMANS 12:1 MSG

The first paragraph of Norman Maclean's book, *A River Runs through It*, begins
with this interesting description:

"In our family, there was no clear line between religion and fly fishing. We lived
at the junction of great trout rivers in western Montana, and our father was a
Presbyterian minister and a fly fisherman who tied his own flies and taught others. He
told us about Christ's disciples being fishermen, and we were left to assume, as my
brother and I did, that all first-class fishermen on the Sea of Galilee were fly fishermen and that John, the favorite, was a dry-fly fisherman."

The most interesting sentence in this paragraph is the first one: "There was no
clear line between religion and fly fishing." There shouldn't be a clear line between our
spirituality and our "fly fishing"—or anything else in our lives. God wants to be a part
of every area of our world, and when we discover how He can and will have His hand
in every part of our daily existence, we experience the blessings He brings—and the
joy of His continual presence.

As Paul instructed: Give your "everyday, ordinary life"—even your fly fishing—
to Him today!

GRACE FOR TODAY:

God desires to be part of every area of our lives.

Good News

God has raised this Jesus to life, and we are all witnesses of the fact.

Acts 2:32

W hat is the Good News of the Gospel? It is the news that is exclusive to the Christian faith. It is the news that our Savior lives. The grave could not hold Him captive. He conquered death—His own and ours as well. The Good News of the Gospel is the good news of eternal life through Jesus Christ.

God's Word commands us to spread the Good News far and wide, to every corner of the earth. We are not to rest until every person has heard and had an opportunity to respond.

Big job. Big responsibility. Big problem. It's an assignment that's simply too big for us. So how does God expect us to do it? He expects us to remember the miracle of multiplication. He expects us to remember that He fed more than five thousand people with a boy's small lunch. He expects us to soak our efforts in prayer and follow His instructions to the letter and look to Him to make it more than enough. That's exactly what the disciples did that day on a Galilean mountainside, and God did the rest.

Have you done your part to spread the Good News of the Gospel? Have you shared your faith with a friend, a neighbor, even a stranger who crosses your path? Did you ask God to use your testimony to transform a heart?

God calls His Good News assignment the Great Commission. It is great, and we are small; but we can all do the part He has given us. Spread the news in your world. Do it today.

GRACE FOR TODAY:

God takes our small efforts to spread the Good News and makes them great.

GIVING THANKS

Even if life has become as tough as it can possibly be, if you are still breathing and your heart is still beating, there is a reason to praise God. No matter what was stolen from you—health, possessions, family, or friends—it was not enough to stop you from living. You are still here, alive. From here, you can go anywhere with God. There are no limits to the greatness you can bring into this world, no matter what state you find yourself in right now. But in order to enter into His presence, something has to happen that would seem to be totally out of harmony with tough times. You have to be thankful.

Have you ever wondered how you can be thankful when it seems like the world is caving in on you? The secret is faith. To have faith means that you completely trust in the word of someone who is faithful. Faith in God means that you believe the promises of the Bible—His Word.

Even if you are still hurting, you can be thankful for God's promises to bring peace and comfort. Even if you are still sick, you can be thankful for a God who heals. Even if you are suffering lack, you can be thankful for a God who provides. The answer to everything you face in life can be declared with thanksgiving when you pray.

> ### GRACE FOR TODAY:
>
> ## God stands behind the great and glorious promises in His Word.

Enter his gates with thanksgiving, and his courts with praise. Give thanks to him, bless his name.

PSALM 100:4 NRSV

LESSONS FROM GOD'S "NO" ANSWER

By Evelyn Christenson

In 2 Corinthians, Paul explained that the Lord told him how a "no" answer would be turned into gain. God was teaching Paul two of life's greatest lessons.

The first lesson Jesus taught Paul was, "My grace is sufficient for you" (See 2 Corinthians 12:9). As long as he had this infirmity (evidently up to the time of his death), there would be grace enough to cover all the difficulties brought on by it. How Paul would need that lesson, not only in his infirmity, but also in the trials, imprisonments, ship- wrecks, and eventual martyrdom that were to come!

Then in His answer, the Lord taught Paul a second powerful lesson. "My strength is made perfect in weakness" (v. 9). (Paul repeated this thought in verse 10 by concluding with, "for when I am weak, then am I strong.") It is not phys- ical strength that counts, but the power of Christ, which pitches its tent over our bodies when we are weak. What was Paul's (or my) maximum strength com- pared with Christ's omnipotence? In comparison to Christ's infinite, limitless power, all the strength we could ever muster, rolled into one gigantic push, would pale like a firefly competing with a nuclear explosion. What did Paul gain when the Lord said "no" to his being at his best physically? What do I gain? The strength of the omnipotent Christ![24]

—ɷ—

MIGHTY FATHER: YOU ARE ALWAYS WATCHING OUT FOR ME, LOOKING AFTER MY BEST INTEREST. WHEN YOU SAY "NO," GIVE ME YOUR STRENGTH TO SURRENDER MY WILL TO YOURS. AMEN.

I will boast all the more gladly about my weaknesses, so that Christ's power may rest on me.

2 CORINTHIANS 12:9

THE APEX OF GRACE

God can always point to us as examples of the incredible wealth
of his favor and kindness toward us, as shown in all he has done for us
through Christ Jesus.

EPHESIANS 2:7 NLT

Jesus Christ is the pinnacle of God's grace. What more could God offer us than His only begotten Son? Jesus' death on the cross was an unimaginable sacrifice for God; however, God lovingly made that sacrifice knowing that it would result in incredible benefits for us. In considering the wonder and magnitude of God's goodness toward us, we must remember that the entirety of His grace is wrapped up in the person of His Son, and it is through Jesus that God's blessings flow to us every day.

GRACE FOR TODAY:

Jesus Christ is the pinnacle of God's grace.

Think of the advantages God affords us through Christ! As the Way, the Truth, and the Life, Jesus reveals the path to godliness and Heaven, shows us ultimate reality, and blesses us with life abundant and everlasting. As the Lamb of God, Jesus pays the price for our sins and gives us His righteousness, so we can withstand God's holy judgment. As our Redeemer, Jesus lifts us from our fallen state and restores us to God's favor. As our solid Rock, Jesus provides our lives with a sure foundation. As our Savior, Jesus delivers us from Satan's grasp. As our Great High Priest, Jesus offers us access to the Father and intercedes on our behalf. As our Teacher, Jesus imparts to us wisdom and knowledge; as our humble Servant, He gives us an example to follow. As our Great Shepherd, Jesus guides and protects us. As God's Son, Jesus makes it possible for us to be adopted into God's family. As the King of Kings, Jesus shares with us His supremacy over the devil, His authority in Heaven, and all His treasures in paradise.

Jesus Christ is our bright Morning Star, our hope of glory. He is the Alpha and the Omega, the Beginning and the End of God's awesome grace.

SWIMMING UPSTREAM

Against all hope, Abraham in hope believed . . . being fully persuaded
that God had power to do what he had promised.

ROMANS 4:18,21

L ife can sometimes seem like a constant barrage of challenges and obstacles. No
sooner do you get past one hurdle then another one pops up to take its place. Yet
challenges can often be blessings in disguise—tools to help you refocus your goals and
pursue new options.

Abraham Lincoln, our sixteenth president, was faced with numerous challenges
that forced him to reconsider his goals. When his first two attempts at becoming a
storeowner ended in failure and left him deeply in debt,
he went into law and eventually opened a successful
practice. When his first attempt at becoming an Illinois
legislator failed, he tried again two years later and won
the job. When he was defeated for nomination for
Congress, he ran again three years later and was elected. When he subsequently failed to gain an appointment
as a senator, he ran for President—and won on two
separate occasions.

Lincoln's triumph over these obstacles did not
come as a result of his overwhelming confidence in his
abilities. He once stated, "Seriously, I do not think I'm
fit for the presidency." But he never let failure derail his progress. When one door
closed, he simply chalked it up to experience and tried another. "I am a slow walker,"
he once said, "but I never walk backwards."

Don't be discouraged when challenges come your way. Take them to God in
prayer and ask Him how you should proceed. He may be calling you to a different
course of action, or He may just want you to persevere. In either event, you can be
assured that during these times He will comfort you with His grace and help you to
understand His will for your life.

> **GRACE FOR TODAY:**
>
> God is always
> waiting to help
> us overcome
> the obstacles in
> our lives.

A CHORD OF THREE STRANDS

In Christ we who are many form one body,
and each member belongs to all the others.

ROMANS 12:5

A man discovered that his boat had become stuck in the soft muddy banks of the lake in which it was moored. Grabbing an old coil of rope, he tied one end to the boat and tried to pull it out, but the rope was too weak and snapped in two. He tried a newer coil of rope, but this also broke. Frustrated, he grabbed a sturdy piece of nylon rope, but this also snapped at the first tug. Finally, the man wound the three pieces of rope together and secured them to the boat. This time, the combined strength of the rope was able to support the weight of the craft, and the boat was freed.

As the author in Ecclesiastes 4:12 NASB notes, "A cord of three strands is not quickly torn apart." When you unite with your fellow Christians to pursue a common goal, you accomplish much more than you ever could on your own. When you join together to serve, you send a powerful message to the world about the incredible grace of God. When you refuse to let differences break apart your relationships, you reveal a strength of character that others will want to model.

Division brings only weakness to the body of Christ and robs you of the joy God wants you to experience. Petty arguments and disagreements damage your relationships with others and hinder the work Christ wants to do in your life. Forgiveness and understanding, however, strengthen your relationships with others and allow you to extend the grace of God into their lives, so that you can truly stand together, united as one.

GRACE FOR TODAY:

The Father, Son, and Holy Spirit live in vital union with one another. We have been called to do the same.

A GOOD FIGHT?

Fight the good fight of faith, lay hold on eternal life, whereunto thou art also called, and hast professed a good profession before many witnesses.

1 TIMOTHY 6:12 KJV

It was the third round, and Jason was giving his all, trying desperately to get the upper hand in the championship boxing match. He was throwing one punch after another, but his opponent seemed unfazed, coming after him with a vengeance. Then it was over. Jason was down, and his opponent had won the match.

Life seems a lot like a boxing match sometimes, doesn't it? You're working hard, throwing punches, but they don't seem to connect. You try hard to raise your children, but they seem to consistently be making poor choices. You give 100 percent at work, but you seem to be overlooked when it comes to promotions. It would be easy to lie there on the mat and decide you're just a loser, down for the count, out of the contest.

But God has a different plan for your life. He has declared you a winner, a champion! The Bible says that even when it seems like you're losing, you're really winning. You see, God adds faith to your fight. He promises that if you raise your children in the ways of God, one day they will see the light (Proverbs 22:6). He promises that if you do your best at your job, you will be rewarded (Proverbs 10:4).

The key is to keep your eyes on Him, to remember that He is fighting each battle alongside you. He has all the courage and strength and endurance you need to live your life as a winner.

GRACE FOR TODAY:

God fights alongside us to ensure that we win the good fight of faith.

PUTTING OTHERS FIRST

The Make-a-Wish Foundation has been granting the wishes of children with life-threatening illnesses since 1980. Most commonly, children wish to meet a celebrity, shake the hand of the president, or go to Disney World.

But Mak Shulist, a critically ill nine-year-old boy, wished instead to enrich the lives of others. Before a brain tumor took Mak's life on April 9, 2004, he requested that the Make-a-Wish Foundation build something for his friends: a rock-climbing wall on the playground of Ellisville Elementary School.

Mak himself never got the chance to climb the wall, but he did get to see it constructed and see how much his friends enjoyed playing on it. Dave Knes, the principal at Mak's school,

GRACE FOR TODAY:

Jesus has given us His life as a selfless example of true giving.

summed up what everyone in the town agreed upon: "We learned a lesson from a nine-year-old—that even when we're going through tough times we should be thinking of other people and not ourselves."

Certainly, if anyone had a reason to be selfish and to request something that he wanted for himself, it would have been Mak. But instead, he followed the selfless example of Jesus—who gave His very life for others—and in turn has become an example for us all.

How selfless have you been lately? Let Mak—and Jesus—inspire you to be a blessing to other people and experience the joy that comes from putting others before yourself.

Since you excel in so many ways . . . now I want you to excel also in this gracious ministry of giving.

2 CORINTHIANS 8:7 NLT

REMOVED HINDRANCES

By Evelyn Christenson

I'm fascinated by street sweepers—those massive lumbering machines which loosen and vacuum up debris on the roads. Knowing the magnitude of the task to which the Lord called Paul on the Damascus Road, doesn't it seem logical that He would have sent His supernatural "street cleaner" to dislodge and remove all the hindrances in Paul's pathway? He could have swept the path clean before sending Paul onto it, or at least vacuumed the obstacles as they confronted Paul. But the New Testament tells us that God did neither. We see rather that they were left there—deliberately.

The whole list, which Paul adds to the "infirmities," was left in his path intentionally so that he could learn and grow from them. Left so that the power would be Christ's omnipotence and not Paul's puny human strength. From man's point of view they were losses, but in God's hands they were turned into gigantic gains.

Which one of us at some time in life has not wished for, even longed for, a life like Paul's? Full of adventure, fruit, rewards! Changing the world in which he lived! Then influencing people all over Planet Earth! Could the secret be that Paul learned and accepted God's "gaining through losing" principle? God's "so that's"?

What did Paul lose? Being delivered from infirmities, reproaches, necessities, persecutions, distresses. What did he gain? Christ's grace and power and strength—resting on Him![25]

—∞—

HEAVENLY FATHER: MY TRIALS SEEM OVERWHELMING RIGHT NOW. I NEED YOUR HELP, YOUR STRENGTH, YOUR GRACE TO TURN THEM INTO GAINS FOR MY LIFE AND FOR YOUR KINGDOM. AMEN.

Who shall separate us from the love of Christ? Shall trouble or hardship or persecution or famine or nakedness or danger or sword? . . . In all these things we are more than conquerors through him who loved us.

ROMANS 8:35,37

WHAT'S THE PLAN?

"I know the plans I have for you," declares the Lord, "plans to prosper
you and not to harm you, plans to give you hope and a future."

JEREMIAH 29:11

I n Lewis Carroll's story, *Alice in Wonderland*, the main character finds herself at a fork in the road with no clear idea of how to proceed. Noticing a large Cheshire cat in a nearby tree, she turns and asks him if he knows which way she should go from that point.

"That depends a good deal on where you want to get to," he replies.

"I don't much care where—" she says.

"Then it doesn't matter which way you go," he responds.

Perhaps you can relate to poor Alice. With more possibilities for places to go and potential directions to take, it can be difficult to narrow down one specific path. In fact, research indicates that 50 percent of today's college students change their major up to three times during the course of their studies, while U.S. Department of Labor studies show that the average adult changes careers three to four times during their lifetime.

Not knowing what direction to take in life can be frustrating, but it is important to remember that God always knows what you should be doing. He has a plan for your life and understands which path will bring you fulfillment. He extends His grace to you day by day as He gradually unfolds the incredible plans He has in store.

Remember that God always has your best interests at heart. When you submit to His will and allow Him to choose the course, He will open doors and place a calling upon your life. He will give you discernment and wisdom to know which way to go and take you to heights that you've never dreamed were possible to attain.

> GRACE FOR TODAY:
>
> "[God] who gives the day will show the way, so I securely go."
>
> JOHN OXENHAM

To the Victor Goes the Crown

I press on toward the goal for the prize of the heavenly call
of God in Christ Jesus.

PHILIPPIANS 3:14 NRSV

In the days of ancient Rome, generals fought valiant battles against their foes knowing that if they successfully defeated their enemies, they would be rewarded with a
special victory celebration upon their return. These celebrations, known as "tri-
umphs," consisted of elaborate parades through the
streets of Rome in order to honor the general's heroic
deeds.

> **GRACE FOR TODAY:**
>
> We must keep our eyes on Jesus and press on toward our heavenly prize—eternal life. Jesus will give us the victory!

As the general rode upon a chariot drawn by two
white horses and waved to the cheering crowd, a servant behind him would hold up a laurel crown over his
head to indicate his victories over the enemies of Rome.
In some instances, a special monument would be built
to better celebrate the triumph and mark its significance
for generations to follow.

You fight a different sort of battle in your Christian
life—a more important type of struggle against those
things in this world opposed to the love of God. Like
the Roman generals, you fight knowing that you will be
rewarded for victory, but the rewards you will receive
for fighting the good fight are of a spiritual nature and will never fade away. For even
the impressive monuments constructed to honor the great Roman generals have since
fallen into ruin and disrepair, but God's reward of eternal life to those who serve Him
is forever.

Sometimes, the struggles in life can get you down and leave you feeling defeated.
When such moments occur, focus on the grace of God and remember that He has
already given you the ultimate victory in life. All you have to do is continue to serve
Him and keep your eyes on the "prize."

JUMP IN WITH BOTH FEET

**Without wavering, let us hold tightly to the hope we say we have,
for God can be trusted to keep his promise.**

HEBREWS 10:23 NLT

Have you prayed for something—something important to you—but the answer hasn't come? There you are waiting . . . and waiting . . . and waiting, but nothing changes. Maybe you were pretty enthusiastic at the start, thinking God would surely answer your prayer with a resounding "yes." But still life goes on as if you had never prayed at all. You haven't even received an insight or heard His still, small voice speaking inside your heart assuring you that help is on the way. Now you feel your confidence slipping away, your faith wavering.

It's a difficult thing, and we all go through it. The important thing is to hang on. The answer will come—maybe not in the way you expect, maybe not from the source you expect, maybe not in the time you expect. But it will come!

We serve a reasonable God. He has a reason for everything He does. Perhaps He wants to stretch your faith—see how much you trust Him. Or He's out to test your commitment to the thing you're praying for. Maybe there are other considerations that you don't know about. It could be any or all of these things—or something completely different.

Whatever His reason, you can rest easy knowing that He knows best, He sees all. He won't let you down. His promises are certain, His ways entirely sovereign. Keep trusting. As surely as the sun rises in the morning and sets again at night, the answer will come.

GRACE FOR TODAY:

God answers our prayers in His own time, in His own way, and always for our good.

THE WEIGHT OF THE WORLD

"When the earth and all its people quake, it is I who hold its pillars firm," [declares the Lord.]

PSALM 75:3

I n today's society, with twenty-four-hour news channels and the Internet constantly reporting on global events, you soon begin to feel the weight of the world on your shoulders. The temptation is to think you should bear it—that is, keep abreast of every development, investigate every issue, worry about what's happening everywhere around the planet. With all the resources and technology available in the twenty-first century, you might figure it's reasonable to try to carry the world like Atlas.

However, in Greek mythology Atlas was a Titan, a massive giant. On his huge, muscular shoulders the earth appears manageable; and standing under that burden, he seems rather heroic. An inspiring image, perhaps, but it might be good to put things in proper perspective.

From our point of view, the surface of the world is pretty bumpy. Mount Everest is nearly thirty thousand feet high, while the Grand Canyon is over a mile deep. Standing next to either landmark will make you feel quite small. But the earth is so large that despite its most impressive features, relatively speaking, it's as smooth as a marble. Now can you picture yourself beneath it?

The Maker of the universe, who pinched the earth a bit to mold Mount Everest and lightly scratched it to form the Grand Canyon, holds this planet in the palm of His hand. God is big enough to see the whole picture as His plan for humanity unfolds, yet He is also aware of the smallest details of each person's life. He graciously commands His children not to worry about global events but rather to pray about them, and in so doing He lifts the weight of the world from their shoulders, freeing them to worship Him and focus on fulfilling the unique, individual purposes for which He created them.

GRACE FOR TODAY:

God alone can bear the weight of the world, and He graciously lifts it from our shoulders.

A WORD TO LIFT YOU UP

A famous author tells a story of the discouragement he encountered when he began writing his first novel. After typing three pages of his first draft, he discovered that he didn't like his lead character, the story wasn't moving him emotionally, and he couldn't connect with the subject matter he had chosen. So he crumpled up the pages in disgust and threw them into the wastebasket.

When he came home the next night, he found that his wife had taken the pages out of the trash and read them. She wanted to know the rest of the story and wondered why he had stopped writing. When he rattled off his above concerns, she simply smiled and said that she would help him with it. "You've got something here," she said. "You really do." The story went on to become the author's first best-selling novel.

Sometimes, all you need to get through a troublesome patch in your life is a little encouragement from a friend. It is amazing how a kind word can change your whole perspective on a situation and motivate you to keep moving ahead. When you turn to God and ask Him to provide you with His grace, He will put people in your life to lift your spirits and help you persevere.

In the same way, when your friends struggle with problems, reach out and encourage them. Let them know you care about them and can relate to what they are going through. Although it may not seem like much, you never know what an incredible gift of grace your few simple words could mean to them.

> **GRACE FOR TODAY:**
>
> God encourages through others and then asks us to let Him encourage others through us.

May our Lord Jesus Christ . . . encourage your hearts and strengthen you in every good deed and word.

2 THESSALONIANS 2:16-17

DISCIPLINED BY GRACE

By Gene Getz

Shortly after I graduated from Moody Bible Institute in Chicago, I moved to Billings, Montana, where I continued my college work and was involved in a Christian radio ministry. I traveled from Chicago to Billings on the Northern Pacific Railroad, a twenty-four-hour trip. I remember getting on the train in Chicago with a book that someone gave me, titled *Disciplined by Grace* by J. F. Strombeck (no longer in print, but it should be). With plenty of time to read, I completed the book by the time I arrived in Billings.

Actually, the book was a careful study of Titus 2:11–12. For a person who had been reared in a legalistic religious system and "disciplined by rules," the message of that book set me free—not to do what I wanted to do, but to live a holy and righteous life because of what God had done for me. It is because of His mercy and grace that I presented my body and mind to Christ and determined to conform my life to His and not the world (Romans 12:1–2). And that has been my goal ever since. Though I have failed God many times, yet He has remained faithful.[26]

—⁓—

SWEET FATHER IN HEAVEN: THANK YOU FOR YOUR MERCY AND GRACE—ENOUGH TO COVER ALL MY FAILINGS AND ENABLE ME TO LIVE A HOLY AND RIGHTEOUS LIFE. YOU HAVE DONE FOR ME WHAT I COULD NOT DO FOR MYSELF. AND FOR THAT I AM SO GRATEFUL. AMEN.

The grace of God that brings salvation has appeared to all men. It teaches us to say "No" to ungodliness and worldly passions, and to live self-controlled, upright and godly lives in this present age.

TITUS 2:11–12

WHEN WISDOM IS NEEDED

If any of you is deficient in wisdom, let him ask of the giving God [Who gives] to everyone liberally and ungrudgingly, without reproaching or faultfinding, and it will be given him.

JAMES 1:5 AMP

We are created in the image of God; redeemed from our sins and brought into right-standing with the Creator of the universe. We have also been empowered by the Holy Spirit to accomplish the impossible. But there are days, and we all have had them, when our efforts just don't measure up.

It is at those times when even our noblest efforts fall short that we tend to feel the loneliest and most separated from God. But we are not. God is always right there, waiting for us to acknowledge that we need Him.

We all make mistakes. We all fall short of the mark. We all make a mess of things. Not always, but often. God knows that it's because we're human. When those times come, we must be willing to make a clean breast of things and start again. We will never be completely defeated as long as we are willing to admit our shortcomings and receive His forgiveness.

If you're feeling discouraged because your best-made plans have come crashing down around your ears, go to the One who knows and understand you. Tell Him you're sorry and ask Him to help you build again—this time on a foundation of wisdom and counsel, this time following His guidance and leadership.

> **GRACE FOR TODAY:**
>
> When we take our failures to God, He will forgive us and provide the wisdom we need to make our failure a success.

CIRCULAR LOGIC

Take delight in the Lord, and he will give you your heart's desires.

PSALM 37:4 NLT

God has promised that if you make Him your heart's desire, He'll give you your heart's desire. Logically, this promise goes round and round, but what a wonderful whirlwind to get caught up in!

You can chase after other desires your whole life long, and you may or may not obtain them. The hard truth of the matter is that even if you do, you'll lose them all eventually. Nothing on this earth lasts, including us. Pursuing worldly things instead of God will trap you in a different type of spiral, one that pulls you downward, more like a whirlpool.

You may be experiencing something between these two extremes. In seeking both God and the things of this world, perhaps you've wound up drifting aimlessly around in a lazy, lukewarm eddy, a light breeze riffling your hair. You may be wondering right now, *Where has all the thrill and excitement gone from my spiritual life, from my walk with the Lord?*

God wants us to relish Him, to revel in His goodness and grace, and His Spirit is grieved when we seek Him only halfheartedly, hoping not so much that He will reveal more of himself to us but that He will give us some material thing our hearts truly desire.

GRACE FOR TODAY:

God grants the heart's desire of everyone whose heart's desire is God.

Are you ready to get caught up in God's love? If so, like Elijah you'll have to leave this earth behind. God is always willing to give you himself, and if you truly delight yourself in Him, you can enjoy Him both now and forever. What's more, God will one day bring it all full circle by fulfilling His promise that if you seek Him first, He will give you the world.

CLEANSING RAIN

The Lord is close to the brokenhearted and saves those who
are crushed in spirit.

PSALM 34:18

Sometimes God's grace falls like rain; sometimes it trickles down like tears.

The Bible doesn't say when Adam and Eve first wept, but is there any doubt they did? At some point after sinning and being cast from the Garden of Eden, they who had walked with God through Paradise, never knowing a hint of sorrow, must have cried long and hard. After the Fall, tears became part of the human experience. But tears are not part of God's curse; they are a gift of grace to help us endure it. Tears are a cleansing, healing rain that enables men and women, who were created to live in a perfect world, to survive and persevere in a world that's broken.

Tears are similar to laughter, in that God uses them to minister to you physically, mentally, emotionally, and spiritually. They provide a sweet release, washing away heartache, soothing sorrow. After a good, healthy cry, you feel better, renewed. The source of your grief hasn't gone, but you are more ready to face it and carry on.

Ultimately, the source of your anguish is the same as Adam and Eve's. It's a yearning for the wholeness and perfection you were designed for—in your environment, in yourself, in your relationships with others, in your fellowship with God. So don't hold back your tears. When you must cry, fall into your heavenly Father's loving arms and pour out your sorrow, your frustration, your loneliness, your confusion. He is near, He understands, and He cares. In Heaven, your true home, the Lord will fill the void in your heart. He can do it, because He is the true object of your longing. There, God will wipe away your tears forevermore, because in Heaven, as once in Eden, there is no need to cry.

GRACE FOR TODAY:

Tears are not part of God's curse; they are a gift of
grace to help us endure it.

LIFE'S A BALANCING ACT

There is a time for everything, a season for every activity under heaven.

ECCLESIASTES 3:1 NLT

John peered anxiously over at the clock on the wall. It was thirty minutes past five o'clock, and he still had a stack of work on his desk to go through. Being a highly motivated individual with a strong desire to succeed, John was tempted to pick up the phone and tell his wife that he would be late. Instead, he put on his coat, turned off the light, and headed for home.

John had learned from experience the value of having balance in his life. He knew that when he focused all of his attention in one area, something else always suffered. When he worked late nights at the office, his family and home life suffered. When he spent too much time loafing around or watching television, his friendships often suffered. When he found himself so caught up in the day's events that he neglected his quiet time with God, his spiritual life suffered.

Balance was not something that John found easy to maintain. He routinely had to evaluate his life to see if any area was being neglected. He had to push himself to do things with his friends when all he felt like doing was staying home and taking a nap. He had to discipline himself to slow down enough so that he could spend some time each day in prayer.

As John shut his office door, he thanked God for all the ways He was helping him to set boundaries in his life, and for His grace in helping him to stay on track and maintain balance in his life.

GRACE FOR TODAY:

God gives us the wisdom we need to bring balance to every area of our lives.

CARDBOARD FIGURES

It took Noah more than a hundred years to build the ark; how long do you think it took him to become a decoration for a nursery?

How real to you are the people of the Bible? Think of young David standing before Goliath, Daniel in the lions' den, Samson straining against the pillars of the pagan temple. Consider all the heroes of faith listed in Hebrews 11. Do they seem like actual people to you, or do you tend to regard them as two-dimensional figures, cardboard characters from some Sunday school lesson long ago?

We are inclined to reduce people to the barest minimum—a physical characteristic; an identity with a certain nation, race, or culture; an accomplishment; a failure. We do it to the people who inhabit the pages of the Bible, to the ones who dwell in the pages of history, and to those who live in the world around us.

> ### GRACE FOR TODAY:
> ## God is intimately acquainted with us and our stories.

Praise God, He always regards each of us as real, flesh-and-blood people, eternal beings stamped with His image, people with thoughts, feelings, souls. Take a look at all the names in the Bible, all the long genealogies. God cares deeply about everyone represented there. Whether or not any details accompany an individual's name, the Lord is intimately acquainted with that person and with his or her story.

Your name may never be recorded in the history books, or you could become the stuff of legend. With one regrettable mistake you could become infamous across the globe—or merely within your family. Regardless, God will never see you as the rest of the world does. He knew you and loved you before time began (Ephesians 1:4–6); He knows you and loves you now. To God you are, and always will be, nothing less than a real person.

Man looks at the outward appearance, but the Lord looks at the heart.

1 SAMUEL 16:7 NKJV

"BUY A HOT DOG, MISTER?"

By John C. Maxwell

A man lived by the side of the road and sold hot dogs. He was hard of hearing, so he had no radio. He had trouble with his eyes, so he read no newspapers. But he sold good hot dogs.

This man put up signs on the highway advertising his wonderful hot dogs. He stood on the side of the road and cried, "Buy a hot dog, Mister?" And people bought his hot dogs. He increased his meat and bun orders, and he bought a bigger stove to take care of his trade. He made enough money to put his son through college.

Unfortunately, the son came home from college an educated pessimist. He said, "Father, haven't you been listening to the radio? Haven't you been reading the newspaper? There's a big recession on. The European situation is terrible, and the domestic situation is worse."

Whereupon the father thought, "Well, my son's been to college. He reads the paper, and he listens to the radio; he ought to know." So the father cut down his meat and bun orders, took down his signs, and no longer bothered to stand out on the highway to sell his hot dogs.

Of course, his sales fell overnight. "You're right, son," the father said to the boy. "We certainly are in the middle of a big recession."

Confidence shakers see the negative side of everything. When they get you to buy into it, the very thing that was helping you be successful becomes your downfall. Our confidence has a great reward. If we keep it and build on it, we will be more than recompensed. Confidence in oneself is the cornerstone to success.[27]

―― ⁂ ――

DEAR FATHER: FORGIVE ME FOR ALLOWING CONFIDENCE SHAKERS TO ROB ME OF MY ASSURANCE THAT I'M DOING WHAT YOU'VE CALLED ME TO DO. BY YOUR GRACE, RESTORE MY CONFIDENCE THAT I MIGHT BEGIN AGAIN. AMEN.

Do not throw away your confidence; it will be greatly rewarded.

HEBREWS 10:35

THE LIVING GOD

The eyes of the Lord are on the righteous and his ears
are attentive to their cry.

PSALM 34:15

Have you ever acquired some coveted possession, or accomplished some sought-after goal, and then tried to sustain yourself on the joy it brings? It's the oddest thing. You get a thrill as you sit in your new sports car for the first time, running your hands over the steering wheel and thinking, *This is great!* Soon the thrill is reduced to a tingle, and your thoughts to, *This is nice.* Before long you're climbing in and out of the car without thinking about it much at all. And eventually you're looking at next year's model and thinking, *Wouldn't that be great!*

This is an age-old phenomenon. Psalm 115 speaks of the false gods of the ancient world, pointing out that although these idols had intricately formed mouths, eyes, ears, noses, hands, and feet, they couldn't speak, see, hear, smell, feel, or walk. People were worshiping and praying to the lifeless work of their own hands! Now, we don't spend much time carving images in wood and stone anymore. Our handiwork consists of all our belongings and achievements. And the Bible makes it clear that the products of human hands are powerless to satisfy us. If we look to them to nourish our souls, they'll disappoint us every time.

> GRACE FOR TODAY:
>
> We serve a living God, who can and does relate to us personally.

We need so much more in this life than the work of our hands. We need God's presence, His touch. Unlike all other "gods," the Lord sees us and hears us. He is the living God, and He can relate to us personally. Whereas the false gods in your life will fail you, God will come through. He sees your needs, hears your prayers, rises from His throne, and extends His mighty hands to help you, guide you, protect you, and comfort you. True fulfillment is found in His vibrant, loving embrace.

ACTS OF GOD

Pure and lasting religion in the sight of God our Father means that
we must care for orphans and widows in their troubles,
and refuse to let the world corrupt us.

JAMES 1:27 NLT

Whenever a homeowner's insurance policy is filled out, one of the first things the policyholder wants to know is whether or not it will cover "acts of God." These include hurricanes, tornadoes, major storms, and even earthquakes—all those things that cannot be controlled by any person are attributed to God. In truth God created a perfect world. These natural disasters are the "natural" result of His creation blighted by sin.

So what is a true act of God? These acts were abundant in the life of Jesus. He gave healing, comfort and provision to those who could not feed themselves. He gave love to those who were lonely and freedom to those who were afflicted. Today, He desires that we as Christians continue His blessed work. He wants us to pour out the acts of God on this earth.

Your life can exemplify the "acts of God." Through your love toward your neighbor, you can bring new meaning and depth to this often misused term. You can bring the spiritual and natural provision so desperately needed by multitudes of people. You can put a smile on the face of a child, or joy in the heart of a senior. All you have to do is be prepared to be a blessing, and God will grant you everything you need in order to commit His acts.

> **GRACE FOR TODAY:**
>
> God's acts toward us are all acts of grace to meet our needs in a sin-blighted world.

A LIFE-OR-DEATH DECISION

See, I have set before you today life and prosperity,
and death and adversity.

DEUTERONOMY 30:15 NASB

P icture for a moment a machine throbbing away in a factory. It functions without thought or reason, simply repeating the task it was programmed to do. It is total-ly predictable and has no control over its own actions. Aren't you glad God didn't choose to create us that way?

Instead, He gave us life and freedom to live that life any way we choose, whether it be for Him or for ourselves. That's a big responsibility—one He gave to no other part of His creation. It is, in fact, one of the ways that we reflect His image in us. We are free moral agents. That's the way God wanted it. The rest of His creation obeys Him without thought, without reason, quite like the machine that has no control over its actions. We are different. He has given us the right to choose Him just as He has chosen us.

What will you do with the freedom God's given you? Will you use it to make choices that glorify God and bring joy and peace to your life and the lives of those around you? Will you use it to surrender yourself to your Creator? Will you use it to give your love to the One who loved you first and best?

He's given you the right to walk away, but remember God is the One who gave you life. Walking away means putting yourself on the path to death. That's no small thing. Only you can decide.

GRACE FOR TODAY:

God has given us the right to choose life over death.

A FOUNDATION FOR FAITH—THE CHURCH

We are surrounded by such a great cloud of witnesses.

HEBREWS 12:1

Consider all the heroes of the Bible mentioned in Hebrews 11, the "Faith Hall of Fame," as well as the numerous godly people described in the Scriptures but not included in this list. Contemplate all the great Christian writers and thinkers from two thousand years of church history, whose works have endured to encourage and inspire us today. Think about the many leaders of the faith now living whose pastoral, publishing, radio, television, and Internet ministries help us keep our minds and hearts focused on God and bolster our faith in Him. Finally, to this impressive gathering add one more group, the biggest of all: the countless unnamed believers who have walked this earth since its creation, each of whom could offer compelling personal testimony to the existence and grace of God. Are you starting to get a picture of the vast, diverse multitude described in Revelation 7:9?

This adoring throng will not appear out of thin air at some future point in time. The Lord has been amassing this huge crowd of worshipers since the dawn of history, from every corner of the world. It is His universal church, and it stands today in Heaven and on earth, as it exists at this very moment, as both a silent and a not-so-silent witness, shoring up our confidence that God is real.

You are not alone on this journey called faith! Every time you read the Bible or a piece of classic Christian literature, every time you hear a dear old hymn from the choir or a contemporary song of worship on the radio, every time you hear a member of your congregation give a moving testimony about the love of Christ, consider it a gift of grace from your heavenly Father, a blessing to strengthen your faith.

GRACE FOR TODAY:

God offers us evidence each day, through the witness of His people, that He is real.

THROUGH YOU, HE LIVES AGAIN!

The motion picture *Gandhi*, seen and loved by millions of people, starred the actor Ben Kingsley as the central character of Gandhi, the man. Rarely has an actor made so impressive a film debut as Kingsley did in this motion picture. Kingsley spent months preparing for the role, visiting many places in India that Gandhi had frequented. He even learned to spin cotton thread on a wooden wheel, as Gandhi had done while holding long, spiritual conversations with the people of India.

The physical resemblance between Gandhi and Kingsley proved startling. After filming a scene in a village south of Delhi, Kingsley stepped out of his car, and an elderly peasant knelt to touch his feet. Embarrassed, Kingsley explained that he was merely an actor playing Gandhi. "We know," replied the villager. "But through you he will surely live again!"

Gandhi was not able to "live again" through the movie that bore his name. However, Jesus Christ actually physically rose from the dead and today lives within each of His followers who are called by His name. Christians are commanded to "be" the hands and feet of Jesus in the world around them. Through His faithful followers who do His will, Christ can "live again" on the earth—not only in the hearts of those who love Him, but in their actions and decisions as well.

> GRACE FOR TODAY:
>
> Through those who love and follow Him, Christ "lives again" in the world.

This is how we know we are in him: Whoever claims to live in him must walk as Jesus did.

1 JOHN 2:5-6

BEFORE IT'S TOO LATE!

By John C. Maxwell

Too often people wait too long to forgive other people. Forgiveness should be given as quickly and as totally as possible. Do it now. Don't be in the position of the young man who needs and wants his parents' forgiveness, but because they are physically unable to communicate, he cannot be sure that they understand him. Every day he goes to the hospital and asks, but he gets no response. Because of his procrastination he will never experience the joy of their forgiveness and reconciliation.

One of the most striking scenes of the last decade was Hubert Humphrey's funeral. Seated next to Hubert's beloved wife was former President Richard M. Nixon, a long-time political adversary of Humphrey, and a man disgraced by Watergate. Humphrey himself had asked Nixon to have that place of honor.

Three days before Senator Humphrey died, Jesse Jackson visited him in the hospital. Humphrey told Jackson that he had just called Nixon. The Reverend Jackson, knowing their past relationship, asked Humphrey why. Here is what Hubert Humphrey had to say: "From this vantage point, with the sun setting in my life, all of the speeches, the political conventions, the crowds, and the great fights are behind me. At a time like this you are forced to deal with your irreducible essence, forced to grapple with that which is really important. And what I have concluded about life is that when all is said and done, we must forgive each other, redeem each other, and move on."

Do you know how to die victoriously? Quit keeping score of the injustices that have happened to you. If you are at odds with anyone, take the first step; confront the problem and ask for forgiveness.[28]

—m—

HEAVENLY FATHER: I CHOOSE TO FORGIVE AND BE FORGIVEN. HELP ME AS I MOVE FORWARD ON THIS PATH TO FORGIVENESS. AMEN.

Be kind and compassionate to one another, forgiving each other, just as in Christ God forgave you.

EPHESIANS 4:32

A LIFETIME OF SECOND CHANCES

If we confess our sins to God, he can always be trusted to forgive us and take our sins away.

1 JOHN 1:9 CEV

I f the parable of the prodigal son reflected the long–term relationship of most of us with God, it would continue with the wayward son slipping out the back door of his father's house soon after the feast, his stomach full, on his way to check out what-ever else the world might have to offer. And if this story accurately portrayed God's boundless grace, it would tell of the father once again taking up his longing vigil.

Surely Jesus chose the best way to describe God by comparing Him to a loving, merciful father. In what relationship in life, other than that of a parent and child, is a person given so many second chances? Children rebel and disobey, and their parents, while doing their best to discipline them, forgive and forgive. The cycle starts in the toddler years and extends through adoles-cence right up to adulthood, nearly twenty years. Who but a father or mother would put up with so many willful infractions for such a long time? Surely not a coach or employer.

> **GRACE FOR TODAY:**
>
> God will love us wherever we roam, and He'll always be waiting for us to come home.

If you are a parent, you have a special insight into God's heart. You know something of the depth of such love that would wait for the return of a wandering child. Deep down, a father will love his son even if his son winds up on the streets. A mother will love her baby even if her baby ends up in jail. They will do whatever is in the best interest of their child, perhaps allowing him to suffer the consequences of his actions for a time. But they will never cease loving. Likewise, God will love you wherever you roam, waiting for you to come home, run-ning to you for the thousandth time at the first sign that you have turned back to Him.

CHERISH HIS LOVE

The Lord appeared to him from afar, saying, "I have loved you with an everlasting love; therefore I have drawn you with lovingkindness.

JEREMIAH 31:3 NASB

When two people are in love, their days are consumed with thoughts of each other. Their conversations are long and filled with affection. And no matter how much time they spend together, they always want more.

It could be that you once had such a relationship with God. You were excited about being with Him, telling Him all about your day, basking in the warmth of His presence. You spent much time in His Word, learning all you could about Him. But for one reason or another, your passion for God has diminished. Maybe the cares of this life got in the way of spending time with Him. Maybe He didn't answer your prayers in the way you thought He should. Maybe you've blamed Him for some tragedy in your life.

No matter what has come between you, God wants you to know that His love for you is still burning strong. He misses the way you used to talk to Him, the way you trusted Him. He misses being part of your life.

All it takes to rekindle those loving feelings you once had for God is for you to open your heart to Him again. A new conversation begins with just one word. Tell Him you're sorry for letting other things get in the way of your relationship. Tell Him you want to start over. Tell Him you still love Him. Don't worry; He'll hear you—He's never stopped listening.

> GRACE FOR TODAY:
>
> God loves us just as much now as He did the day we first met Him.

THE COMFORTER

I will pray the Father, and he shall give you another Comforter, that he may be with you for ever.

JOHN 14:16 ASV

There isn't any other way to say it—life is tough. It's easy to feel overwhelmed at times with the demands of family and work and just getting along in this world. That is exactly why God has graciously given us His Holy Spirit.

We tend to think of comfort as something we need when we are facing a tragedy or an illness, when we lose our jobs or have to deal with some serious financial need. We reserve our prayers for comfort for those times when we are really hurting and have no place to turn. Unfortunately, that means we shortchange ourselves.

God's Holy Spirit has been given to us for all the minutes and days and weeks of our lives. He is there to bring us comfort in the little things as well as in the big ordeals. He is God's gift of grace, the gift of His own Spirit to warm and console us in all the conditions of our lives. He is there for us when we struggle with the aches and pains of aging, and He's there for us when the family business goes belly up.

If you have been suffering in silence, understand today that God wants to help you with every detail of your life. Don't sweep the little things under the rug. Let Him strengthen and comfort you. His grace is sufficient for you—in every way.

GRACE FOR TODAY:

The Holy Spirit of Christ is a constant comfort to us through all the ups and downs of our lives.

THE FAMILY OF GOD

[Jesus replied,] "Whoever does the will of My Father in heaven is My
brother and sister and mother."

MATTHEW 12:50 NKJV

B illy was attending his first day in junior-high school. An opening assembly
introduced all the homeroom teachers. Miss Smith was introduced first. She
was an "easy" teacher, so the kids cheered. Mr. Brown also met with thundering
approval. But Mr. Johnson was known to be a very strict disciplinarian. As the jeers
cascaded down on him, the pain was evident on his face.

The scene was devastating to the brand-new seventh grader, and suddenly Billy
stood up in the middle of the bleachers and shouted: "Shut up! That's my father!"
Instantly, the booing stopped.

After school, Billy went home, and when he saw his father, he began to cry. "Dad,
I told a lie at school today," he confessed. Billy told his dad how he had said Mr.
Johnson was his father and how he had yelled at all the other kids to "shut up" and be
nice to the man. His dad said: "It's all right, son. You just got the family members mixed
up. Mr. Johnson's not your father—he's your brother."

Jesus specifically told us who His family was—the family of God. One day, when
He was busy in ministry, He was interrupted when one of His disciples told Him that
His mother and brothers were waiting to speak to Him. What was Jesus' reply?
"Whoever does the will of My Father in heaven is my brother and sister and mother"
(Matthew 12:50 NKJV).

In God's family, we are all brothers and sisters, and when one of us hurts, we all
hurt. Billy may not have gotten it perfect, but he did understand the concept: When we
see other people—especially fellow Christians—suffering or in pain, we are to do
everything we can to help them out. After all, they're part of the family too.

GRACE FOR TODAY:

God has brought us into His family. We are all
brothers and sisters in Him!

HUMBLE HEIRS

Isn't it wonderful to be around people who are humble and gentle, who don't have anything to prove, who don't exalt themselves at your expense? They exhibit a quiet confidence in the Lord, whom they adore and to whom they belong. They are children of the King, princes and princesses in God's eternal realm, and they know He will raise them to their proper places at the proper time.

Like Jesus, humble people are here to serve, not to be served. In their quiet way they minister to you powerfully, because they know how to listen well, and they are willing to take time to do so. Unassuming people are a joy to be with, because you can be yourself around them, you can open up and share your hopes and dreams, your fears and concerns. You don't have to be afraid to admit to them your weaknesses and failures, because they have a healthy awareness of their own. They are accepting and gracious and willing to demonstrate God's mercy and forgiveness.

Unpretentious people treat you with politeness, courtesy, and respect. When you're with them, you feel you have been elevated somehow, in a very real and personal sense. In subtle ways they build you up, strengthening your faith in God—and in what God can do in and through you. Such people leave you feeling refreshed; you depart from them with a new sense of vitality and hope.

Thank God for His meek ones! Give Him glory that someday His humble children will inherit the earth. Praise Him that you will spend eternity in the fellowship of those who are like Christ, the One who taught us all the meaning of blessed humility.

> ### GRACE FOR TODAY:
> ## God's grace flows powerfully through those who are meek.

If you humble yourself, you will be honored.

MATTHEW 23:12 CEV

THE DESIRES OF YOUR HEART

By Dr. Charles Stanley

When the time came for me to buy my daughter a car, I asked her what she wanted. She had been praying, and she knew the exact year, model, color, and interior of the car she wanted. So we began looking. I had taught her to be specific in her prayers, but I had no idea she would be so specific. Regardless of what kind of car we saw or how good the price was, she stuck by what she originally asked God for. This went on for months.

Then one night my son was looking through the want ads, and he found a car just like Becky was looking for. It was the right make, color, model, and year. We went to look at it that night, and after talking with the owner for just a few minutes, we knew it was the right car. It didn't take much prayer to know if we were making the right decision; all the praying had been done.

God encourages us to pray specific prayers. Once we decide on something, we must stick with it in our prayers; otherwise we demonstrate a lack of faith. The psalmist does not say, "He shall give thee the needs of thine heart." But rather he writes, "He shall give thee the desires of thine heart" (Psalm 37:4 KJV). We must understand that what we are asking for is not really the issue. It is the attitude of our heart that matters. God wants to bless His children, but the relationship and method must be right.[29]

—❧—

DEAR FATHER: THANK YOU FOR CARING ABOUT EVERY ASPECT OF WHO I AM, INCLUDING MY HOPES AND DESIRES. I OFFER THOSE DESIRES TO YOU. TRANSFORM THEM BY YOUR GRACE IN ACCORDANCE WITH YOUR PERFECT WILL FOR MY LIFE. AMEN.

[Jesus said,] "I tell you, whatever you ask for in prayer, believe that you have received it, and it will be yours."

MARK 11:24

A FOUNDATION FOR FAITH—CREATION

From the time the world was created, people have seen the earth and sky and all that God made. They can clearly see his invisible qualities—his eternal power and divine nature.

ROMANS 1:20 NLT

O nly God can make a flower. Silk blossoms, humankind's best effort to dupli-cate this awesome feat, may appear quite realistic, yet they are merely life-less facsimiles. People may be able to cultivate new varieties of flowers, but in the end we are only altering the seeds and plants God created in the first place. Despite all our modern knowledge and technology, no one on this earth is able to produce—from scratch—a single living, growing flower capable of producing energy through photosynthesis, nourishing other living things, and reproducing itself.

GRACE FOR TODAY:

God left His fingerprints all over creation, to undergird our faith in Him.

Here at the beginning of the twenty-first century, science has finally evolved to the point where it can manufacture a humanlike robot that can climb steps. That's quite an accomplishment, yet it utterly pales in comparison with God's greatest creation. A two-year-old child can master a flight of stairs! And that's just the beginning of the incredible capabilities with which God has imbued the human race. Think of our capacities for reason, imagination, language, music, art, literature, and invention (after all, we can make pretty good robots). Not only that, but we have the ability to feel a wide range of emotions, to love each other, to worship and adore our Creator. Finally, and most telling, we are eternal beings. We will continue to exist long after all the robots in the world have broken down and corroded into dust.

The Bible says that creation bears constant witness to God's existence (Psalm 19:1). As part of creation, human beings are the greatest testimony to the Lord's infinite wisdom, power, and love. We can look at each other, and at ourselves, and see the undeniable stamp of His divine image. On a daily basis, God graciously gives us, in nature and throughout His creation, overwhelming evidence that He is real.

A LEAP OF FAITH

Those who hope in the Lord will renew their strength,
they will soar on wings like eagles.

ISAIAH 40:31

Wilbur and Orville Wright looked down the hillside as strong winds swept across the sand dunes of Kitty Hawk, North Carolina. It was not the best day to try out their new aircraft, but the two were pressed for time and knew they had to seize the moment. Trusting in their design and their preparations, they determined to brave the windy conditions and rolled the aircraft down the hill.

The Wright brothers were willing to risk their lives because they had faith in their invention and believed it would not crash. This was not an unfounded faith, for they had performed numerous experiments to ensure they had accounted for every possible contingency that might arise. Though they couldn't be absolutely certain their plane would actually fly, they had reasonable assurance—based on their tests and observations—that things would go as planned.

When you trust in the grace of God, you exhibit a similar type of faith. As you face a difficult situation and rely on God to get you through it, you base your faith on the promises in His Word. You have an assurance He will guide you through the problem because you understand His loving nature and because you know He has helped you through other difficult moments in your life. Faith is simply trusting in something greater than yourself.

The Wright brothers soared into the history books because they had faith they would succeed. When you put your trust in Christ, He will fill you with His grace as you soar through the situations that arise in your life.

> GRACE FOR TODAY:
>
> Our faith is based on God's Word—which cannot fail!

YOUR LIFE—A WORSHIP SERVICE

I urge you, brothers, in view of God's mercy,
to offer your bodies as living sacrifices, holy and pleasing to God—
this is your spiritual act of worship.

ROMANS 12:1

Have you ever considered your life to be a worship service? No, that doesn't mean you have to spend every minute in church. It just means that you worship God constantly by keeping Him always in your consciousness and involving Him in the details of your everyday life.

Too often we think of worship as singing hymns or listening to sermons. We know how to worship together, and we feel comfortable with that. We even recognize that reading and studying the Word, devoting ourselves to prayer and praise, engaging in godly activities are worship. And they are. But there are still other aspects of worshipping God.

The word "worship" means, among other things, "devotion." When our lives are devoted to God—every second of every day—they become a worship service, wholly pleasing to Him. When our thoughts are constantly being intermingled with God's thoughts, when our actions become extensions of His actions, when our love is purified by His love, we become instruments of worship.

God glories in the worship we give to Him at church. He rejoices when He sees us reading His Word. He revels in our prayers and praise, but He wants more. He wants all of you, all of the time. He wants you to worship Him with your life, day in and day out.

GRACE FOR TODAY:

God has already given us the grace we need to make our lives a living demonstration of worship.

HE LIVES IN ME!

This is the secret: Christ lives in you, and this is your assurance
that you will share in his glory.

COLOSSIANS 1:27 NLT

One day a teacher was asking her fourth-grade class to name the person whom they considered to be the greatest human being alive in the world on that particular day. One boy said: "John Elway. He led the Broncos to a Super Bowl win this year!" Another little girl said: "Mother Teresa. She cares for people who are sick, and she doesn't get paid for it at all." Another little girl raised her hand and exclaimed: "I think it's the President of the United States. America is the greatest country in the world!"

But little Timmy had a different response: "I think it's Jesus Christ, because He helps everybody and is always ready to help them." The teacher smiled and said, "Well, I certainly like your answer, Timmy, but I asked you to tell me who you think the greatest living person is."

To which little Timmy replied: "Jesus Christ is alive! He lives in me right now!"

To a world that does not know Christ, we are called to show forth His light. Christians carry Jesus with them everywhere they go, for He is alive on the inside of them.

This type of experience may be difficult to describe to people who have never yet encountered the living Christ for themselves. The best way to demonstrate Jesus to others is to let Him live through you and shine His light through your life for others to see.

Is Jesus alive in you today? How can you share the reality of His presence with those around you?

GRACE FOR TODAY:

The Christ who lives in us is the hope of the world!

GRACE UNDER FIRE

Knowing His people need protection as they face intense spiritual warfare in this world, the Lord has supplied them battle gear—His own armor. He has also provided them a fortress—His very name. Ephesians 6:10–18 describes this armor in vivid imagery, that of a belt, a breastplate, footwear, a shield, a helmet, and a sword. Proverbs 18:10 and Psalm 18:2 portray this fortress just as graphically, describing it as a rock, a mighty tower, a stronghold.

Don't get lost in the metaphors, however! When the enemy is near and the fight is joined, mental images of swords, shields, helmets, and castles will do you no good at all, unless you use them for their intended purpose: to remind you of the real weapons and stronghold of God. If you've memorized the Scripture passages above, the words that should be highlighted in your mind's eye are truth, righteousness, the gospel, peace, faith, salvation, God's Word, prayer, and God's name. This is the armament and the fortress with the power of God to save. These are the defenses the Lord has graciously given you for your protection.

God's weapons are potent, and His stronghold is secure. But they must be appropriated. Truth will be useless to you unless you've learned it and can remember it and rely on it in the heat of battle. You can't try to put on righteousness as the war rages; you must be wearing it beforehand. Similarly, faith will afford you adequate safety in the tumult only insofar as you've reinforced it during times of calm. God's Word will serve you well if you regularly study it and meditate on it and commit it to memory. God's name will be your blessed, eternal refuge if you always honor it and strive to ascribe it glory.

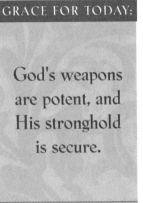

GRACE FOR TODAY:

God's weapons are potent, and His stronghold is secure.

God's name is a place of protection—good people can run there and be safe.

PROVERBS 18:10 MSG

AN ENCOURAGEMENT TO PRAY

By Dr. Charles Stanley

Some people question whether we should ask God for material things. The answer is simple. Wise parents do everything in their power to satisfy their children's needs. This goes for material needs as well as nutritional and spiritual needs. The material gifts we give our children are proof that God wants to give to us in the same way, but to a greater degree. Do we have a privilege that God has deprived himself of? No! In fact, there is no way we can outgive God, materially or any other way.

Another hang-up people have is in regard to their unworthiness to have God answer their prayers. But the basis of all God's answered prayer is His love for us. Calvary settled the question of worth once and for all. According to His love, we are worthy of the greatest gift He had to give—His Son. After that, anything else we ask for is secondary.

Why do we have so much trouble believing God for the minor things in life? It is Satan who says, "Who do you think you are, to ask God for anything?"

To this question there is only one answer: "I am a child of the King. I am so worthy in the eyes of God, He sent His only begotten Son to die for me. If He died for me, certainly He will give me whatever I need."[30]

―◆―

HOLY FATHER: BY YOUR GRACE, YOU HAVE GIVEN ME EVERY GOOD GIFT, ESPECIALLY THE GIFT OF YOUR SON. NOT ONLY HAVE YOU GIVEN TO ME, YOU HAVE ALSO MADE ME WORTHY TO RECEIVE YOUR GIFTS. WHAT A WONDERFUL FATHER YOU ARE! AMEN.

[Jesus said,] "Ask and it will be given to you; seek and you will find; knock and the door will be opened to you. For everyone who asks receives; he who seeks finds; and to him who knocks, the door will be opened."

MATTHEW 7:7-8

THE MIRACLE OF FORGIVENESS

Dear friends, let us love one another, for love comes from God.

1 JOHN 4:7

Lewis Grizzard often wrote about growing up in a little Methodist church in Georgia and how precious it was to him in his childhood. Once, he said, a couple of rowdy brothers in town who were the town juvenile offenders started coming to the youth group at the church. On the first night they went, they beat up two fifth graders and threw a hymnal at the lady who was the youth leader. She ducked just in time.

Afterward, she looked them squarely in their devilish eyes and said, in a voice that was as soft as an angel's: "I don't approve of what you boys did here tonight, and neither does Jesus. But if He can forgive you, I guess I'll have to." Then she handed them a plate of cookies.

As Grizzard said, "The last I heard—both those boys grew up, and they rarely miss a Sunday at church. That was the first miracle I ever saw."

The miracle of forgiveness can do amazing things in the lives of people—especially for those for whom it is the least expected! In His famous Sermon on the Mount, Jesus commanded us to forgive other people in the same way that His Father forgives us of our sins. (See Matthew 6:14–15.) The apostle John exhorts us to "love one another, for love [and forgiveness] comes from God" (1 John 4:7). The Sunday school teacher had it right: If Jesus can forgive people of their sins, surely we can do the same!

GRACE FOR TODAY:

God is the author of forgiveness—one of the greatest gifts of His grace.

DIVINE INSPIRATION

The people walking in darkness have seen a great light.

ISAIAH 9:2

W hen Paul encountered the Lord on the road to Damascus, he saw a brilliant flash of light. Nowadays God uses somewhat less dramatic means to get our attention, but He still meets us along our journey every now and then, sending little bursts of grace to encourage us in this sometimes dark world.

A man who had been depressed for a few days was disinterestedly watching his four-year-old daughter stick bright, colorful letters on a black felt board. Suddenly three letters in the middle—one red, one yellow, and one blue—leaped out at him. The little girl had spelled out the word "God." Immediately he felt the Lord's presence and sensed that it was His way of encouraging him, as if to say reassuringly, "I'm here."

During a break between speakers at a Promise Keepers convention in the Pontiac Silverdome, a man whose faith hadn't seemed very vibrant in a while sat in the upper level, watching the attendees toss around Frisbees and beach balls. Just then a large Styrofoam airplane gracefully glided by, far above the crowd. At once he was conscious of the Holy Spirit moving through the stadium, joyfully inviting him, "Come soar with Me."

GRACE FOR TODAY:

> God meets us along our journey with gifts of love and encouragement.

Driving along the expressway, a man wounded by a broken engagement in his past struggled with whether or not to propose to his new girlfriend. "Give me a sign, Lord," he said. "I need to know what You want me to do." Glancing up at that moment, he saw a billboard advertisement featuring a giant diamond ring. He shook his head and laughed, and he popped the question within a week. She said yes, and they've since celebrated their fifteenth anniversary.

LEARNING TO LIVE

What, then, shall we say in response to this?
If God is for us, who can be against us?

ROMANS 8:31

Young lions are amazingly confident when they are learning to hunt. Still small in size, they find a prey and stalk it. They creep up on it, and then they pounce. They rarely capture the prey, but in those rare instances that they do, they normally have no idea what to do with it. The skill of the kill is not in them yet, so they do all they can to subdue it, usually without success. During this time, the adult lions are nearby watching as the younger lions chase their terrified prey. They stay where they are until the young lions need them—and then they rise up and finish the job.

The older lions know how important it is for the younger lions to learn to hunt. It isn't a game; it's imperative to their survival. In the jungle, if you don't hunt, you don't eat.

You may have challenges in your life right now—challenges that you are working as hard as you can to conquer. God is nearby, watching, waiting to help. But He recognizes that there are some things He cannot do for you. You must learn to do them for yourself. That might be getting out of debt, working to improve your marriage or an important relationship, managing your health, any number of skills you need to survive in this world. If He stepped in and miraculously supplied your every need, you would soon become a weakling, unable to function on your own.

Now that doesn't mean He won't come to Your rescue when you've done all you can do. At just the right time, He'll step in and help you finish the job. You can depend on that.

GRACE FOR TODAY:

God does not do for us what we must learn to do
for ourselves. But He's always there to help
when we need Him.

He Will Take Care of You!

[Jesus said:] "I'll be with you . . . day after day after day."

MATTHEW 28:20 MSG

A community once held an Easter pageant in which different people in the community played the various characters. Jesus' character was given to a big, burly oil-field worker, primarily because he was the only one strong enough to carry the heavy wooden beam that was to be Jesus' cross.

As they came to the part in the performance in which Jesus was being led away to be crucified, a little man who was simply part of the jeering crowd got caught up in the emotion of the moment. He joined in the shouts of "Crucify Him! Crucify Him!" and as the man playing Jesus was being led away, carrying the cross upon his back, he had to walk right in front of this little man, who was still shouting at the top of his lungs. The little man was so consumed by the moment that he actually spit on Jesus. The big, burly oil-field worker stopped, wiped his face dry, looked at the little man, and then uttered the most memorable line in the entire play that day: "I'll be back to take care of you after the Resurrection!"

For us today, those words are true, but they're not a threat—they're a promise! Jesus will take care of us after the Resurrection! He has promised to be with us always, taking care of us and providing for our needs. Even now, He is preparing a place for us in Heaven, where we will live with Him forever, and one day we will see Him face to face in that place.

In what ways has Jesus cared for you today?

GRACE FOR TODAY:

Closer is He than breathing, and nearer than hands and feet.

ALFRED LORD TENNYSON

BRAGGING RIGHTS

When the Red Sox made their historic comeback to beat the Yankees in the final game of the 2004 American League Championship Series, baseball fans in Boston finally had something to feel good about. No other team had ever overcome a three-game deficit to win in the postseason. Best of all, Boston had defeated its arch-rival, New York, seemingly reversing the legendary "curse" that had haunted the Red Sox ever since they traded Babe Ruth to the Yankees in 1920. Sure enough, the Red Sox went on to win the World Series for the first time in eighty-six years. Boston's team earned bragging rights for the entire city, and Bostonians rejoiced, wearing their Red Sox caps proudly and lauding their heroes.

Jesus Christ won the greatest victory of all time on a hill outside Jerusalem two thousand years ago. He achieved something no human being could ever do: He conquered Satan, sin, and death forever. With one loving act of self-sacrifice, Jesus opened the way for anyone with faith in Him to be reunited with God. On the cross, Christ took the punishment for humanity's sins and secured eternal life for all believers. Was there ever a finer champion?

Through Christ, God offers you this triumph. Ephesians 2:8-9 says, "It is by grace you have been saved, through faith—and this not from yourselves, it is the gift of God—not by works, so that no one can boast." You cannot claim to have won the victory yourself, through your own righteousness, any more than a resident of Boston can say that he personally won the World Series. But if you've identified yourself with Jesus, God invites you to share in the celebration and reward, to bear Christ's name proudly, and to boast endlessly about your awesome Lord.

GRACE FOR TODAY:

God provided for our salvation, and now He invites us to share in the reward.

Let him who boasts boast in the Lord.

1 CORINTHIANS 1:31

God's Answers

By Dr. Charles Stanley

When God answers our prayers, He either answers with "yes," "no," or "wait." When He answers "yes," we are prone to shout, "Praise the Lord!" We tell everybody what a great thing God has done for us.

But when God says "no," we have a hard time finding reasons to praise Him. We look for the sin in our lives that kept Him from granting our requests, because surely if we had been living right He would have answered "yes." But not one shred of scriptural evidence shows that God will say "yes" to all our prayers just because we're living right. God is sovereign. He has the right to say "no" according to His infinite wisdom, regardless of our goodness.

But God only says "no" and "wait" when it is best for us (Romans 8:28). He does it many times for our protection. Sometimes God wants to answer our prayer, but the timing is not right.

We don't like waiting around, especially when it looks like a unique opportunity might slip away. We don't like to hear God say "no," especially when everything in us says "yes, yes, yes!"

But deep in our hearts we really want God's perfect will for our lives. And we must remember that God's answer is always His ultimate best for us. If He says "no," then the answer is no. God is more interested in our character, our future, and our sanctification than He is in our momentary satisfaction. His answers are always an act of grace, motivated by His love.[31]

—⁓—

HEAVENLY FATHER: I WANT YOUR PERFECT WILL FOR MY LIFE—EVEN WHEN IT MEANS YOU MUST SAY "NO" TO SOMETHING I'VE ASKED OF YOU. I KNOW THAT YOUR PLAN FOR MY LIFE IS FAR BETTER THAN MY OWN. HELP ME AS I RESOLVE TO WALK IN THAT DIFFICULT TRUTH. AMEN.

In his heart a man plans his course, but the Lord determines his steps.

PROVERBS 16:9

BEING FOUND IS WONDERFUL!

"[The father said,] 'We had to celebrate and be glad, because this brother
of yours . . . was lost and is found.'"

LUKE 15:32

A little seven-year-old boy once went to a circus, where there were over
20,000 people in the crowd. Jimmy and his older brother, Steve, went to buy
some cotton candy, with the admonishment from their parents that they stay close
together.

After Steve got his own cotton candy, he stepped aside for Jimmy. Just then, loud
laughter came from the arena. Steve didn't mean to leave his little brother alone, but he got caught up in the excitement of the crowd and wanted to see what the fuss was all about.

Jimmy got his cotton candy, and then he turned around to look for his big brother—who was gone. In that moment of panic, nothing looked familiar. He was lost! He wondered if he'd ever see his family again. He started to run, desperately trying to fight back the tears.

But after a few moments of terror, Jimmy felt a gentle touch on his shoulder, and he turned around to see his father right behind him. It's hard to describe the feelings that little boy had when he saw his dad at that

GRACE FOR TODAY:

Even when we were lost to ourselves, God knew exactly where we were.

moment. Now a grown man, Jim relates: "I learned a valuable lesson that day: Being
lost is terrible. Being found is wonderful!"

No wonder "Amazing Grace" is America's favorite hymn! For every Christian,
the words "I once was lost, but now am found" can be related to. Without Jesus, we
wander around, lost in the crowd, panic rising at every turn. But when He rescues us,
what a wonderful feeling it is!

LOST AND FOUND

[Jesus said,] "Whoever wants to save his life will lose it, but whoever loses his life for me will find it."

MATTHEW 16:25

A man trying to explain to his friend the ramifications of faith and nonbelief took a piece of paper and drew a simple graph. First he made a horizontal line across the middle of the paper. "Everything above this line is a gain," he said. "Everything below it is a loss." Then he drew an arrow on the left side of the page, from the horizontal line to the bottom. "This is possibility A, the worst-case scenario. God exists; you reject Christ. Your earthly life is void of God's blessing and fellowship, and like everyone you eventually lose it. You also lose your eternal life. An incalculable loss."

To the right of the arrow he made a tiny mark downward from the horizontal line. "Here's possibility B: God doesn't exist; you accept Christ. Without God, there is no blessing, divine fellowship, or eternal life anyway, so your earthly life is all you lose."

Drawing another small mark farther to the right, this time upward from the horizontal line, he said, "Possibility C: God doesn't exist; you reject Christ. Again, there's no blessing, divine fellowship, or eternal life. You still lose your earthly life, but at least you can live it the way you want to."

> **GRACE FOR TODAY:**
>
> God's grace equals blessing, fellowship, eternal life— incalculable gain!

To the far right he made an arrow from the horizontal line to the top of the paper. "Finally, the best-case scenario by far. Possibility D: God exists; you accept Christ. You enjoy God's blessing and fellowship forever, in this life and beyond. When your earthly life is over, you gain an eternity of love, joy, peace, pleasure, and reward. Incalculable gain." He smiled at his friend. "This arrow represents God's endless grace, which is freely available for you if you put your faith in Jesus Christ. What have you got to lose?"

GOD'S TRAFFIC LIGHT

Wait patiently for the Lord. Be brave and courageous.
Yes, wait patiently for the Lord.

PSALM 27:14 NLT

S erving God at times is like sitting at a traffic light that seems to be stuck on red.
Although you know where you want to go and when you want to get there, as
long as the light remains red, you have to sit and wait . . . and wait . . . and wait some
more. As cars in other lanes move swiftly through the light, you may wonder why
you don't get to move ahead like everyone else. People behind you may honk impa-
tiently at you and "encourage" you to just run the light. You may even be tempted to
do so—after all, you surely shouldn't have to wait this long.

Sometimes, the toughest thing that God will ask you to do is to sit at that red light
and wait upon Him. Since God's timing will not always match your own, you may
have to alter certain expectations in your life and wait for God to reveal His purpose.
You may have to remain for a while longer in a job situation that is less than ideal or
pass up certain relationships until God brings the right person into your life. You may
even have to wait on the sidelines as friends struggle with particular problems.

Waiting will require you to trust in God's plan and believe that He is actively
working in your life, especially when others speed past you or "encourage" you to just
move ahead without His direction. However, as you wait upon the Lord, try to just
relax and enjoy the moment. Rest in His grace, and look with hope towards the future,
knowing that He will bless you for your obedience to Him.

GRACE FOR TODAY:

When we are waiting, God's plan and His perfect
timing are worthy of our trust.

"PRECIOUS LORD"

Even when the way goes through Death Valley,
I'm not afraid when you walk at my side.

PSALM 23:4 MSG

Tommy Dorsey's popular gospel song, "Precious Lord," was composed out of a devastating experience in his life. In 1932, as he was singing in a church, his wife went into labor and died. The pastor of the church handed him a telegram with four heartbreaking words on it: "Your wife just died." Tommy discovered that she had given birth to their firstborn son, but later that night, the baby died too. Tommy Dorsey buried his wife and infant son in the same casket. Then he fell apart. He felt God had done him an injustice. But one day he sat down at the piano and started playing a new melody, and the words just came to him: "Precious Lord, take my hand. Lead me on, let me stand. I am tired. I am weak. I am worn. Through the storm, through the night lead me on to the light; take my hand, precious Lord, lead me home."

Maybe you have felt that life has dealt you an unfair hand, and you wonder where God is or what He is up to. It's easy to fall into these thoughts and feelings when you are in the midst of depression and despair. But He has promised to never leave us or forsake us. Take Christ's hand when you walk through the valley of death; He will take your hand, walk by your side, and show you the way through.

GRACE FOR TODAY:

Charles Spurgeon once said: "The refiner is never very far from the mouth of the furnace when his gold is in the fire."

JUSTICE SERVED

In the American legal system, justice is personified by the image of a woman holding a scale. The woman is blindfolded, indicating that she is impartial; the trays of the scale are level, indicating that all is well. When a person breaks the law, the scale is tipped. When that person is punished with a fine, community service, prison time, or in some cases death, the penalty offsets the offense, the scale returns to its proper balance, and Justice is satisfied.

The Bible also uses a scale to symbolize justice. Except God, who sees all yet remains perfectly fair, holds the scale—and it's His holy sense of right and wrong that must be satisfied. It was the Lord who instituted the law of eye for eye, tooth for tooth, even life for life, to keep the scale in balance (Exodus 21:23–25). And although the sins of humankind have thrown the scale off-kilter, God has sworn to set things right in the end.

His vow comes as a blessing to you. Like every person, you have an innate sense of right and wrong, which is in line with God's and reflects His image in you. Regularly, if not daily, you are assaulted by events that offend your sense of justice. The media reports iniquities across the globe; coworkers, friends, and family members share how they are mistreated by others; and you experience hurtful behavior firsthand.

Thanks to the Lord's promise of ultimate justice, you don't have to seek vengeance for wrongs committed against you or your loved ones, trying to balance God's scale yourself. You can rest in the knowledge that He will deal with all the evil in this world, either through divine judgment or—better yet—by the grace made possible by Jesus' death on the cross.

> **GRACE FOR TODAY:**
>
> God's pledge of ultimate justice frees us to forgive others.

[God] will judge the world with justice and rule the nations with fairness.

PSALM 9:8 NLT

WHAT SHALL WE PRAY?

By Dr. Charles Stanley

When we go to God, instead of asking, "Lord, please do this and that," let's ask Him to show us how to pray. Let's ask the Holy Spirit to pray through us from beginning to end. Then we can be assured of praying according to His will. We will pray for things we would never think to pray for otherwise. As we pray, God will show us a side of prayer we have never seen.

When our hearts are clean and we have committed ourselves to obey Him, yet we have not a clue as to what to pray, God takes the responsibility for showing us. He may use Scripture, or He may use circumstances. If our request isn't in keeping with His will, He will redirect our attention on Him, and we will lose interest in what we were asking for. Regardless of how He shows us, we must believe that He will. Often we will have to wait. But it is during these times of waiting that we begin to really know God.

As we find God's will in our prayers, He confirms it by filling our hearts with the peace of the Holy Spirit. We can know without doubt that we are on His track in our prayers. When this is true, we can pray with the assurance that Christ is praying with us to the same end. Peace in our hearts is God's seal of approval on our prayers.

God desires to give us direction in our prayers. He has promised in His Word to do so. Our responsibility is to seek His direction through Scripture. Once we have found His promise to us, we must dig in and wait while thanking Him for what is already ours. For "if God be for us" (Romans 8:31) in our prayers, who or what can stand against us?[32]

—∞—

HEAVENLY FATHER: SHOW ME HOW TO PRAY FOR MYSELF AND ALSO FOR OTHERS. I DON'T WANT TO JUST SAY WORDS; I WANT MY WORDS TO MATTER.

Do not worry about anything, but in everything by prayer and supplication with thanksgiving let your requests be made known to God. And the peace of God, which surpasses all understanding, will guard your hearts and your minds in Christ Jesus.

PHILIPPIANS 4:6–7 NRSV

GOD'S TEAM

I can do all things through Him who strengthens me.

PHILIPPIANS 4:13 NASB

Many people consider Michael Jordan to be the greatest basketball player of all time. One night, he scored sixty-three points in a single game. A Chicago Bulls teammate of his, who was neither a star nor a starter, was later asked: "What's been the highlight of your NBA career?"

With his tongue firmly implanted in his cheek, he answered: "It was the night Michael Jordan and I combined for sixty-five points!"

While Michael Jordan's teammate was joking, in a way he was absolutely right. Without the rest of the team supporting him and providing the backup he needed, Michael Jordan would never have been able to achieve such high scores and amazing accomplishments. But on the other hand, by being a part of Michael Jordan's team, the other player became part of a victory that might not have otherwise been his.

The Bible declares that with Christ, you can do all things! If you are simply looking at your situation without considering Jesus Christ as your teammate, you may be right to despair. But when Jesus comes on board your team, anything is possible! Allow Him to grab the ball and run with it. Follow His lead and obey what He tells you to do. You will be surprised what you will be able to accomplish, the two of you together.

> **GRACE FOR TODAY:**
>
> **When we allow God to play on our team, there is no limit to what we can accomplish!**

SPIRITUAL MENTORS

They invited him to their home and explained to him
the way of God more adequately.

ACTS 18:26

Before Jesus ascended into Heaven, He commanded His followers to "go and make disciples" (Matthew 28:19). Sometimes the leaders of the early church carried out this command by preaching to large groups of people, as when the apostle Paul went to Athens and spoke in the synagogue, the marketplace, and the Areopagus.

At other times, however, this discipling process took on a more personal manner, as when Philip sat in a chariot with an Ethiopian official and explained a passage of Scripture to him, or when Priscilla and Aquila invited Apollos into their home for a bit of spiritual mentoring.

God still uses this more intimate style of ministry today, making—and molding—disciples through one-on-one encounters between people who know Him well and those who don't know Him at all, or need to know Him better. Wherever you are in your relationship with the Lord, He will grace your life with Christians more spiritually mature than you, who will lovingly challenge, encourage, and help you to grow in your faith.

> **GRACE FOR TODAY:**
>
> God provides spiritual mentors to disciple us, so that we in turn can disciple others.

Pray for these relationships, welcome them, and cherish them! The Bible promises that if you spend time with the wise, you too will become wise. And as the Lord uses spiritual mentors to teach you and guide you, He will begin to provide you with opportunities to take others under your wing. Then you will experience the wonderful blessing of being used by God to create and develop new disciples. Even as you learn to soar more gracefully with Him, you'll rejoice to see your protégés start to spread their wings and fly.

IF I SHOULD DIE BEFORE I WAKE

If you confess with your mouth that Jesus is Lord and believe in your heart that God raised him from the dead, you will be saved.

ROMANS 10:9 NLT

As a child, did you ever pray the "Now I lay me down to sleep" prayer? Most of us felt a twinge of apprehension when we got to the part that goes, "If I should die before I wake, I pray the Lord my soul to take." A little scary to our childish minds, right? Was our soul going to be snatched away while we slept? We probably weren't thinking about where "The Lord" might be taking it. But the day comes for each of us when those questions must be asked and answered.

Can you be sure you will open your eyes in Heaven if you should die before you wake? According to God's Word, you can be absolutely certain. Ephesians 1:7 says, "In him we have redemption through His blood, the forgiveness of sins, in accordance with the riches of God's grace." Christ's sacrifice on the cross for us has purchased sure passage, an eternal assurance for our souls. All He asks us to do is appropriate His grace and place ourselves in His care.

If you have not yet claimed God's gracious gift of salvation and assured your place in Heaven, why wait? It was never His plan for you to fear death or live with uncertainty about your eternal destination. Reach out to Him; exchange your sins for His grace; give yourself to Him heart and soul. You'll never wonder again, and odds are you will sleep much better.

GRACE FOR TODAY:

God has provided a place for us in Heaven. All we have to do is claim it.

YOU ARE VALUABLE TO GOD

[Jesus explained,] "There will be more joy in heaven over one sinner who repents than over ninety-nine respectable people who do not need to repent."

LUKE 15:7 GNB

A teenage boy was once playing basketball in his driveway. Somehow, he lost a contact lens. He looked for it for a couple of minutes before he was ready to give up the search and resume playing, but he thought he'd better go tell his mom what had happened first.

His mother came outside, got down on her hands and knees, and began to meticulously go over every inch of the driveway, looking for the contact lens. After crawling around for over half an hour, she finally exclaimed: "Here it is!" Sure enough, she'd found it.

In amazement, her son exclaimed: "Mom, I can't believe you found it! I looked really hard, but I sure didn't see it!"

His mother replied, "That's because we weren't looking for the same thing. You were just looking for a tiny piece of plastic, but I was looking for a hundred and fifty dollars!"

Have you ever lost something valuable to you? When we are motivated to find something, we search even harder for it. Jesus used this illustration to demonstrate the lengths that His Father would go to find and save His lost sheep: When a man loses one of his sheep, he goes out and searches for it until he finds it and then he has a celebration. When a woman loses one of her valuable silver coins, she sweeps the house from top to bottom until she locates it, and then she holds a party. "In the same way," Jesus said, "There will be more joy in heaven over one sinner who repents than over ninety-nine respectable people who do not need to repent!" (Luke 15:7 GNB).

GRACE FOR TODAY:

Our heavenly Father has gone to great lengths to find us and bring us home. That's how much we mean to Him!

SOUL MATES

If you are married, a good deal of God's grace will flow to you through your spouse. The Lord will bless you in many ways through your marriage. In your mate, God has given you a companion, a partner, a helper, a counselor, a supporter, a fellow disciple. He or she can encourage you, care for you, hold you accountable, pray for you, point out your weaknesses, affirm your strengths, console you in times of failure, and celebrate with you in times of success.

Marriage is an opportunity for you to be a member of one of the smallest, yet also one of the most beautiful and compelling, manifestations of the body of Christ. The marriage relationship is a microcosm of the church, encompassing every aspect of what it means for believers to live together in community. All the "one another" commandments in the New Testament—love one another, serve one another, bear with one another, submit to one another—apply to a husband and wife. And a marriage reflects the mysterious nature of the Trinity, in which Father, Son, and Holy Spirit exist together eternally as one.

Most importantly, God will use your spouse to mold you into the image of Christ. This process can be challenging, since it's not always easy and often involves the hard work of resolving conflict with your partner and cooperating with the Holy Spirit to produce change within your heart. Through your mate, the Lord will open your eyes to many truths about yourself—the first being how self-centered a person really is. As you learn to live in harmony with your spouse by making sacrifices and placing his or her interests before your own, God is blessing you by slowly shaping you into the person He intended you to be.

> **GRACE FOR TODAY:**
>
> A good spouse is a gift directly from God's throne of grace.

From the beginning "God made them male and female." And he said, "This explains why a man leaves his father and mother and is joined to his wife."

MATTHEW 19:4–5 NLT

THE VICTORIOUS CHRISTIAN

By Luis Palau

During preparation for one of our evangelistic festivals in South America, a poor, shabbily dressed man attended our counselor-training course. Although the training is open to all spiritually mature Christians, generally the better-educated and socially established lay leaders of local churches attend these classes. This man was also illiterate, so he brought his young nephew to read and write for him.

Although the man attended every class, we didn't expect him to do much counseling. Like many illiterate people, however, he had a fantastic memory and had learned much through the counseling classes.

Following one of the evangelistic meetings, every available counselor was busy except the illiterate man. At that time a doctor walked in, requesting counsel. Before anyone could stop him, the shabbily dressed man took the doctor into a room for counseling.

When our counseling director learned of this, he was a bit concerned. He didn't know if the illiterate man would be able to communicate effectively with the sophisticated doctor. When the doctor came out of the counseling room, our counseling director asked if he could help him in any way.

"No, thank you," the doctor replied. "This fellow has helped me very much."

The next day the doctor returned with two other doctors. Our counseling director wanted to talk to him, but the doctor refused, asking for counsel with the illiterate man. By the end of the festival, that illiterate man had led four doctors and their wives to Christ! He couldn't read or write, but he lived an authentic Christian life.

So often we look on the outside for signs of victorious Christian living. But the outward appearance doesn't count. Outward appearances reveal little of authentic Christian living. What really counts—what really makes a Christian's life vibrant and real—is the power of the living Christ within.[33]

—⁂—

FATHER: HELP ME TO LIVE AN AUTHENTIC CHRISTIAN LIFE—ONE THAT EXHIBITS THE POWER OF THE LIVING CHRIST WITHIN ME. AMEN.

Man looks at the outward appearance, but the Lord looks at the heart.

1 SAMUEL 16:7

TAKING OUT THE GARBAGE

[Jesus declared,] "Don't criticize, and then you won't be criticized."

MATTHEW 7:1 TLB

A woman left her apartment one morning for a trip downtown. She put on her most fashionable outfit and her favorite perfume and went to catch a bus. As she hurried out the back door, she picked up a small sack of garbage in the kitchen to toss it in the container at the curb on her way to catch the bus. But she was so preoccupied, she forgot about holding the sack of garbage. So, she carried it, along with her other packages, onto the bus.

As she took her seat, she noticed this terrible stench. She opened the window, to no avail. Later, as she shopped, she noticed that the terrible stench was in every store she visited. She couldn't escape the smell and eventually concluded, "The whole world stinks!" Only after she returned home and opened her packages did she realize where the odor was coming from.

Before you begin to point the finger at other people, it is always smart to check out your own packages first. The "stink" you smell may not be from others—it may be your own! Jesus had this to say about judging other people: "Don't pick on people, jump on their failures, criticize their faults—unless, of course, you want the same treatment. That critical spirit has a way of boomeranging" (Matthew 7:1–2 MSG). Jesus was right! Make sure you've taken out your own garbage first before you begin to criticize the garbage of the people around you.

GRACE FOR TODAY:

God has given us the power to reject a critical spirit.

LITTLE ONES

Children are God's best gift.

PSALM 127:3 MSG

A four-year-old girl stumbled on the sidewalk and scraped her knee as she raced to get into the family's minivan. Her father held her and consoled her, then strapped her into her car seat. The girl looked at her knee, then told her younger sister, "If you wanna get a boo-boo, you gotta fall down."

Getting ready for a long road trip, a mother was trying to fix the family's small portable television with the built-in videocassette player. She removed the cover and looked around inside the unit, trying to figure out what had caused a tape to jam. Spying something that didn't look right, she reached in and pulled out a Tootsie Roll Pop.

If you are a parent, God will use your children to bring you wisdom, humor, and joy. Through children He will teach you about selfless, unconditional love. As you raise your little ones, striving to meet their constant needs for attention, assistance, and affection, cleaning up after them on a nonstop basis, looking out for their safety and health, and building their character through love and discipline, your heavenly Father is building your character as well.

Most of all, you will learn a great lesson about depending on God. You'll begin to look to Him for the strength, patience, and discernment you need to accomplish the awesome task He's assigned you, that of molding young individuals into people who will know, love, honor, and serve Him and be a blessing to others in this world. And once you've discovered that God is faithful to meet your needs as a parent, you'll have the precious gift of knowing that you can rely on Him to meet all your needs in life.

GRACE FOR TODAY:

Through your children, your Father in Heaven will teach you that you can depend on Him.

HIS TRUTH IS MARCHING ON

Jesus said to him, "I am the way, the truth, and the life. No one comes to the Father except through Me."

JOHN 14:6 NKJV

Have you ever felt as though your belief in God was firm, but your belief He actually hears and answers your prayers was wavering? If so, take comfort in knowing that the God who created the entire world around you, who is all in all, letting nothing exist without the counsel of His own will, cannot lie. Not only is it impossible for God to lie, but it is also impossible for Him to decree a thing that can be overpowered and nullified. This means that there is nothing is this life that can overrule what God has already said in His Word. You have an assurance of victory from a God who cannot help but tell the truth.

Our God is all-powerful. He not only tells the truth but also has the right and the authority to say whatever He pleases concerning you. All you have to do is remain strong in faith, not allowing anything to cause you to waver. Don't let this world fool you into thinking that God might fail you. He won't—He can't! Nothing can keep Him from performing His Word on your behalf.

God's Word is settled forever. It isn't subject to the circumstances of this life. Every tiny bit of His Word will come to pass in His perfect timing. That means you will triumph if you stand strong in faith and trust Him.

GRACE FOR TODAY:

Nothing in this world can overrule what God has said to us in His Word.

The Loving Creator

The heavens declare the glory of God;
the skies proclaim the work of his hands.

PSALM 19:1

The psalmist David was constantly exclaiming the goodness and majesty of his Creator, long before modern-day scientists began to discern what an amazing planet on which we live.

Even today, science has only scratched the surface of unlocking the mysteries of Planet Earth, but here are a few interesting facts they've been able to uncover: The earth is situated at precisely the perfect distance from the sun so that the temperature is neither too hot nor too cold. If the earth only rotated 364 times, instead of 365, our days and nights would be ten times as long, making life impossible. If the axis of the earth were forty-five degrees instead of twenty-three, the core of the planet would become so hot that, again, life would be impossible. Twenty-one percent of the earth's atmosphere is oxygen—if it were 50 percent, a mere striking of a match would set the planet ablaze. But if it were only 1 percent, we wouldn't be able to breathe.

It is hard to imagine that some people who live on this planet, who breathe the air, eat its food, and drink its water, still refuse to believe that there is a God. But as David declared so long ago: "The heavens declare the glory of God; the skies proclaim the work of his hands" (Psalm 19:1). There is Someone in charge of this world, a loving Creator who made it and who continues to sustain it each day.

Are your problems or life circumstances making it hard to see your Creator? Take some time out to gaze up at the sky, to look at the stars, the trees, the flowers around you and allow your loving Father to "declare His glory" to you afresh and anew.

Grace for Today:

Through every flower, every tree, every breath of wind on our faces, God is saying, "I love you."

LEGITIMATE CLAIMS

I f you trust God's promises and act on them, He gives you the right to claim them through prayer. The Lord invites you to boldly come before Him in Jesus' name, request His promised blessings, and then believe and expect that you will receive them. This relationship is possible only because through faith in Christ, you are not an outsider living under God's law; you are a member of His family, abiding in His grace. Your relationship to God is that of a son or daughter of the King, a resident of His palace, an heir to His realm. God has graciously and lovingly granted you that privilege, which He dearly purchased at the cross.

The Lord wants so much to bestow His blessings on you. But He created you with a free will, and you must choose to take the steps necessary to receive them. It begins with trusting His promises enough to act on them. For example, the Bible says that if you live to please the Holy Spirit, you will receive, among many other blessings, joy (Galatians 5:22–23). If you are a Christian and are not experiencing a deep, lasting sense of joy, start by placing your confidence in this promise from Scripture. Commit it to memory. Then learn how to live to please the Spirit. Since the only one who ever was able to accomplish this was Jesus, study His life in the Gospels, observe His ways and emulate them, listen to His words and obey them. Christ and the Holy Spirit will lead you into proper relationship with your heavenly Father, and it is within that relationship that you can prayerfully remind God of His promises and—with all gratitude, humility, and respect—claim them.

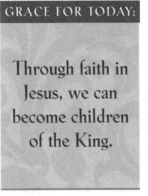

GRACE FOR TODAY:

Through faith in Jesus, we can become children of the King.

Let us have confidence, then, and approach God's throne,
where there is grace.

HEBREWS 4:16 GNB

THE RIGHT FORMULA

By Dr. Charles Stanley

When most of us pray, we add "in Jesus' name" to the end of our prayers. For some it is a habit; for others it is considered a magic phrase that assures an answer. We read John 14:14 and mistakenly decide that the only qualification to having our prayers answered is to say, "in Jesus' name." This is a mistake. For there is another qualification: We must abide.

Praying in Jesus' name is more than a phrase we add to a prayer; it is a character of the prayer itself. To pray in Jesus' name means that we are asking something because it is in character with what Jesus would ask if He were in our circumstances. It means that the prayer is in keeping with His nature and character as He lives His life through us. Since He indwells us, He not only desires to live through us, but to intercede through us as well.

Many times we make what may appear to be mundane requests. But they are real needs to us, and God is willing to meet them. Whether they are for spiritual or material needs, it makes little difference to Him; He is our loving Father who delights in meeting all our needs. But before we add "in Jesus' name" on the end, we must make sure everything in the prayer is in keeping with His character.[34]

—·—

HEAVENLY FATHER: I OFFER MY HEART TO YOU. FILL IT WITH YOUR DESIRES, YOUR CONCERNS, YOUR PRIORITIES. SHOW ME BY YOUR GRACE HOW TO PRAY IN KEEPING WITH YOUR NATURE AND ACCORDING TO YOUR WILL. IN JESUS' NAME. AMEN.

If you remain in me and my words remain in you, ask whatever you wish, and it will be given you.

JOHN 15:7

THE LOVE THAT
SETS US FREE

There was nothing beautiful or majestic about his appearance. . . . He was
. . . a man of sorrows, acquainted with bitterest grief.

ISAIAH 53:2–3 NLT

T
he great plastic surgeon Dr. Maxwell Maltz once met a woman who was concerned about her husband. He had been terribly disfigured in an unsuccessful
attempt to save his parents from a house fire. Not only had he lost both his mother and
his father in the tragedy, but his face and hands were almost unrecognizable.

The man gave up on life and went into hiding, becoming a recluse and planning to
stay that way for the rest of his days. He refused to see
anyone, including his wife. At that point, she traveled
to see Dr. Maltz with a shocking request: "If you disfigure my face, doctor, then maybe he'll let me back into
his life. Please do this for me, doctor. I love him so
much."

Of course, Dr. Maltz could not fulfill her request,
but he was moved by her love. He went to the home of
the disfigured man and knocked on the locked door.
There was no answer. He called out loudly through the
door, "I know you're in there! I am a plastic surgeon,
and I can restore your face." Again, there was no
answer. Then Dr. Maltz called to the man, "Your wife loves you so much that she is
willing to disfigure her own face in order to be with you. That's how much she wants
to help you!" The doorknob slowly opened, and the disfigured man walked through and
found a new life.

Love has the amazing ability to set us free. Jesus modeled this kind of love when
He became disfigured for our sakes, to set us free from the disfigurement of our own
sin. Because of Him, we have been set free to pursue a new life of righteousness and
freedom.

GRACE FOR TODAY:

**God's love
never fails to
set us free to
really live.**

PARABLES

[Jesus] taught by using stories, many stories.

MARK 4:2 MSG

God enriches human experience through stories that are rooted in His truths. Great works of literature such as John Bunyan's *Pilgrim's Progress,* Victor Hugo's *Les Misérables,* J. R. R. Tolkien's *The Lord of the Rings,* and C. S. Lewis' *The Chronicles of Narnia* have an enduring power to teach us about faith and inspire us to live it out. These and other Christian writings are rich with biblical imagery, and scriptural themes run through them like veins of gold through a range of beautiful, rugged mountains. They leave us with the memory of marvelous characters and compelling acts of self–sacrifice, compassion, and trust in God, arousing within us a strong desire to know the Lord and to be righteous and good. How wonderfully God blesses us through His gift of imagination! Truly we would be much poorer had we never met Christian, Jean Valjean, Aragorn, and Aslan.

GRACE FOR TODAY:

God allows us to glorify His name through creative gifts.

Jesus knew the power of a good story. He told parables often, using metaphors to teach important principles about God and the kingdom of Heaven. Fortunately, Christ explained to His disciples the meaning behind His parables, to ensure that the lessons these allegories contained were clearly understood. Of course, Jesus could have taught in a more direct manner, but He recognized that a story inspired by the Holy Spirit has the remarkable ability to touch our hearts as well as our minds, leaving an indelible impression.

Enjoy the masterpieces of Christian literature, and more recent, contemporary fiction that points to the Bible. Allow God to enrich your life through these writings. More importantly, take time to read and study Jesus' parables. God will use them even more powerfully to enlighten and inspire you, for they carry the considerable added weight of being straight from His Word.

PIANO SOLO

Your love has made me happy and has greatly encouraged me.

PHILEMON 1:7 CEV

The ability to encourage others is a gift of the Holy Spirit. God sends His grace to you through the edifying words and deeds of His people.

A church decided to put on a talent show to raise money for missions. One member told his wife this would be a good opportunity to debut a piano piece he composed years earlier. The praise song had become very meaningful to him, and he often used it as a personal time of worship. He could play it in his sleep, but he rehearsed it diligently anyhow. He was nervous about performing in front of an audience, but he wanted to share his song with others.

At the show, he tried to calm his nerves as he waited for his turn to go on stage. When his name was announced, he sat at the piano, cleared his throat, and introduced his song, talking about what he had tried to express while writing it. Then he started to play.

At first things went well, but soon his self-consciousness got the better of him, and he began fumbling the notes. Finally, he got so flustered that he lost his place and had to stop. He apologized and left the stage as the audience applauded his effort.

He was disappointed and frustrated with himself. At home, however, his godly wife reminded him of how much he meant to her and how the Lord had gifted him in many ways. She reminded him, too, that his self-worth wasn't tied to being able to perform well in front of people. Then she kissed him and went to bed.

Encouraged, he sat at his piano and played his song the way it was meant to be played—as an intimate time of communion between him and his heavenly Father.

GRACE FOR TODAY:

God uses the words and deeds of others
to encourage and inspire us.

A Second Opportunity to Get It Right

If we confess our sins, He is faithful and just to forgive us.

1 John 1:9 NKJV

Many of the people whom we today consider to be highly successful could once have been considered failures. But their perseverance caused them to press on and achieve amazing results for the human race.

Jonas Salk attempted two hundred unsuccessful vaccines for polio before he finally came up with the one that worked. Someone later asked him, "How did it feel to fail two hundred times trying to invent a vaccine for polio?" He replied indignantly, "Why, I never failed at anything in my life! My family told me to never use that word. I simply discovered two hundred ways not to make a vaccine for polio."

Winston Churchill, the great orator and leader of Great Britain through a turbulent time in history, was once asked, "What made you most prepared to lead England through World War II?" His reply? "It was the time I repeated a class in grade school." His inquisitive questioner then asked: "You mean you flunked a grade?" Winston Churchill straightened himself up to his full height and replied: "I never flunked in my life. I was given a second opportunity to get it right!"

Aren't you glad that God also gives us "second chances to get it right"? No matter how many times you feel you may have failed Him, you can always come back to Him, seek forgiveness, and try again. The Christian life isn't something that is accomplished overnight; it's a process of learning and growing and following Jesus. And failures may sometimes be a part of that process. But don't give up. With God's help, success is just around the corner.

Grace for Today:

God gives us "second chances" to get it right.

MILESTONES

When things get difficult and your trust in God is being tested, or when you are about to take a step of faith into unknown territory, the Lord will graciously remind you of times in the past when He has proven himself reliable. If you continue to seek the Lord and are attentive to His voice, He will bring to your mind those instances when He helped you endure trying circumstances or provided for your needs after you stepped out in obedience to Him.

People in the Old Testament used to set up stone altars to honor God in the places where He came to their aid. Today many Christians keep journals to record how God answers their prayers. Others make a note in the margins of their Bible whenever the Lord works mightily in their lives. More creative types compose poems, songs, or works of art to commemorate such events. If you find a way to keep track of how and when God blesses you, He will use it powerfully in the years ahead to encourage you to continue living in complete dependence on Him.

This blessing will flow down to your children and the generations that follow, if you faithfully record the marks of God's grace upon your life, preserving them for posterity. After Joshua led the Israelites across the Jordan River and into the Promised Land, God told him to take twelve stones from the middle of the dry riverbed and set them up as a memorial. The Lord intended to use this pile of stones to benefit others in the future, when the Israelites' children and grandchildren would ask about their meaning, learn of how He had miraculously caused the river to stop flowing, and be inspired to place their trust in Him.

> **GRACE FOR TODAY:**
> God will remind you of His faithfulness in the past to encourage you to keep relying on Him in the future.

Samuel took a stone and set it up between Mizpah and Shen, and called its name Ebenezer, saying, "Thus far the Lord has helped us."

1 SAMUEL 7:12 NKJV

SATISFACTION WITH LITTLE

By John MacArthur Jr.

Our needs as human beings are simple: food, clothing, shelter, and godliness with contentment. Scripture says to be content with the bare necessities of life.

That attitude is in marked contrast to the attitude of our culture. People today aren't content—with little or much. My theory is that the more people have, the more discontent they're apt to be. Typically, the most unhappy people you'll ever meet are very wealthy. They seem to believe their needs can never be met. Unlike Paul, they assume their wants are needs. They've followed our materialistic culture's lead in redefining human needs.

You'll never come across a commercial or ad that tells you to eat food, drink water, or go to sleep. Mass media advertises items that are far more optional and discretionary, but you'd never know it from the sales pitch. The appeal isn't, "Wouldn't you like to have this?" but "You need this!" If you expose yourself to such appeals without thinking, you'll find yourself needing things you don't even want! The goal of this kind of advertising is to produce discontent and make a sale.

To protect yourself, pay careful attention whenever you attach the word need to something in your thoughts or speech. Edit any use of it that goes beyond life's bare essentials. Paul did, and you can too. Thankfully regard any surplus as a blessing from God. You will be satisfied with little when you refuse to depend on luxuries the world redefines as needs.[35]

—⁓—

HEAVENLY FATHER: THANK YOU FOR PROVIDING ALL I NEED. GRANT ME YOUR WISDOM AS I SEPARATE MY NEEDS FROM MY WANTS AND SEEK A LIFE OF CONTENTMENT AND THANKFULNESS. AMEN.

I have learned to be content whatever the circumstances.
I know what it is to be in need, and I know what it is to have plenty.
I have learned the secret of being content in any and every situation,
whether well fed or hungry.

PHILIPPIANS 4:11–12

LISTEN FIRST—ASK QUESTIONS LATER

Everyone should be quick to listen, slow to speak and
slow to become angry.

JAMES 1:19

O ne of Gary Larson's "Far Side" cartoons depicts a bearded man standing at
his front door. He is dripping wet, and his clothes are in shreds. His wife
opens the door, and the caption to the cartoon has her saying to the bearded man: "For
crying out loud, Jonah! Three days late, covered with slime, smelling like a fish. And
what story have I got to swallow this time?"

While this cartoon is amusing because we know
the rest of the story, many times we are a lot like
Jonah's wife. We jump to conclusions, making all kinds
of assumptions about other people, without listening
first. King Solomon, arguably the wisest man to ever
walk on the earth, had a lot to say about watching our
words: "A gentle answer turns away wrath, but a
harsh word stirs up anger" (Proverbs 15:1); "A prudent
man keeps his knowledge to himself, but the heart of
fools blurts out folly" (12:23); and "The lips of the
righteous know what is fitting" (10:32). But perhaps
James could have given Jonah's wife the best advice of
all: "Be quick to listen, slow to speak and slow to
become angry" (James 1:19).

> ### GRACE FOR TODAY:
>
> God never
> makes
> assumptions
> about us. He
> always knows
> what is in our
> hearts.

How about you? Are you like Jonah's wife in the cartoon? Or are you more like
the "prudent man," watching your words carefully and taking care to listen to what others have to say before jumping to conclusions? Jonah had a pretty good reason for
showing up the way he did—if only he'd had a chance to explain!

PERISHABLES

Stockpile treasure in heaven, where it's safe from moth and rust.

MATTHEW 6:20 MSG

There really are such things as hidden blessings, or blessings in disguise. See how many you can spot in the next paragraph.

As John hurriedly buttons his shirtsleeves, he sees that the edge of one cuff is starting to fray. He sits on the bed to put on his shoes, which look a little scuffed. One of the laces breaks when he pulls it tight. His wife offers to replace it while he puts on a tie, so he won't be late for work. He picks out a burgundy one; it's kind of faded, but it'll do. On his way down to the kitchen, John almost trips on a toy truck lying broken at the foot of the stairs. The light is out in the refrigerator. John reaches for the milk, then pours it out after checking the expiration date. Grabbing some orange juice and a bagel, he picks up his worn briefcase, yells goodbye, and heads out to the garage. His hands full, he struggles to open the car door, which is showing a bit of rust. Finally, John pulls out of the driveway, but not before noticing a tiny crack in his windshield.

Maybe you see the blessings easily. Some may seem pretty obvious: John is alive; he has a wife, a child, a roof over his head, a bed to sleep in, clothes on his back, modern appliances, food to eat, a car, a job. However, like John, you may not recognize one of life's greatest hidden blessings. Because of God's grace, every hint of brokenness and decay that you encounter each day can serve as a gentle little reminder that waiting in Heaven for you is an inheritance that will never perish, an eternal treasure that far surpasses the fading things of this world.

> GRACE FOR TODAY:
>
> God uses the perishable things of this world to remind us of our everlasting treasure in the next.

FOCAL POINTS

Let us run with endurance the race that is set before us, looking unto Jesus . . . who for the joy that was set before Him endured the cross.

HEBREWS 12:1–2 NKJV

When a couple attends a Lamaze class prior to the birth of their baby, one of the techniques they are taught is to take a special object with them into the delivery room and use it as a focal point. Concentrating intently on this object during each labor contraction helps the mother shift her attention away from the pain and better withstand it. Many couples choose a stuffed animal or a child's toy to symbolize the joy their new baby will bring. Of course, this technique doesn't bring complete relief—far from it—but trying not to think about the pain helps somewhat, and focusing on the happiness to come provides inspiration, a reason to persevere through the suffering. Afterward, as the parents rejoice over their beautiful baby, the pain is quickly forgotten, and the words of John 16:21 are proven true.

God gives you two excellent focal points to help you through your trials as a Christian. First, He encourages you to fix your eyes on Jesus. Take your mind off your own suffering by considering what Christ suffered for your sake. Concentrate on His teachings about how to live a godly life despite hardship and pain. Focus on His example of how to humble yourself before others, how to turn the other cheek, and how to forgive those who hurt you.

Second, God invites you to do as Jesus did and fix your eyes on the promise of Heaven. God set this joy before Christ, and it bore Him through His ordeal. God lays this same joy before you, knowing it will carry you through as well. Moses knew and practiced this technique, as did the apostle Paul. Both kept their eyes squarely focused on their eternal reward in Paradise, where joy washes away all memory of pain.

GRACE FOR TODAY:

God sets the joy of Heaven before us, to carry us through all our trials.

FACING THE MOUNTAIN

[Jesus said,] "Say to this mountain, 'May God lift you up and throw you into the sea,' and your command will be obeyed."

MARK 11:23 NLT

S ir Edmund Hillary was the first person to every conquer Mount Everest, the first man to ever plant his flag at the mountain's peak. What is not often told, however, is that the first time he tried to climb the mountain, he failed.

Not too long after this first failure, he was knighted by the Queen of England, and at that gala occasion, right there on the wall behind the head table, hung a huge picture of Mount Everest. When Hillary was introduced, the people gave him a standing ovation for even daring to attempt the treacherous climb. When they finally ceased applauding, however, Hillary turned his back on the audience, faced that picture of the awesome mountain, and loudly declared, "Mount Everest, you have defeated me once, and you might defeat me again. But I'm coming back again and again, and I'm going to win because you can't get any bigger, Mount Everest, and I can!"

What an attitude! What perseverance! Ultimately, this attitude is what drove Hillary to stand on top of the mountain he had conquered.

What mountain are you facing today? What failure has caused you to think that you might not ever succeed? Turn to it, and with faith in God and in His ability to help you through anything, declare, "You can't get any bigger, mountain, but my faith can!" With God, all things are possible (see Mark 10:27), and your mountain can be removed and cast into the sea, if you persevere.

GRACE FOR TODAY:

All things are possible with God—including conquering the mountain you are facing.

GOD PROVIDES THE VICTORY

When the Israelites called out to God for deliverance from their enemies, the Lord called upon Gideon to lead the people and promised him the victory. Understandably, Gideon was a bit reluctant to believe this promise at first—his tribe was weakest in all of Israel— so he asked God for a sign. God complied, but Gideon was still hesitant, so he asked for another sign to make sure his understanding was correct. God performed this sign as well, and then told Gideon to get moving!

Gideon raised a mighty army and soon felt comfortable the Israelites would succeed. However, God didn't want any doubt about who would be providing the victory, so He instructed Gideon to send 70 percent of his men home, then cut this number down to three hundred. When Gideon defeated the enemy, the Israelites clearly understood it was God who had provided the victory.

Often, it is not until you have exhausted your own means that God provides the victory in your life. Like the Israelites, He wants you to trust in the power of His grace for victory— not your own strength. Doing so requires faith on your part and a willingness to follow everything He commands you to do. You will have to trust in a power greater than your own and believe in the love and protection of Christ.

Victory in life comes through walking with God on a daily basis. Prayer and study in the Word fortifies you against attacks from the enemy and allows God to pour His grace into your life. As you trust in God and remain in His grace, He will give you the confidence and hope to overcome any situation.

> **GRACE FOR TODAY:**
>
> As we walk through life with God, He gives us victory over every obstacle.

It is the Lord . . . who goes with you, to fight for you against your enemies, to give you victory.

DEUTERONOMY 20:4 NRSV

The God of Grace

By Luis Palau

In my ministry, I have counseled many people who are bored with certain aspects of their lives—their jobs, their spouses, their vacations, their friends, their homes. Often these people appear to have great jobs, perfect families, active social lives, and nice homes. Yet inside, they are so bored they can hardly stand it.

I, too, have experienced boredom in my life. One of the most boring periods of my life occurred when I worked for the Bank of London in Argentina. Partly because I spoke English and Spanish, I had tremendous opportunities for advancement. Yet, in spite of what appeared to be a great job, I was bored stiff with the routine.

How can people be bored when their lives seem to be going great? Is there a solution to the problem of boredom? I think Dr. Harold Dodds understands this problem very well when he says: "It is not the fast tempo of modern life that kills, but the boredom, a lack of strong interest, and failure to grow that destroys. It is the feeling that nothing is worthwhile that makes men ill and unhappy."

God doesn't want us to live life halfheartedly. He has exciting plans for us! He wants us to live life to the fullest. That is a part of His grace.

When we seek to please God and walk according to His will, we will not be bored. We will live full lives. We can take God's promise to heart.[30]

―❦―

LOVING FATHER: I BELIEVE THAT YOU HAVE AN EXCITING PLAN FOR MY LIFE, A PLAN MORE WONDERFUL THAN ANYTHING I COULD IMAGINE. I ASK YOU TO TAKE MY BOREDOM AND GIVE ME YOUR ENTHUSIASM. SHOW ME HOW TO LIVE WHOLEHEARTEDLY. AMEN.

"I know the plans I have for you," declares the Lord, "plans to prosper you and not to harm you, plans to give you hope and a future."

JEREMIAH 29:11

A GOOD WORD

No matter what happens, always be thankful, for this is God's will for you who belong to Christ Jesus.

1 THESSALONIANS 5:18 TLB

At the peak of his career, Mark Twain earned five dollars a word for the magazine articles he wrote. One of his critics sent him a five-dollar bill in an envelope, enclosed with a note that read: "Dear Mr. Twain, Please send me a good word."

On a sheet of paper, Mark Twain responded with this "good word": "Thanks!"

The word "thanks" is a good word, because being grateful helps us to hold on to the good things in life, to recognize them and appreciate them for who and what they are. When we say thanks, we are acknowledging that we can't make it on our own. We are dependent on other people, and that's not a bad thing! It's the way God has made us.

"Thanks" is also a good word because being grateful opens us up to happiness—and to God. A young woman with a crippling disease was left paralyzed and almost without a voice. An insensitive social worker asked her one day if she wouldn't just as soon be dead. With a radiant face that beamed with happiness, the girl whispered from her wheelchair: "I would not have missed being alive for anything. I thank God for every minute—even the most impossible ones."

Be thankful today for the blessings that God has put into your life: family, friends, shelter, clothing, productive work, joy in the little things, and even the struggles that bring you closer to Him. If you want to give someone a good word today, say "Thanks."

> **GRACE FOR TODAY:**
>
> When we offer Him our grateful hearts, God gives meaning and purpose to even the most impossible minutes and hours of our lives.

A True Friend to the End

The heartfelt counsel of a friend is as sweet as perfume and incense.

PROVERBS 27:9 NLT

There is nothing quite like the feeling of knowing that you have a close friend who will always be by your side. Someone with whom you can share the intimate details of your life and know that he or she will listen and understand. Someone whom you can depend upon to give you good advice and support you in the love and grace of God. Someone whom Proverbs 18:24 says "is a friend that will stick closer than a brother."

In the Bible, David and Jonathan were two of the more unlikely individuals to share this type of friendship. David was a shepherd boy who had been anointed by God to assume the throne of Israel. Jonathan was the son of the king and in the line of succession. Yet the two put aside any feelings of jealousy between them and formed a bond that would last their entire lives.

Even when things got bad between David and King Saul, Jonathan remained David's friend. Though this friendship created tension in Jonathan's own relationship with his father, he trusted in the will of the Lord and had the courage to remain loyal. Though Jonathan knew that he and David would have to part ways, he committed to forever being David's friend.

It takes a great deal of courage to reveal your true self to others and share your life with them. Yet when you open up yourself to others, you allow God to fill you with His grace, and you experience His love. And as others experience trials in their lives, you also enable God to use you as a means of extending His grace directly into their lives.

> **GRACE FOR TODAY:**
>
> God gives us courage to reveal our true selves to Him and to others.

BELIEVE BEFORE YOU SEE

Jesus said, "So, you believe because you've seen with your own eyes.
Even better blessings are in store for those who believe without seeing."

JOHN 20:29 MSG

For ages, mankind has sought evidence of the existence of God. In fact, biblical artifacts are among the most sought-after treasures for anthropologists and historians. There seems to be a belief that, if they can find some relic or perhaps some evidence of an ancient city of the Bible, it would dispel all of their doubts and help them truly believe.

But history has shown us that the finding of such historical objects does not increase faith. Instead, it simply raises more questions. The truth that God is real cannot be proven by the latest scientific expedition. It must be experienced. He is more than a fact; He's a personal God, who reveals himself to us on a personal level.

Precious Christian, God is real. He is real to those who go to Him in faith. He is real to those who trust Him enough to believe what He says, instead of what they see. The unbelieving world tells us that seeing is believing. But with God, we must believe before we see.

Someday, someone may actually locate Noah's Ark on Mount Ararat's icy face. Someone may come up with convincing evidence that the Shroud of Turin once was wrapped around our Savior's body. But those things will always be conjecture. The only real proof is our lives transformed by faith in a living Lord.

GRACE FOR TODAY:

God has given us His living presence in our hearts as
the eternal proof that He exists.

I SEE MYSELF IN YOU

All of you together are Christ's body, and each one of you is
a separate and necessary part of it.

1 CORINTHIANS 12:27 NLT

There is an old rabbinic story in which the rabbi asks, "Children, how can we determine this moment of dawn, when the night ends and the day begins?"

One person responded, "When I see the difference between a dog and a sheep?"

"No," said the rabbi.

A second person asked, "Is it when I can see the difference between a fig tree and a grapevine?"

"No."

"Please tell us the answer," said the students.

The old rabbi responded, "You know when the night ends and the day begins when you can look into the face of any human being and have enough light to recognize that person as your brother or your sister; when you can say, 'I see myself in you.' Up until that time it is night, and the darkness is still with us."

"I see myself in you." What important words for Christians to understand today! Paul wrote that as believers, we are all together part of Christ's body, which means that if one of us stubs his toe, the others among us hurt along with him. No wonder he also wrote, "When others are happy, be happy with them. If they are sad, share their sorrow. Live in harmony with each other" (Romans 12:15–16 NLT). When your brothers and sisters in Christ sorrow or rejoice, share those troubles and joys with them—and they will do the same for you. See yourselves in each other—and then you will know that the night has ended and the dawn has come.

GRACE FOR TODAY:

Through our faith in Jesus, God has made us all part
of the Body of Christ.

THOSE GRACEFUL RELATIVES

Looking back, Elaine could remember moments in her life when her family simply drove her crazy. Her father could be stubborn and liked to joke around at her expense. Her mother could be overprotective and tended to nag her about the slightest things. Her sisters could talk for hours about the most irrelevant subjects. Then there was her Aunt May, who liked to drop by unannounced, along with her four cats.

Growing up, Elaine often looked forward to the day when she would go off to college and gain her independence. Yet after living a year on her own, she found herself missing some of those little things that used to irritate her. She missed the spirited debates she had with her dad and his quick wit. She missed having a person like her mom around who was truly concerned about her well-being. She missed the long conversations with her sisters and the opportunity to be involved in their lives. She even missed old Aunt May—but not the allergic reaction she had to her cats.

However, no matter how far Elaine was removed from her family, she knew that she would always have a place in their hearts. She could count on them to be there when she needed encouragement and motivation to get through difficult times. She could also depend on them to tell her the truth about a situation, even if she didn't want to hear it.

It took time away from home for Elaine to realize that her family was a gift that God had provided to her through His grace. As she picked up the phone to call them, she thanked God for the incredible influence they had been in her life.

> **GRACE FOR TODAY:**
>
> **Family is God's way of encouraging us in hard times and speaking the truth to us when we have trouble hearing His voice.**

Grandchildren are the crowning glory of the aged;
parents are the pride of their children.

PROVERBS 17:6 NLT

WE CAN BELIEVE THE PROMISES OF GOD

By Luis Palau

Jesus' death and resurrection are our guarantee that God is faithful, that He hears our prayers, and that all His promises are true. Paul clearly explains this to the Corinthians because if they have any doubts about his integrity as God's messenger, they probably doubt God's message too.

I have a hunch that many Christians today, like the Corinthians, occasionally have trouble believing God's promises. Oh, the promises sound nice. Sometimes they even cheer us up. Yet I think many of us have, at least unconsciously, questioned whether God is faithful to keep His promises. We'll sometimes catch ourselves thinking, *Are the promises of God really true?*

None of God's promises ever has failed! The great evangelist D. L. Moody confidently stated, "God never made a promise that was too good to be true." Think about that! No wonder Jesus says not to worry about tomorrow (Matthew 6:25). God did not create us to be self-sufficient. He created us to depend on Him. We don't have to rush around trying to solve all our problems and trials in thirty seconds. We don't have to exhaust all of our human problem-solving options before we turn to God as a last resort. Every trial we face is an opportunity for God to demonstrate His loving faithfulness to us.

God has been faithful to His people in the past and promises to be faithful in the future. Thus, we have no need to worry. We can rest assured that the God who is faithful will fulfill every promise we claim in the name of Jesus.[37]

—⌇—

HEAVENLY FATHER: TEACH ME TO LOOK AT MY TRIALS AS OPPORTUNITIES TO SEE YOUR GRACE AND FAITHFULNESS POURED OUT IN MY LIFE. BEGINNING TODAY, I WILL EXCHANGE EACH WORRY FOR ONE OF YOUR GRACIOUS PROMISES. AMEN.

God, who has called you into fellowship with
his Son Jesus Christ our Lord, is faithful.

1 CORINTHIANS 1:9

WHAT DOESN'T KILL ME . . .

Those who hope in the Lord will renew their strength.

ISAIAH 40:31

Experiments were done during space flights to test the effects of weightlessness on the aging process. Both carpenter ants and honeybees were used in the studies, and both species were found to age more rapidly and die more quickly in a weightless environment. It seems they needed the pull of gravity to make their bodies work and maintain their physical vitality.

That's a great parable for us humans! If things are too easy, we grow flabby. Everyone understands that it's the weight on the bar that builds up the lifter's muscles. We all need some level of difficulty to keep us strong. It's the awareness of this fact, however, that can give us an entirely new perspective.

"This has been the period of my greatest growth in life," a man once said. The significance of his statement lay in the fact that he had lost his job six months earlier, and two months after that, his wife was diagnosed with cancer.

Don't despair of the struggle you are facing. With the right attitude, problems and tragedy can become our teachers, not our enemies. Without them, our spiritual "muscles" would grow weak and flabby. A man once quipped, "What doesn't kill me will make me stronger." We may chuckle at his statement, but in many ways, he was right! Learn to exercise your faith, even in the disappointments and difficult circumstances of life. You'll be amazed at the strength you'll show!

> **GRACE FOR TODAY:**
>
> God's grace allows our problems to become our teachers rather than our enemies.

MAKING THE MOST OF LIFE

Think about what is true . . . what is noble, right and pure . . . what is lovely and worthy of respect.

PHILIPPIANS 4:8 NIRV

"Life is what you make of it," or so the slogan goes, and current research seems to support this claim. People who choose to view life events in positive ways expect favorable results and derive meaning from negative circumstances tend to be happier than those who do not. Happier people, in turn, tend to be more loving, forgiving, trusting, sociable, and helpful towards others.

According to a 2001 study conducted by the American Psychological Association, contented people also have good self-esteem and the ability to see the positive things in their lives. They have a good network of friends and at least a few close ones with whom they can share intimate details. They feel good about their jobs and believe they are effective in their chosen activities. They also consider their faith to be the most important influence in their lives.

When you allow God to be your foundation and focus on serving Him, He will give you contentment through His grace. He will reveal just how much He loves and values you and build your self-esteem. As you concentrate on His grace and comprehend the blessings He has provided, you will gain new hope and optimism for the future. With a new focus on others, you will understand the joy of loving others and sharing with them. You will discover the gifts God has given and seek to use them for His glory—and He will bless whatever you do.

If life is truly "what you make it," choose to make it a good one. Learn to rely on the grace of God and His provision for your life, and always put your faith in Him.

> **GRACE FOR TODAY:**
>
> When we focus our lives on Him, God gives us the gift of true contentment.

IS ANYONE THIRSTY?

As a deer longs for a stream of cool water, so I long for you, O God.

PSALM 42:1 GNB

Few of us can ever understand what it is like to be really thirsty. Water is plentiful and accessible to us almost all the time. But in some places in the world, people suffer from thirst daily. They know what it's like to walk miles down dusty roads to get the one thing that will end their craving. They know what it's like to carry the precious liquid back on their heads and shoulders, careful not to spill a drop. Though we often take it for granted, water is life itself. Without it, there is only death.

God wants us to seek Him as we would seek water—as though we cannot live without Him. He wants us to view Him as our very life. And when we feel ourselves becoming thirsty spiritually, He wants us to search until we find the living water that will satisfy.

You see, spiritually speaking, this world is a dry, barren desert. It cannot sustain us—only God can keep our spirits alive and well. But God has left us several wonderful sources of water to quench our spiritual thirst. He has given us the Holy Scriptures—the Bible—from which to drink of His goodness and mercy. He has given us vital communion with the "living water"—Jesus Christ—through prayer and praise. And that's just the beginning. He's also given us the water of Christian fellowship and His wonderful, thirst-quenching Presence.

Don't live with spiritual thirst. Drink daily from the pure stream of God's grace.

GRACE FOR TODAY:

God has provided life—giving water for
our thirsty souls.

SOMEONE ALWAYS FORGETS

The King will reply, " . . . Whenever you did this for one of the least important . . . you did it for me!"

MATTHEW 25:40 GNB

Halford Luccock once told about a young man who lived and worked in a pretty tough environment. He tried to hold on to his faith, even when people were cruel to him. He was not always appreciated for his religious views, and people often made fun of him. They were always challenging him and his commitment.

One day a particularly abusive person shouted at him, "You fool! Can't you see that if there were a God who cared a penny for the likes of you, He would tell someone to come along and give you what you need—decent food, a bed of your own, at least a chance to make good?"

The young man calmly replied to the man's insult: "I reckon God does tell someone. But someone always forgets."

God does tell someone—the believers, His children, His Church—to feed the hungry, to clothe the naked, to provide shelter for the homeless, to visit the widows, to pay attention to prisoners. God does tell someone. But that "someone" often forgets.

Jesus promises to bless those who obey His commands to be His hands and feet in a lost and hungry, lonely world. He even goes so far as to say that when we show kindness to "one of the least of these," we have shown kindness to Jesus himself! (See Matthew 25:31–46.)

Don't "forget" about the needs of the people around you. When you serve them, you are serving Jesus, and He loves to bless those who selflessly give of themselves to others.

GRACE FOR TODAY:

God promises great blessing for those who are willing to become His hands and feet.

A SECURE HOPE

People use the word "hope" to express some form of wish or desire that they would like to have happen. This desire could be an aspiration for the immediate future, as in "I hope you remembered to pick up food for dinner," or it could describe a more general feeling about the future, as in "I am hopeful for you now that you have graduated." It could also represent the object upon which expectations are centered, as in "You are the team's best hope for winning the trophy."

While each of these uses of the word "hope" incorporates some form of positive outlook for the future, each also implies a degree of uncertainty on the part of the speakers. After all, they may doubt that you remembered to pick up food, wonder if the future will really improve now that you've graduated, or be uncertain as to whether you really are good enough to win the trophy for the team.

Such is not the case when the Biblical authors refer to "hope." In 1 Peter 1:13 NASB, when the writer states, "fix your hope completely on the grace to be brought to you at the revelation of Jesus Christ," he means that when you hope in Christ, you not only desire good things to happen in the future (such as the grace of God to come upon you) but you expect it to occur.

When you believe in the grace of God, accept His love, and place your hope in Him, you can expect Him to faithfully remain by your side throughout your life. You can depend upon the promises in His Word and rest in the knowledge that He will keep you safe in His loving arms.

> **GRACE FOR TODAY:**
>
> ## When we hope in Christ, we can depend on Him and His promises.

Faith and understanding rest on the hope of eternal life.
Before time began, God promised to give that life.

TITUS 1:2 NIRV

THROW AWAY THE MASK

By Luis Palau

When we live in godly sincerity, we don't wear masks. We don't try to act like fine Christians. We don't build up a "Christian" façade to impress other people. Godly sincerity simply means we are who we are in Jesus Christ. It means we walk in the light of the Lord, no longer putting on a show to deceive others.

Christians have no reason to live behind a mask. Christians are admonished to "walk in the light, as he is in the light" (1 John 1:7). This means we are to walk before God and man with the same transparency—or, as Paul says, sincerity—that Christ showed in His life. And by accepting the grace of God, we can do so.

When we place ourselves under the control of the indwelling Christ, we then are able to boast about our conscience and live in godly sincerity. When our hearts are transparent before God, we suffer no guilt from sin; we can boldly proclaim the message of Jesus Christ.

We don't have to put on any kind of spiritual show because the power and authority of the Holy Spirit are at work within us.

Nothing is more humbling than the expectation of standing before the Lord Jesus in judgment. On that day, all façades will be exposed. Everyone who has hidden behind a mask will be revealed. But those who know the all-sufficient Father, and are controlled by His grace, can live with a clear conscience and godly sincerity until that day.[38]

DEAR LORD: I RECEIVE YOUR GRACE AS I LAY DOWN MY MASK AND RESOLVE TO WALK IN SINCERITY AND TRUTH. I KNOW THIS IS POSSIBLE ONLY BECAUSE OF JESUS AND THE WORK OF REDEMPTION. THANK YOU FOR RECEIVING ME JUST AS I AM. AMEN.

If we walk in the light as he himself is in the light, we have fellowship with one another, and the blood of Jesus his Son cleanses us from all sin.

1 JOHN 1:7 NRSV

A TRUE FRIEND

There are "friends" who pretend to be friends, but there is a friend who sticks closer than a brother.

PROVERBS 18:24 TLB

"**A**manda, why don't you hang out with Stacy anymore?" a friend asked.

"Would you hang out with someone who flirts with your boyfriend whenever she gets a chance? Someone who copies everything you do—your clothes, your hairstyle, even the way you laugh?" Amanda asked.

"I guess not," admitted the friend.

GRACE FOR TODAY:

God is our model for true friendship. He promises never to betray our trust, and He will always be there when we need Him.

"Would you want to hang out with someone for whom, no matter what you did for her, it was never enough? Would you want to hang out with someone who talks bad about you behind your back?" Amanda continued.

"No way," the friend agreed.

"Neither did Stacy," Amanda said sadly.

Amanda learned a hard lesson that day—that for a person to have friends, he must "show himself friend- ly" (Proverbs 18:24 KJV). Amanda had been a "friend" who liked to call herself a friend, but who really didn't know the meaning of the word.

What kind of friend are you? Are you someone who takes advantage of your friends, or are you a friend who "shows herself friendly"—who provides kindness, love, and support, a shoulder to cry on in sad times, and shared laughter and joy in the good times? Don't be like Amanda, whose friend eventually deserted her. Instead, fos- ter deep, solid friendships based on mutual trust and sharing—in other words, be like Jesus, the "friend who sticks closer than a brother" (18:24 TLB).

BLESSINGS IN DISGUISE

We know that in all things God works for the good of those who love
him, who have been called according to his purpose.

ROMANS 8:28

D iscovering you have made a mistake is never a fun experience. Mistakes can
be aggravating wastes of time that leave you feeling frustrated and angry. Yet
mistakes can often turn out to be a blessing in disguise. In fact, some of the most practical inventions in the past century originally began as mistakes.

In 1849, for example, Jean-Baptiste Jolley accidentally spilled oil from a lamp on
his wife's tablecloth. Fearing the oil would destroy the cloth, he frantically wiped it up,
only to discover that the tablecloth became cleaner with
each swipe. With a bit of tinkering, he invented a sol-
vent that would clean fabric better than soap and water,
thus founding the dry cleaning business.

In the 1940s, engineers at General Electric rejected a material known today as "silly putty" because it
made a poor rubber substitute. Likewise, in the 1960s,
engineers at 3M looking for a way to make a powerful
glue rejected a substance that would later be used in
Post-It Notes because it bonded weakly and pulled
apart too easily.

> **GRACE FOR TODAY:**
>
> God turns even
> our mistakes
> into something
> good.

At times it can seem like all you are doing is mak-
ing mistakes and that your efforts are not bearing any fruit. However, when you follow God and seek to do His will, He will take your "mistakes" and turn them into
something good. He will use your efforts for His glory and bless you when you persevere in the tasks He has prepared for you.

You may not be able to see progress now, but God sees the whole picture and
knows the end result. So submit your efforts to God and rest in His grace, knowing
that He will bless the work you have done for His kingdom.

CAN HE SHAKE YOUR HAND ON IT?

The integrity of the upright shall guide them.

PROVERBS 11:3 ASV

Honor is not a word we hear much about these days. It used to be that a hand-shake would cinch a deal, and a man's word was his bond. But today, even a contract doesn't always do the job. Not so long ago, goods and services were sold at face value, but now, we have to read fine print before we buy anything, from anyone. Honor has taken a backseat in this present world—but not with God.

What God has spoken in His Word is indisputable. He will do exactly what He says He will do, no matter what is happening in this world. He will bless us. He will provide for us. He will love us. He is a God of honor. And He wants us to be people of honor. He wants us to be His holy children, without reproach in this world, keeping our promises just as He keeps His.

How can we expect those around us to believe our message of God's love and grace and faithfulness if they can't trust what we tell them concerning the simple affairs of daily life? It would be difficult to share the love of Christ with those we have short-changed. It's even hard to pray with our spouses and children when we haven't kept our word to them.

Honor may not be the norm for most, but it should always be the rule of the day for Christians. Ask God to show you those areas where the walls of honor in your life need shoring. He's promised to help you walk honorably in this world—and He always keeps His promises.

GRACE FOR TODAY:

God always keeps His word, and He wants to help us keep ours.

The "Bozone Layer"

Getting wisdom is the most important thing you can do!

PROVERBS 4:7 NLT

Recently The Washington Post's Style Invitational asked readers to enter a contest. They were to take any word from the dictionary, alter it by adding, subtracting, or changing just one letter, and supply the word with a new definition. Here is just a sampling of the winning entries:

Inoculatte: To take coffee intravenously when you are running late.

Intaxication: Euphoria at getting a tax refund, which lasts only until you realize that it was your money to start out with.

Reintarnation: Coming back to life as a hillbilly.

Dopeler Effect: The tendency for stupid ideas to seem smarter when they come at you rapidly.

Bozone: The substance surrounding some of us that stops wisdom from penetrating. Unfortunately, unlike the ozone layer, the bozone layer shows little sign of breaking down.

Sadly, this last definition is too often true for both ourselves and the people around us! But attaining wisdom, despite our possible "bozone" layers, should still be a priority in our lives. The wisest man who ever lived, King Solomon, once wrote of the importance of wisdom: "Sell everything and buy Wisdom! Forage for Understanding! . . . Above all and before all, do this: Get Wisdom! Write this at the top of your list: Get Understanding!" (Proverbs 4:5, 7 MSG).

The wisdom that Solomon was urging others to attain can come only from a healthy fear of God and obedience to His commands. When you follow God's ways, you will be well on your way to gaining wisdom in your life!

GRACE FOR TODAY:

God offers his wisdom without reservation to all who ask for it.

WHEN PRAYER ISN'T ANSWERED

You have read all of the scriptures about God's faithfulness, learned of His promises to help, and seen God take care of situations in the past. But this time is a different story. You prayed sincerely. You believe what you have asked for is in God's will. You have been patient and searched your own heart. But nothing has happened.

What do you do when prayer doesn't seem to work? And, how do you answer all the questions and doubts that have arisen in your heart and mind? The answer is unwavering faith—faith that hangs on through the toughest questions and the longest waits. Faith that surrenders your understanding to His matchless wisdom.

GRACE FOR TODAY:

By His grace, God transforms our puny faith into an unwavering faith strong enough to move the mountains in our lives.

Well, you may be thinking, *That's fine for the apostles and the great men and women of the faith. But what about me? I'm just a struggling Christian. How do I get my hands on unwavering faith?*

The answer is that you already have it—not one bit less than any believer before you has had. That's true because all faith is a gift of God's grace. Even when we think our faith is weak and puny, we have enough to move mountains. (See Matthew 17:20.)

So let go of your little faith and let God replace it with great faith, unwavering faith, faith that expects miracles no matter how long the wait.

Let us hold fast the confession of our hope without wavering,
for He who promised is faithful.

HEBREWS 10:23 NASB

LIVING A LIFE OF FAITH AND TRUST

By John MacArthur Jr.

George Müller knew a lot about faith—the best way anyone can know anything: He lived it. His early life was one of gross wickedness. By the time he was twenty, the age he became a Christian, he had already done time in jail. But then his interests and attitude radically changed.

After Müller spent years training for the ministry, he went to England to do missionary work among Jewish people. When he and his wife moved to the British seaport of Bristol in 1832, they were horrified to see masses of homeless orphans living and dying in squalid, narrow streets, and foraging for food in garbage heaps.

The Müllers, with an unshakable belief in the Bible, were convinced that if Christians took Scripture seriously, there were no limits to what they could achieve for God. They set out to feed, clothe, and educate destitute orphan children. At the end of their lifetimes, the homes they established cared for more than 10,000 orphans. Unlike many today who say they "live by faith," the Müllers never told anyone but God of their need for funds. He always abundantly provided through their thankful prayers and humble waiting on Him.[30]

———

HEAVENLY FATHER: I KNOW MY GREATEST EFFORTS AMOUNT TO NOTHING WITHOUT THE PROVISION OF YOUR GRACE. I TAKE HOLD OF IT NOW AS I STEP OUT IN FAITH TO WALK IN YOUR PLAN FOR MY LIFE. AMEN.

You've been raised on the Message of the faith and have followed sound teaching. Now pass on this counsel to the Christians there, and you'll be a good servant of Jesus.

1 TIMOTHY 4:6 MSG

WHAT A MISSION FIELD!

[Jesus] said to his disciples, "The harvest is plentiful but the
workers are few."

MATTHEW 9:37

S cholar and author D. A. Carson tells of a time when he and a friend were going
to the beach for some much-needed peace and quiet. When they got there, however, they found that the beach was covered with hordes of high-school kids, celebrating their upcoming graduation with lots of beer and loud music.

Carson wrote: "Deeply disappointed that my evening's relaxation was being shat-
tered by a raucous party, I was getting ready to cover my disappointment by moral
outrage. I turned to [my friend] Ken to unload the
venom, but stopped as I saw him staring at the scene
with a faraway look in his eyes. And then he said,
rather softly, 'High-school kids—what a mission
field!'"

So many times it is easy to overlook the opportunities for mission that God lays directly into our paths.
The tired-looking clerk at the grocery store, the less-
than-hygienic man who services your car, even the
grouchy boss in your workplace—each of these people
are precious to Jesus and someone for whom He died.
You need not pack your bags and head overseas to find
a mission field ripe and ready for harvest. All you real-
ly need to do is look around you and ask the Lord to give you His heart of compassion
for the lost.

When Jesus looked at the crowds around Him one day, He had compassion on
them because they were like "sheep without a shepherd." That's when He turned to
His disciples and said: "The harvest is plentiful but the workers are few. Ask the Lord
of the harvest, therefore, to send out workers into his harvest field" (Matthew 9:37-
38).

Pray to the Lord of the harvest today to show you the mission field He has for
you. You probably won't have to travel far.

> GRACE FOR TODAY:
>
> God promises to
> share with us
> His love and
> compassion for
> the lost.

A UNIQUE CREATION

Try to do your best in using gifts that build up the church.

1 CORINTHIANS 14:12 NIRV

I f you've ever had the experience of getting picked on in school because you didn't fit in with the other kids, you probably have learned the value of conformity. No one enjoys the loneliness associated with being left out of a group or cast aside. Blending in with the crowd often seems the easiest and safest way to avoid such confrontation.

You've probably heard the statement that "no two snowflakes are alike," but you may not know why this is the case. Snowflakes, in fact, begin as similar-looking droplets of water. However, as the snowflakes fall, each is affected differently by slight variations in temperature, which causes it to develop unique crystalline patterns. The longer the snowflake remains in the air, the greater its complexity and individuality.

As a part of God's creation, He has given you unique talents and gifts. Like the snowflake falling from the sky, as you move through this life you encounter various situations that cause you to grow and develop these gifts in different ways. When you continually strive to be like everyone else, you suppress these gifts and deprive others of the abilities you have to help them.

> **GRACE FOR TODAY:**
>
> God has given each one of us unique talents and gifts and the privilege of sharing them with others.

The beauty in snowflakes lies not in their conformity with each other, but in the intricate details that separate one from the next. The beauty in your life is not the degree to which you resemble others, but the intricate details of your life that distinguish you from them. You can choose to play it safe and conceal this beauty in your life, or you can choose to take a chance and use the distinct talents God has given you to share His grace with others.

FOLLOW THE LEADER

Obey those who rule over you, and be submissive,
for they watch out for your souls.

HEBREWS 13:17 NKJV

G eese and other large migratory birds often fly in a type of "V formation," with one bird leading the flock while the others trail closely behind. Flying in this formation, scientists have recently learned, reduces the air resistance on the birds trailing the leader and allows them to conserve energy by gliding more often. By using this technique, a flock of geese can actually lower their heart rates and travel 70 percent farther than other birds flying in isolation.

The interesting thing about this formation is that the goose at the head of the "V" is not always the leader. As one goose at the front tires and begins to lag, another back in the ranks comes forward to take its place at the head of the formation. In this manner, the followers often become the leaders to the benefit of the entire flock.

Although God is the ultimate authority over mankind, He has chosen to delegate His power to different individuals in various leadership roles, including parents, teachers, and church leaders. When you submit to these individuals, you also submit to the authority of God, and your life benefits as a result.

Good leaders can be a powerful influence on your life. Following their advice can allow you to learn from their experience and grow as an individual. Submitting to their authority will also help you learn humility, which God requires from all those who want to follow Him.

Respect the leaders God has placed in your life and view their guidance as an act of God's grace. Besides, like the goose at the head of the V-formation, you never know when God will call you up from the ranks and put you into a leadership position.

GRACE FOR TODAY:

God has placed His leaders in our midst and given
care over our souls.

HE KNOWS WHAT IT'S LIKE

Let [Jesus] have all your worries and cares, for he is always thinking
about you and watching everything that concerns you.

1 PETER 5:7 TLB

When Damien was in high school, his father suddenly passed away—two days before his graduation. He was a brand-new Christian at the time, and the experience was devastating to his faith. He longed to hear God speak, to know what He had to say about the situation, to learn to deal with his grief. Damien prayed—and then he waited for God to speak.

On the day of the funeral, the church was packed. Damien sat with his mother and two sisters in the front row. The priest tried to speak comforting words, but Damien was too numb to hear them. He was struggling to pay attention to the service, hoping that God would speak to him and give him the explanation he so desperately needed.

Suddenly the service was over. The family lined up in the foyer to receive the condolences and sympathy of the congregation as they filed past. Damien stood numbly accepting their words, but still nothing was sinking in, despite the hugs, shed tears, and offers of help and encouragement. And then Damien saw his friend, Kim. She was Damien's age; they were in youth group together. And Kim had buried her own father just months before.

Kim walked over to Damien with tears in her eyes and, without saying a word, simply pulled him into her arms for a hug. In that moment, Damien heard God speak. Kim knew exactly what Damien was going through—and so did God. Damien knew then that he would be okay.

If you want to hear God's voice in your life, you need look no farther than the One who knows exactly what you're going through. Jesus knows what it's like to be human; He knows what it's like to suffer; and He cares. Allow Him to speak to your heart and embrace you in His arms of love.

GRACE FOR TODAY:

There is one who always knows what we're going
through—His name is Jesus.

FOCUS ON WHAT IS TRUE

Before the days of radar and global positioning satellites, sailors relied upon the stars to navigate their ships to safety. One star, known as "Polaris" or the "North Star," was especially important to sailors, for it always remained fixed in the same place in the sky—due north. By using a sextant, sailors could use the North Star to determine the latitude of their ship on a map, and thus chart the proper course they wished to take.

However, finding the North Star took a bit of skill, for the sky was filled with many stars that looked exactly alike. If sailors focused their sextants on the wrong star—something other than the true North Star—they could miscalculate the position of the ship and lose many days traveling in the wrong direction. Only when the sailors focused once again on the true North Star could the error be corrected and the ship set back on course.

Keeping your life focused on God can be difficult to accomplish in a world today that encourages its members to base their lives upon wealth, relationships, and personal ambition. Each day, you are confronted by messages that promote the joy of having money, or the security of having someone to depend upon, or the importance of moving up the corporate ladder. Yet when you focus on these things, you base your life upon something that is unstable, and your path is sure to go astray.

Material wealth will fade away, and people will always disappoint you; but the grace of God will never fail. When you focus on Him and obey His Word, He will guide your way and make all your paths straight.

> GRACE FOR TODAY:
>
> **Material wealth fails to satisfy, but God will never disappoint us.**

Those who live according to the Spirit set their minds on
the things of the Spirit.

ROMANS 8:5 NRSV

COLORED PENCILS

By Luis Palau

Many of us would give anything to live with a clear conscience. We don't realize that all we have to do is admit that we have sinned and need His forgiveness. Once that's done, God will clear out all the skeletons locked away in our closets.

When I was in middle school in Argentina, I stole a box of colored pencils that belonged to a boy named John Payne. Stealing those pencils didn't bother me at first. Later, though, when I began walking closer with the Lord, my conscience wouldn't let me forget the incident.

Years later, I came to the United States. When a friend asked if I could preach at his church, I told him I'd be happy to. He then asked, "Can you have dinner with one of the elders prior to the meeting?"

"Sure," I replied. "What's his name?"

"John Payne."

When I arrived at the house, I realized it was the same John Payne. As we reminisced, I finally said, "John, this is very embarrassing for me, but when we were in school in Argentina, I stole a box of pencils from you. Will you forgive me and let me pay you back?"

"Luis," he said, "it's forgotten. I'm a grown man. What would I do with a box of colored pencils? I forgive you. Forget about it."

That was exactly what I needed to hear. It felt so good to be free from that burden on my conscience.

Let's not wait to clear up problems that keep us from enjoying all the blessings the Lord has for us. Let's get down on our knees and clear up anything that's preventing us from being free.[40]

—⁂—

FATHER: BY YOUR GRACE, FORGIVE MY MISDEEDS AND HELP ME FREE MY CONSCIENCE OF OLD OFFENSES THAT KEEP ME FROM PEACE AND FREEDOM. AMEN.

Our conscience testifies that we have conducted ourselves in the world, and especially in our relations with you, in the holiness and sincerity that are from God. We have done so not according to worldly wisdom but according to God's grace.

2 CORINTHIANS 1:12

THE MOST IMPORTANT QUESTION

There is salvation in no one else! Under all heaven there is no other name for men to call upon to save them.

ACTS 4:12 TLB

For years, Billy Graham has presented the gospel to thousands of people through his crusades and television broadcasts, and one of his favorite questions to ask whomever he came in contact with has always been: "If you died tonight, do you know for certain that you would go to Heaven?"

In January of 2000, leaders of Charlotte, North Carolina, invited Billy Graham to a luncheon. Initially, Reverend Graham hesitated to accept the invitation because of his struggle with Parkinson's disease. But he eventually agreed to go and speak just a few words—and in his address that day, he answered for himself the question he had asked so many other people:

GRACE FOR TODAY:

Because of God's grace, we can know who we are and we can know where we're going.

"See the suit I'm wearing?" Billy Graham began. "It's a brand new suit. My wife, my children, and my grandchildren are telling me I've gotten a little slovenly in my old age. I used to be a bit more fastidious. So I went out and bought a new suit for this luncheon—and for one more occasion. You know what that occasion is? This is the suit in which I'll be buried. But when you hear I'm dead, I don't want you to immediately remember the suit I'm wearing. I want you to remember this: I know who I am, and I also know where I'm going!"

Everyone, including Billy Graham, will eventually stand before God, but for those who have accepted Christ as their Lord and Savior, it is not a frightening experience to be dreaded, but a joyful reunion to be anticipated. Thank God that we can know who we are—and where we're going!

The Place for Grace

We are all one body, we have the same Spirit, and we have all been called
to the same glorious future.

EPHESIANS 4:4 NLT

In a survey conducted in 1995, a group of Christian believers were asked to give the main reason why they chose to attend their church and return there week after week. The survey concluded that two of the top five reasons concerned the theological teachings of the church and the quality of the sermons delivered by the pastors. However, the other three answers all concerned the degree to which people felt a sense of community in the church. When people found a church where the congregation cared about each other, were friendly to visitors, and were involved in helping others, they tended to go back.

When you hear the word "church," the first image that probably springs into your mind is a building with a tall steeple where people sit quietly listening to a sermon each Sunday morning. Yet the church is something much more. It is a place where you can come together with others to encounter the grace of God and experience true Christian community. A place where you can hear the Word of God and be inspired to make a radical change in the way you think and act. A place where you and others can celebrate the joy of belonging to the family of God through worship. And a place where you can actively demonstrate the grace of God by serving and helping others.

> **GRACE FOR TODAY:**
>
> By God's grace we have been given support and encouragement through a community of believers.

When you share your burdens with others in the Christian community, you will be strengthened and revitalized by the support and encouragement you receive. You will experience the grace of God in a genuine way and be able to share that grace as you help others who rely on you for support.

THE FOUNTAIN OF YOUTH

That's what baptism into the life of Jesus means. When we are lowered into the water, it is like the burial of Jesus; when we are raised up out of the water, it is like the resurrection of Jesus. Each of us is raised into a light-filled world by our Father so that we can see where we're going in our new grace-sovereign country.

ROMANS 6:3-5 MSG

Throughout the ages, people have sought new ways to regain their youth. It's natural enough to long for the days when our minds were sharp, our lives simple, our bodies light and agile, and our faces not yet lined by the passing of time. No wonder the fable of a "fountain of youth" intrigued explorers and lingers in our corporate consciousness even in modern times.

Imagine for a moment what such a wonder would mean. Can you see yourself immersing yourself in its sparkling waters and coming up feeling like a child again? Suddenly, the world looks new and fresh, and you have the energy to explore it all. Wouldn't that be great?

You should be happy to know that there is a fountain of youth. It is the fountain filled with blood flowing from the hands and feet and side of Jesus, our Savior. When we immerse our old sinful, dying selves in this amazing stream, we are raised to newness of life, pure and holy by the grace of God. So important is this process that we are asked to undergo the writ of baptism, which is a physical acting out of what has happened spiritually.

Even if someone found the mythical Fountain of Youth tomorrow, it would only apply to our physical bodies. It would do nothing to end the cycle of death—only God can do that. Won't you come wash in His fountain?

GRACE FOR TODAY:

God has blessed us with a Fountain of Youth that provides us with a whole new life.

PERSECUTION—OR OPPORTUNITY?

"As far as I am concerned, God turned into good what you meant for
evil . . . so that I could save the lives of many people."

GENESIS 50:20 TLB

John Rucyahana, the Anglican bishop of Shyira, Rwanda, served as a pastor in
Uganda during the brutal reign of dictator Idi Amin. Amin targeted 200,000 political opponents, Christian leaders, and members of certain ethnic groups for extermi-
nation.

One day the government soldiers came for John. He remembers, "One put the
cold barrel of a gun against my ear and held his finger on the trigger. They put me in a
vehicle and made me sit on a sack of explosives. As we began moving, I thought, *Even
the slightest jolt, and I'm dead."*

The soldiers finally released John, figuring that they had successfully intimidated
him, and that he would no longer speak out.

What the oppressors meant for evil, though, God used for good. Two days after
John's harrowing brush with death, the sun rose in the sky over a beautiful Sunday
morning. That day, John walked into the cathedral to find it packed—people were even
standing in the aisles. The word had spread as to what had happened to John, and from
miles around, people had come to find out what John would say. Would he continue to
speak out for Christ, even under the threat of further persecution?

John did speak for Christ that day, and because of his ordeal, he was able to reach
many more people with the Gospel than would ever have been possible had he not been
a target of persecution. From that day forward, the people of Uganda witnessed with
their own eyes the strength and conviction of a man who was persecuted for Christ,
and many were won to the Lord because of it.

What about you? What persecutions are you facing right now? Turn all of your
life's circumstances—both good and bad—over to Him, and let Him make of them an
amazing witness to other people.

GRACE FOR TODAY:

God uses the difficult circumstances in our lives to
touch other people with His love.

INSPIRED BY GOD

You've undoubtedly experienced the frustration of working on a tricky problem that you can't seem to solve. No matter how many times you pace the floor or tap your head, the answer just doesn't seem to come. What's even more aggravating is that you know the solution is out there—you just can't seem to grasp it at the moment.

Elias Howe experienced this type of frustration when he struggled for weeks trying to make his sewing machine work. No matter what he tried, he couldn't figure out how to make the thread pass through the cloth in the right way needed to make a proper stitch. Exhausted by his efforts one night, he fell asleep at his workbench and had a dream that men with spears were chasing him.

When he awoke, he remembered something odd about the spears the men were carrying—they had holes at the end! Howe realized that his machine needed a needle with a hole near its point (instead of the base) so that the thread would pass through the cloth first. The inspiration to solve the problem had come when Howe relaxed and fell asleep.

The best way to solve any problem is to step back and give it to God. When you do, you will be amazed at the many ways He will provide inspiration. Ideas will pop into your head from books you've read. Conversations with others will spark new solutions to help you solve problems. Even the buildings and signs you pass each day on your way to work will spark new insights. Yet this insight can occur only when you refuse to worry about a problem and allow God to give you His grace and provide the inspiration.

> **GRACE FOR TODAY:**
>
> ## When we release our concerns to God, He inspires us with ideas to help us solve our problems.

No eye has seen, no ear has heard, no mind has conceived
what God has prepared for those who love him.

1 CORINTHIANS 2:9

GOD'S GIFT OF HOLINESS

By Luis Palau

In our own power and wisdom, it's impossible for us to understand and live out the concept of holiness. Yet God is holy and demands that His people be holy too.

In the midst of the world's degenerate moral condition, it's tough for Christians to live in holiness. Those who live in holiness are truly set apart from the world. But if we are to have a conscience about which we can boast, we must live in holiness.

God, however, does not forget. He will not tolerate sin. When we commit immorality or other unholy actions, we dishonor God and will reap the penalty of our sin. When we stubbornly continue in our sin, we devastate our own lives and that of others. But when we walk in holiness, transparent before the Lord, our lives will reflect His power and authority.

Living in holiness is not impossible; Jesus' death and resurrection paid the penalty for our sins, making holy living possible. The Holy Spirit, living within us, gives us the power to follow Christ's example of holy living so that we can have fellowship with a holy God. This is why Paul can speak of living with a clear conscience.

The wonderful news is that we can begin holy living at any moment. The blood of Jesus Christ truly cleanses us from all sin and restores our relationship with God.[41]

—⁓—

PRECIOUS SAVIOR: THANK YOU FOR THE GIFT OF HOLINESS. TEACH ME TO LEAD A LIFE THAT IS PLEASING TO YOU AS I CALL UPON THE POWER OF YOUR GRACE. AMEN.

Make every effort to live in peace with all men and to be holy; without holiness no one will see the Lord.

HEBREWS 12:14

THE WRONG TARGET

I press on to take hold of that for which Christ Jesus took hold of me.

PHILIPPIANS 3:12

M att Emmons had the gold medal in sight. He was one shot away from claim-ing victory in the 2004 Olympic 50-meter, three-position rifle event. He didn't even need a bull's-eye to win. His final shot merely needed to be on target.

Normally, the shot he made would have received a score of 8.1, more than enough for a gold medal. But in what was described as "an extremely rare mistake in elite competition," Emmons fired at the wrong target. Standing in lane two, he fired at the target in lane three. His score for a good shot at the wrong target? Zero. Instead of winning a medal, Emmons ended up in eighth place.

> **GRACE FOR TODAY:**
>
> God has called each one of us to fulfill His perfect plan for our lives.

What are your goals in life? Are you aiming at the right target? At the end of your life, what are the things that will ultimately matter? It is possible to set goals in life—and achieve them—but if they are the wrong goals, in the end, they lead to nothing. The apostle Paul wrote about a goal that really mattered: "Forgetting what is behind and straining toward what is ahead, I press on toward the goal to win the prize for which God has called me heavenward in Christ Jesus" (Philippians 3:13-14).

In the end, only the goal of following Christ and going where He leads will bring a prize that really matters. No matter what else you are aiming for in your life, put Jesus first. When the final score is tallied, you won't regret it.

THE REAL DEAL

Teach me knowledge and good judgment, for I believe in your commands.

PSALM 119:66

Despite modern technological advances, most works of art that are revealed to be forgeries today are detected not through technology, but through the skill and judgment of experts in the field. These experts carefully study the painting in question and look at microscopic details in the work, then compare these findings to other paintings by the same artist. If these minute details do not match, or if they reflect differing styles and techniques, the painting is determined to be false.

Discerning the authenticity of a particular painting can be quite a difficult task. Some of the more cunning forgers were gifted artists who carefully studied the techniques of the artist they were forging and practiced it to near perfection. However, while these forged works may look identical to the genuine painting on the surface, a discerning expert can always tell the difference.

The same is true in your life. Often, people in the world will approach you with ideas that look good on the surface, but upon closer inspection prove to be false. Knowing whether these ideas are from God or other sources can be difficult to discern. Fortunately, you don't have to rely upon your own judgment in such situations, for you have experts in the church to help you, the Word of God to guide you, and the ability to ask God directly about it through prayer.

When you seek God for discernment, the Bible says that He will provide you with the wisdom you need to uncover the truth. He will protect you from the false ideas that come your way, and through His grace He will bring you closer to Him as you seek to serve Him and understand His will for your life.

> **GRACE FOR TODAY:**
>
> When you seek God for discernment, He graciously gives you the wisdom and the understanding to know the truth.

LET YOUR MONEY REMIND YOU

Those who trust in the Lord are like Mount Zion,
which cannot be shaken but endures forever.

PSALM 125:1

Have you looked at your money lately? Whether you have a lot or very little, every cent you possess has a simple phrase that should remind you of how you ought to live your life. Pressed upon every dollar bill, nickel, dime, and penny is the phrase, "In God We Trust."

In today's society, it is so easy to trust in the money we possess. The message that the world puts out is to get as much of it as we can, so that we can be happy, secure, lacking no good thing. We are urged to trust in it for today and even for tomorrow—when we retire.

Now there's nothing wrong with using money wisely and saving for the future, but money alone can't bring us security or happiness—not to those who have it and not to those who constantly seek it. Ironically, the money itself tells us to place our trust elsewhere—in God.

Trusting in God brings you all the things that money cannot buy. It opens up Heaven and gives you access to everything that God promised in His Word. It brings solutions for the problems in your life. It offers contentment despite the circumstances you may be facing. It is the only path to peace and happiness.

Don't place your trust in money. Instead, let your money talk. Let it remind you that silver and gold are a flimsy, temporary substitute for the security that comes from knowing God.

GRACE FOR TODAY:

God has provided all the security we will ever need
for this life and for the life to come.

BEAUTY FOR ASHES

To all who mourn . . . he will give beauty for ashes.

ISAIAH 61:3 NLT

O ne of the most beautiful wildflowers in Alaska is the fireweed. The delicate, purple–pink blossoms have a number of uses. As a tea, fireweed is good for upset stomachs, coughs, and asthma. Applied in other ways, it treats bites, cuts, and eczema. The blossoms may also be used to make flavorful jellies and honey.

It is interesting how the fireweed blossom got its name: It is the first plant to bloom in that part of the country after a fire. When the smoke clears and the earth cools, these flowers emerge from the blackened earth. The fireweed covers the damaged landscape like a stunning quilt, trading beauty for ashes.

As Christians, we have the opportunity to allow God to raise up beautiful blossoms—just like the fireweed—out of the ashes of our lives. Without a fire, the fireweed does not bloom, and without adversity, the strength and beauty of a life wholly devoted to God cannot shine. But just as He promises, He will give "beauty for ashes; joy instead of mourning; praise instead of heaviness" (Isaiah 61:3 TLB).

Are you in the midst of the "fires" of life? Do you fear that nothing beautiful could ever come out of the circumstances in which you find yourself? Trust in God and wait for the fireweed to blossom in your life. Beauty can come from ashes, and when it does, it will be a witness of God's power and love to all those around.

GRACE FOR TODAY:

God takes the broken things in our lives and turns them into strength and beauty.

BLESSED ARE THE PEACEMAKERS

When two of his siblings started arguing at the annual Bakerton family picnic, Eric knew that it would be a long day. As the most level-headed and even-tempered of his family, he knew that they would again rely upon him to help resolve this disagreement. Thus, in his usual manner, Eric listened patiently as his siblings approached him with their respective sides of the story. He then asked them to consider the other side of the issue and to think about their own actions.

In this sense, Eric was a peacemaker because he was willing to work with his siblings to bring about a resolution to their conflict. It was a role at which he excelled not because of an absence of conflict in his life, but because he had honestly submitted his life to God and adopted His way of approaching stressful situations. Because of this surrender, God had given him peace.

When conflict did arise, the grace of God in Eric's life allowed him to calmly listen to others without getting angry and upset. It allowed him to see where they were coming from and to better understand how his actions had affected them. It provided him with the humility to admit when he was wrong and ask for forgiveness. It also allowed him to restore peace to the relationship.

As Eric watched his two siblings begin to reconcile an hour later, he felt blessed that God had given him this gift of peace in his life. For he knew that it was a gift he could share with others again and again, so that they too would experience the grace and peace of God in their lives.

> **GRACE FOR TODAY:**
>
> **God gives us peace and calls us to be peacemakers.**

Those who are peacemakers will plant seeds of peace and reap a harvest of goodness.

JAMES 3:18 NLT

REACT TO PROBLEMS WITH THANKFUL PRAYER

By John MacArthur Jr.

Instead of praying to God with feelings of doubt, discouragement, or discontentment, we are to approach Him with a thankful attitude before we utter even one word. We can do that with sincerity when we realize that God promises not to allow anything to happen to us that will be too much for us to bear (1 Corinthians 10:13), to work out everything for our good in the end (Romans 8:28), and to "perfect, confirm, strengthen and establish" us in the midst of our suffering (1 Peter 5:10). These are key principles for living the Christian life. Go beyond memorizing them to letting them be the grid through which you automatically interpret all that happens to you. Know that all your difficulties are within God's purpose and thank Him for His available power and promises.

Being thankful will release you from fear and worry. It is a tangible demonstration of trusting your situation to God's sovereign control. And it is easy to do, since there are so many blessings to be thankful for: knowing that God will supply all our needs (Philippians 4:19), that He stays closely in touch with our lives (Psalm 139:3), that He cares about us (1 Peter 5:7), that all power belongs to Him (Psalm 62:11), that He is making us more and more like Christ (Romans 8:29; Philippians 1:6), and that no detail escapes Him (Psalm 147:5).[42]

—◊—

DEAR LORD: I THANK YOU FOR ALL THE BLESSINGS YOU'VE POURED OUT ON MY LIFE. I THANK YOU THAT YOUR POWER AND PROMISES ARE WORKING YOUR GOOD PURPOSE IN MY LIFE, NOT ON THE BASIS OF MY OWN WORTHINESS, BUT BY YOUR REMARKABLE GRACE. AMEN.

Do not be anxious about anything, but in everything, by prayer and petition, with thanksgiving, present your requests to God.

PHILIPPIANS 4:6

A WINNING SEASON

The Lord your God . . . turned the curse into a blessing for you, because
the Lord your God loves you.

DEUTERONOMY 23:5

E very year, a company held an interoffice softball game between the marketing
department and the support staff. One year, the support staff whipped the marketing department soundly, but the next day the marketing department demonstrated
how they earned their keep by posting this memo on the bulletin board:

> **GRACE FOR TODAY:**
>
> God is able to
> turn every
> "curse" into
> eternal blessing.

The marketing department is pleased to announce
that we came in second place in the recent softball season, after losing but one game all year. The support
department, however, had a rather dismal season, winning only one game.

How about you? What attitude toward life do you
most often have? Do you see the glass more often as
half empty or half full? Studies have shown that people
with a positive attitude generally are healthier, live
longer, and lead more satisfactory lives than those with
a negative perspective.

So the next time life tries to get you down, allow God to turn your "curse" into a
blessing. Look for the good in the situation, no matter how deep you have to search.
Just like the marketing department made the decision to view their situation as a positive one, you may also need to choose a different perspective. But your outlook on life
is important—it may even determine whether you have a "winning" season or a "losing" one!

DON'T WORRY ABOUT IT

Cast all your anxiety on [God] because he cares for you.

1 PETER 5:7

A healthy concern about something that is coming up in your life can be a good thing. It can compel you to give some serious thought to the situation and motivate you to get an action plan together so that you can work towards handling it when it arrives. But all too often, this healthy concern turns into excessive brooding and stewing over the problem, which is a more destructive behavior called "worrying."

Excessive worry is problematic. Studies show it slows decision-making processes and can impair thinking, learning, and memory. When you worry, you shut off what is happening in the present to fixate on things that have happened in the past or that may happen in the future. When worrying occurs, you disengage from what is going on around you and miss out on what God is doing in your life at the moment.

Worry takes up a great deal of energy but doesn't produce any worthwhile results. In one study, researchers found that over 70 percent of the things their subjects worried about either never happened or were completely out of their control. In fact, worry will never change what has occurred in the past nor alter what will happen in the future.

> **GRACE FOR TODAY:**
>
> God takes our worries and makes them into opportunities to pour out His love and grace on our lives.

In Matthew 6:34, Jesus says, "Do not worry about tomorrow; for tomorrow will worry about itself." When something arises that causes you to worry, commit it to the Lord in prayer and depend upon His grace to get you through the situation. Determine to view challenges and obstacles not as stumbling blocks, but as opportunities for God to work in your life and demonstrate His mercy and grace.

NO REASON TO FEAR

I can do everything by the power of Christ. He gives me strength.

PHILIPPIANS 4:13 NIRV

Following the stock market crash in October of 1929, America plunged into the Great Depression. Twenty-five percent of the workers in the United States lost their jobs, thousands of families lost their homes, and many more couldn't afford to even buy food. Millions of Americans were hopeless and fearful of what would happen next.

In the midst of this nightmare, the public elected a new president by the name of Franklin Delano Roosevelt. Crippled by polio at the age of 39, he seemed an unlikely candidate at first to bolster the nation and inspire confidence. Yet the frailty in his limbs masked the inner courage he possessed—a courage he conveyed in his inaugural address by boldly stating, "The only thing we have to fear is fear itself."

As Roosevelt well knew, the fear regarding the uncertainty of a situation is often more detrimental than the actual situation itself. Fear can leave you feeling helpless, without hope, and unable to see any way out of your current situation. It cannot only rob you of all joy and excitement in life, but it can also prevent you from realizing your dreams.

However, when you give up your worries to God and trust in the power of His grace, He will fill you with the courage to overcome your fears. He has promised in His Word to never leave nor forsake you, and you can rest assured knowing there is nothing He is not able to overcome. So approach your day with confidence in knowing that you are a beloved child of God. Be courageous in the face of adversity and remember that He has promised to always be by your side.

GRACE FOR TODAY:

God promises to give us the courage to
overcome our fears.

The Longest Night

God has said, "I will never leave you; I will never abandon you."
Hebrews 13:5 GNB

One Native American tribe had a unique practice for training young braves. On the night of a boy's thirteenth birthday, he was placed in the middle of a dense forest—alone—to spend the entire night. Until that time, he had never been away from the security of his family or his tribe, but on this night he was to prove himself to be a man. He was blindfolded and taken miles from anyplace familiar to him. When the blindfold was removed, he was in the woods—alone—all night long.

Every time an animal howled, he probably imagined a wolf leaping out of the darkness. Every time a twig snapped or the wind rustled the leaves, he probably wondered if a wild animal was about to pounce. It was likely the most terrifying night of the young boy's life.

But when the first rays of sunlight began to penetrate the depth of the forest, the boy began to look around and see flowers, trees, and the outline of the path. And to his surprise, at the end of the path he could see the figure of a warrior, just a few feet away, armed with a bow and an arrow. It was the boy's father—who had been there throughout the entire night.

Your heavenly Father is always present with you, no matter how dark or frightening the circumstances in which you find yourself. Although His presence may be unseen, He is standing watch over your life, armed and ready to protect you, even as you go through the tests of life.

Grace for Today:

God is watching, standing guard through every dark
night of our lives.

A SIMPLE ACT OF KINDNESS

After spending nineteen years in prison for stealing a loaf of bread, Jean Valjean, the main character in Victor Hugo's novel *Les Miserables*, was a deeply bitter man upon his release. Shunned by society as he traveled from place to place, the only person to show him any real compassion was a priest named Bienvenu, who took him in and gave him food, clothes, and a warm place to sleep.

For the priest's kindness, Valjean stole an expensive silver candlestick from him and fled away in the night. When he was later caught by the police and brought back to the church, Valjean expected he would be arrested and sent back to prison. Yet when he was brought before Bienvenu, the priest explained not only that the candlestick had been his gift to Valjean but that Valjean had forgotten the other matching candlestick. Valjean was freed, and this single act of compassion forever changed his life.

You never know how the simplest act of kindness you perform will forever change someone's life. When you intervene and allow God to use you as His instrument, you demonstrate the grace of God to those without hope and give them strength to carry on. Yet compassion requires great commitment, for opportunities will often arise when you are busy or tired, and you will be tempted to turn the person away. You may feel taken advantage of at times or you may worry that your efforts are not helping at all.

Fortunately, when you determine to lead a compassionate life, God will lead you to other compassionate individuals who can support and encourage you when you need it most. Working together, you can truly spread the grace of God into the lives of everyone you meet.

> **GRACE FOR TODAY:**
>
> **God pours out His compassion on us and then makes us instruments of compassion to others.**

As God's chosen people, holy and dearly loved, clothe yourselves with compassion, kindness, humility, gentleness and patience.

COLOSSIANS 3:12

RUNNING THE RACE

By Warren W. Wiersbe

In the races, each runner was to stay in his assigned lane, but some runners would cut in on their competitors to try to get them off course. This is what the Judaizers had done to the Galatian believers: they cut in on them and forced them to change direction and go on a "spiritual detour." It was not God who did this, because He had called them to run faithfully in the lane marked "Grace."

The believer who lives in the sphere of God's grace is free, rich, and running in the lane that leads to reward and fulfillment. The believer who abandons grace for law is a slave, a pauper, and a runner on a detour. In short, he is a loser. And the only way to become a winner is to "purge out the leaven," the false doctrine that mixes law and grace, and yield to the Spirit of God.

God's grace is sufficient for every demand of life. We are saved by grace (1 Corinthians 15:9-10). Grace enables us to endure suffering (2 Corinthians 12:9). It is grace that strengthens us (2 Timothy 2:1), so that we can be victorious soldiers. Our God is the God of all grace (1 Peter 5:10). We can come to the throne of grace and find grace to help in every need (Hebrews 4:16). As we read the Bible, which is "the word of His grace" (Acts 20:32), the Spirit of Grace (Hebrews 10:29) reveals to us how rich we are in Christ.

"And of His fullness have all we received, and grace for grace" (John 1:16). How rich we are![45]

—⁂—

FATHER GOD: KEEP ME RUNNING IN THE LANE MARKED "GRACE." AND IF I SHOULD EVER LOOK TO MY OWN GOODNESS TO GAIN SALVATION, PULL ME QUICKLY BACK FROM MY DETOUR. I WANT TO LIVE EACH DAY FULLY DEPENDING ON YOU. AMEN.

I strain to reach the end of the race and receive the prize for which God, through Christ Jesus, is calling us up to heaven.

PHILIPPIANS 3:14 NLT

A CHICKEN NAMED TED

Put on the new self. This is the new being which God, its Creator, is constantly renewing in his own image.

COLOSSIANS 3:10 GNB

You probably know Ted Giannoulas, even if you've never heard his name. He has been the San Diego Chicken for over thirty years. But unfortunately, Ted is getting older. At the age of fifty, being The Chicken has been his entire life—his whole identity. He never allows his face to be photographed unless he is in costume. He has no family. In short, no one knows the real Ted.

At first, he loved his alter ego. "I discovered an untapped personality in that suit," he once said. "It gave me freedom. I no longer had to be Ted." But there was a price to pay. Dave Raymond, who for years wore the costume of the Philly Phanatic, said, "[Giannoulas] was the first and the funniest [of the mascots], and I have nothing but respect for him. But if you're not careful, you can lose yourself in that suit." Ted himself says sadly, "I have plenty of Chicken stories. I'm afraid I don't have any Ted stories."

Many people go through life trying to be someone other than who God created them to be. But ultimately, they lose themselves in the process.

God has made you to be an amazing, unique individual—there has never been, nor will there ever be, another person like you. Don't waste your life hiding, as Ted did, in a Chicken costume, or behind some other mask or façade. Ask God to show you your true identity in Christ, and then discover the wonderful plans He has in store for your life. You won't regret it!

> **GRACE FOR TODAY:**
>
> God has made each one of us His own unique creation.

TEAR DOWN THE WALLS

[Jesus said,] "Let your good deeds shine out for all to see, so that everyone will praise your heavenly Father."

MATTHEW 5:16 NLT

One of Pablo Picasso's most famous masterpieces is the work he created in 1937 called Guernica. An enormous painting, it hung for years on a wall in the Museum of Modern Art in New York, where people were allowed to view and appre-ciate all of its intricate details from close up. Only one incident marred its history in the United States, when in 1974 a political protestor splashed the masterpiece with red paint.

Although no permanent damage was done, when the painting was moved to the Prado in Madrid, Spain, authorities decided to protect it from any further harm by setting it fourteen feet behind a glass enclosure. No longer could patrons admire the artist's work from close up, and the glare off the glass also created difficul-ty in observing the whole painting from afar. Guernica was certainly safe from harm, but it no longer had the same impact on people.

The pain you have experienced in your life has probably caused you to set up some walls in your life. While these walls certainly protect you from further harm, they also prevent people from getting to see the intricate details of your life. They cut you off emotionally from others and deprive them of the opportunity to see the beauty that God has created within the real you.

C. S. Lewis noted, "To love at all is to be vulnerable." The only way to experi-ence true fellowship and honestly let people love you for who you are is to let them get in close. This involves tearing down the walls that protect your life. But once you accept this risk of vulnerability, God will cover you with His grace and bring healing to your life.

GRACE FOR TODAY:

We must allow God to tear down walls that block others from seeing His beautiful gifts in us.

JESUS IS COMING SOON

You yourselves know very well that the day of the Lord will come
like a thief in the night.

1 THESSALONIANS 5:2 NRSV

E very fifty years or so, someone makes a loud prediction about when Jesus will return. We know they're wrong because—here we are, still waiting. The Bible says that Jesus will return—and soon—but it also says that we will not be told when. We are urged to live as house servants waiting for their master's return. We are to be ready—every moment of every day—to see Him face to face, either here or as He receives us in death.

If you've never given your heart and life to God, then now is the time to do it. You must not delay. What a tragedy it would be if Jesus returned to find that you had not availed yourself of His gracious gift of salvation. Offer Him your sinfulness and receive in exchange His white robe of righteousness. It was purchased just for you on the Cross of Calvary. No matter what you've done in the past, God's grace will wash you clean and adorn you like a bride on her wedding day. Be ready.

If you are already a Christian, ready your soul by embracing His grace and mercy for your daily walk here on earth. Be quick to forgive and to ask for forgiveness. Love Him with all your heart, and love your neighbor as yourself. Don't let anything keep you from preparing for that special day of the Lord. Keep always in mind the glories of heaven.

Jesus is coming soon. Will you be ready?

GRACE FOR TODAY:

When Jesus returns, He will receive us into His
presence for eternity.

THE FAITHFULNESS OF GOD

Blessed be the God and Father of our Lord Jesus Christ, the Father of
mercies and God of all comfort.

2 CORINTHIANS 1:3 NASB

Evelyn Husband lost the love of her life—her husband, space shuttle commander
Rick Husband, in a national tragedy. A year later, she shared her message about
God's healing hand with the nation.

On that fateful day, Evelyn stood with the other families of the space shuttle
Columbia's crew at the landing site in Cape Canaveral, Florida, waiting for her husband to return home. The shuttle was just minutes from landing when NASA's
Mission Control lost contact with the shuttle crew. The next few moments were a blur
of events: video images of Columbia breaking apart over the Texas skyline, NASA
officials scrambling to move the family members away from the view of television
cameras. Evelyn remembers looking over at the horrified expressions on the faces of
her son, Matthew, and her daughter, Laura, then ages seven and twelve.

Since that day, however, Evelyn has been able to proclaim a simple but powerful
message: Even in the midst of intense suffering, God is faithful. "Deep inside, I knew
God was going to walk me through this somehow," she declared. "I knew it because
He'd walked with me through other crises earlier in my life."

How have you seen God's faithfulness proven in your life? Maybe you haven't
lost a husband in a space-shuttle accident, but no doubt you have experienced other
crises and tragedies that came without warning. But just as God has walked with you
through those trying times, He will continue to walk with you in the days ahead. No
matter what the future may bring, God will be there to see you through.

GRACE FOR TODAY:

"When you have nothing left but God, then for the
first time you become aware that God is enough."

—MAUDE ROYDEN

GET MOVING!

Although the skies were clear over the southern coast of Florida, the typically crowded beaches and restaurants were eerily quiet. A few determined folks still wandered the streets, but the majority of the population had literally hit the road. Thousands of cars jammed the main interstate, backing up traffic in some places for more than nineteen miles. An enormous hurricane named "Frances" had been predicted, and it was on a direct course to hit the state.

When the call to evacuate went out to the more than 2.5 million Floridians, the majority packed their bags and moved to safety—especially those who had endured similar hurricanes in the past. Yet thousands more refused to leave their homes and valuables unattended, deciding instead to place their trust in the strength of their concrete buildings.

After all, they had been in hurricanes before. How bad could this one be?

Many people have a similar reaction when God gives a call to action in their lives. Some refuse to see the warning signs, insisting that skies are clear and the storm won't get that bad. Others are afraid to act because they are unsure of what they should do. Many more are simply unwilling to hand their lives over to God and leave behind the security of their current situations.

It's often easier to plan to do something than to actually do it. Yet all the plans in the world won't help you if you're just sitting there when the hurricane hits. When God calls you to action, remember, He does it out of grace and because of His great love for you. His desire is to guide you through what's coming ahead.

> **GRACE FOR TODAY:**
>
> When God calls us to action, He is graciously guiding us through trouble on His best route for our lives.

[Lord,] I hurry and do not delay to keep your commandments.

PSALM 119:60 NRSV

TO DIE IS GAIN

By Gene Getz

When Paul wrote to the Philippians, he knew his chances of being executed were great. That is why he said, "For to me, to live is Christ and to die is gain" (Philippians 1:21). He was rejoicing in his situation no matter what, for he was convinced that he would be delivered (v. 19).

The idea of "deliverance" had a twofold meaning for Paul. Either he would be "delivered" from prison to spend more time with the Philippian Christians, or he would be "delivered" from faltering in his Christian testimony as he faced the threat of death at the hands of the emperor. In actuality, there was a third alternative, for if his life were taken, then he would be "delivered" from his earthly "home" to spend eternity with Christ—which, Paul stated emphatically, "is better by far" (v. 23). In other words, Paul knew that as a Christian he would win no matter what happened. "I eager-ly expect and hope," he wrote, "that I will in no way be ashamed, but will have sufficient courage so that now as always Christ will be exalted in my body, whether by life or death" (v. 20).

Paul's eternal perspective enabled him to face these problems and troubles with great courage and comfort. In the light of eternity, he called them "momen-tary troubles," and "so," he said, "we fix our eyes not on what is seen, but on what is unseen. For what is seen is tem-porary, but what is unseen is eternal" (2 Corinthians 4:17–18).⁴⁴

—᚜᚛—

FATHER GOD: MAY I SEE MY ADVERSE CIRCUMSTANCES AS "MOMEN-TARY TROUBLES." HELP ME, BY YOUR GRACE, TO FIX MY EYES ON ETERNITY. AMEN.

I eagerly expect and hope that I will in no way be ashamed, but will have sufficient courage so that now as always Christ will be exalted in my body, whether by life or by death.

PHILIPPIANS 1:20

THE TRUE MEANING OF HOPE

In [God's] great mercy he has given us new birth into a living hope
through the resurrection of Jesus Christ from the dead.

1 PETER 1:3

When Jerome Groopman diagnosed patients with serious diseases, the Harvard Medical School professor discovered that all of them, without exception, were looking for a sense of genuine hope. That hope was more important to them than anything he could ever have prescribed as a physician.

> **GRACE FOR TODAY:**
>
> By God's grace, we have a hope of a heavenly life beyond the one we are living here on earth.

After writing a book titled *The Anatomy of Hope*, Groopman was asked for a simplified definition of the term. He replied: "Basically, hope is the ability to see a path to the future. When someone is facing dire circumstances, they need to see a potential path that can get them where they want to be. Once they see that, there's a tremendous emotional uplift that occurs."

The doctor confessed: "Hope has been, is, and always will be the heart of medicine and healing. None of us can live without hope. Even with all of the medical technology available to us now, we still come back to the profound human need to believe we can reach a future that is better than our life in the present."

Thank God that as Christians we have a hope in a life to come that is so much better than "life in the present"! All of our hopes and dreams for our lives here on earth can never compare to the life that is awaiting us in Heaven. So even as you go about pursuing earthly goals and dreams, don't forget to look at the eternal perspective once in a while. The "living hope" from God trusts in a heavenly life beyond this one—a life with a very bright future.

A BLUEPRINT FOR LIFE

The unfolding of your words gives light;
it gives understanding to the simple.

PSALM 119:130

I f you want to build a house, you will first need a set of "blueprints." Blueprints are detailed scaled drawings that describe how the house should look when it is completed. They act as guidelines to show you how to construct the home from the foundation up. They describe all the systems that will need to be included—such as heating, plumbing, and electrical. Without these vital guidelines to follow, you wouldn't know if the house you are building is stable.

The Bible is the blueprint for your life. When you open its pages, you discover teachings that outline the way God wants you to live. You find stories that provide concrete examples of the benefits of following God's path and the consequences involved when you choose your own course. You learn about the foundation upon which your life should be built and the "systems" that need to be in place to live a Christian life—such as worship, prayer, and fellowship. You also gain the wisdom to determine when an error has been made and how to correct it.

GRACE FOR TODAY:

God has graciously given each of us a blueprint on which to build our lives.

Reading God's Word on a daily basis takes patience, perseverance, and commitment, which perhaps is why studies show that only 36 percent of adults typically read it at all during the week. Parts of the Bible can be complicated and difficult to comprehend. However, if you faithfully study God's Word, He will give you the wisdom you need to understand His message for your life. He will reveal new insights to you through the stories and parables. He will bless you and cover you with His grace as you strive to build your life upon the blueprints He has provided.

THE MISSING PIECE

Since you are eager to have spiritual gifts,
try to excel in gifts that build up the church.

1 CORINTHIANS 14:12

T he body of Christ can often resemble a large jigsaw puzzle that was just dumped out of the box onto the table. The pieces can seem jumbled together without any sense of cohesion, but as you examine the various shapes, you soon begin to figure out how certain pieces will join to others. Connecting one part to the next, the "big picture" gradually comes into focus as you begin to see how other pieces fit into place.

Every person in the family of God is given a specific gift. This could be a gift of teaching, music, leadership, writing, fellowship, or even compassion. It could be the transformation of a talent you already have or a completely new ability God gives to you. Of course, like the jumbled puzzle on the table, it may not be clear at first how your specific gift will "fit in" with the others that people have in the church. You may even be hesitant to use your gift out of fear that others will think it silly or unimportant.

However, it is important to remember that every gift from God is significant for His purposes. When you fail to contribute your gift, you withhold pieces necessary to complete the "big picture" that makes up the body of Christ. Like that frustrating last piece that is missing, withholding your gift leaves gaping holes in the body that could be used to bless others.

Rely upon the grace of God and trust that the gifts He has given will fit together to make the body of Christ stronger as a whole. Go to Him in prayer and ask Him how He wants you to use those gifts for His kingdom.

GRACE FOR TODAY:

God has entrusted each of us with a unique gift that
will strengthen and inspire the body of believers.

Banking on God's Promises

"God, you're my refuge. I trust in you and I'm safe!"

PSALM 91:2 MSG

A ctor Jimmy Stewart found comfort in Psalm 91. When the United States entered World War II in 1941, Stewart enlisted in the Army Air Corps and prepared to go overseas. Stewart's father choked up when he tried to bid him farewell, so he wrote a note for his son to read en route. After being shipped out, Jimmy read the words his father had been unable to say aloud:

My dear Jim boy,
Soon after you read this, you will be on your way to the worst sort of dan-ger. Jim, I'm banking on the enclosed copy of the 91st Psalm. The thing that takes the place of fear and worry is the promise of these words. I am staking my faith in them. I can say no more. I only continue to pray. Goodbye, my dear. God bless you and keep you. I love you more than I can tell you.
Dad

Jimmy Stewart returned home safely, a decorated war hero, unharmed even though his record included twenty combat missions. During the height of battle, Stewart said he learned to lean on the words of his tattered copy of Psalm 91, especial-ly verses one and two, which speak of God as a refuge and a fortress.

God can be your refuge and your fortress as well. No matter what battles you may face today, lean on Him and trust in His protection. Learn to say of the Lord, "He is my refuge and my fortress, my God, in whom I trust" (Psalm 91:2). He will be there for you—you can "bank on it!"

GRACE FOR TODAY:

God promises to be a refuge and a fortress to His children.

LET GOD BE YOUR PILOT

A seasoned pilot was suddenly caught in the midst of a terrible storm. As the clouds closed in and visibility was reduced to less than twenty feet, he quickly lost all sense of direction. Unsure of whether he was going left, right, up, or down, he decided to completely rely on his instruments for guidance. At times, his instincts told him that he was going the wrong way, but he ignored these feelings and continued to rely upon his instruments. Just as he got to one hundred feet off the ground, he broke out of the clouds and successfully landed the plane.

When the storm clouds form in your life, you can often lose perspective and become unsure of which direction to turn. Situations emerge that you have never faced before and for which you have no experience to handle. During such times, you may be tempted to trust in your own instincts and "wing it." Yet if you do this, you are flying blind.

In the same way the pilot trusted his instruments to guide him through the storm, you need to trust the Lord to help you through times of uncertainty in your life. Only God knows exactly where you are, where you need to go, and what route you need to take to get there. However, He can't guide you if you are stubbornly insisting on following your guidance system. You have to let go of the controls and completely trust in Him.

When you trust God, He will guide you through the storm, bring you to safety, and bless you with His grace in the process. He will build your faith and strengthen you, so that you can handle the next storm that is just over the horizon.

> **GRACE FOR TODAY:** We must trust God, for He will guide and protect us and give us His grace to make it through every hardship.

[God says,] "I am with you . . . [I will] help you . . . [I] will take good care of you."

ISAIAH 41:10 NIRV

HIS BURDEN IS LIGHT

By Warren W. Wiersbe

The yoke of religion is hard, and the burdens heavy; Christ's yoke is "easy" and His burden is "light." That word easy in the Greek means "kind, gracious." The yoke of Christ frees us to fulfill His will, while the yoke of the law enslaves us. The unsaved person wears a yoke of sin (Lamentations 1:14); the religious legalist wears the yoke of bondage (Galatians 3:13). The believer is no longer under law; he is under grace (Romans 6:14). This does not mean that we are outlaws and rebels. It simply means that we no longer need the external force of law to keep us in God's will, because we have the internal leading of the Holy Spirit of God (Romans 8:1–4). Christ died to set us free, not to make us slaves.

There are some believers who are frightened by the liberty they have in God's grace; so they seek out a fellowship that is legalistic and dictatorial, where they can let others make their decisions for them. This is comparable to an adult climbing back into the crib. The way of Christian liberty is the way of fulfillment in Christ. No wonder Paul issues that ultimatum: "Do not be entangled again in the yoke of bondage." Take your stand for liberty.[45]

—⁂—

DEAR FATHER: THANK YOU FOR THE GRACE YOU'VE GIVEN ME TO LIVE IN LIBERTY, FREE TO FULFILL YOUR PERFECT WILL FOR MY LIFE. AMEN.

[Jesus said,] "Are you tired? Worn out? Burned out on religion?
Come to me. Get away with me and you'll recover your life.
I'll show you how to take a real rest. Walk with me and work with me—
watch how I do it. Learn the unforced rhythms of grace.
I won't lay anything heavy or ill-fitting on you. Keep company with me
and you'll learn to live freely and lightly."

MATTHEW 11:28–30 MSG

A BOOMERANG BLESSING

[Jesus said,] "Give, and it will be given to you."

LUKE 6:38 NKJV

Vernal Simms, senior pastor of Morris Brown AME Church in Philadelphia, grew up in a family of nine children, in a rough Boston housing project called Columbia Point. Although he was a hardworking student, paying for college seemed impossible. But his mother's favorite expression was, "Pray, and the Lord will make a way somehow." Vernal decided to take his mother's advice and pray for a way to attend college.

He packed up his things and headed to college for orientation, but he didn't have the money to stay. He'd have to turn around and make the 100-mile trip back home unless his prayer was answered. But then an heir to a corporate fortune heard about his plight and decided to pay for both his college and seminary education.

GRACE FOR TODAY:

We can never outgive God!

After Vernal graduated, he went to his benefactor's office to thank him and ask what he could do in some small way to repay the man for his kindness. The man replied, "Help somebody." Those were the most profound words ever spoken into Vernal's life, and he has spent the last twenty years ministering to both the drug-ridden, crime-infested inner city as well as the well-manicured suburbs. As he says, "The blessing of God is like a boomerang. As I've tried to help others, the blessings just keep coming back to me!"

Just as Vernal's benefactor asked of him, when you receive tremendous blessings from God, all He asks in return is that you "help somebody" with what He has given you. But when you obey His request and begin to help others, something amazing happens. As you give into the lives of other people, the blessings "boomerang" back toward you! A minister once said, "You can't outgive God!" No matter what you give to Him, He always gives more in return.

GRACE FOR ALL SEASONS

[Jesus said,] "In this world you will have trouble. But take heart! I have overcome the world."

JOHN 16:33

As the days begin to warm in springtime, trees burst into bloom and sprout new green leaves. When the days become hot in the summer, the leaves grow larger and take on a darker hue. In the autumn, the days shorten and the leaves turn vibrant shades of red and gold. Winter soon follows, and the leaves begin to fall off the limbs to the earth below.

The reason this occurs each year is because God has designed the tree to adapt to the changing seasons. Trees need sunlight to grow, so in the spring they sprout green sunlight—collecting leaves. In the fall when the days shorten, the trees begin to conserve energy for the long winter ahead and drop their leaves. All of these events are a natural reaction on the part of the tree to change.

Whether changing your career, moving to a new location, or getting married, change always brings new challenges, uncertainty, confusion, and unwanted periods of instability in your life. In a culture that promotes safety and security, change can be a frightening prospect.

GRACE FOR TODAY:

God uses change in our lives to encourage us to grow spiritually.

Yet change is necessary because it brings growth. In the same way the trees must change with the seasons to maintain their growth, you must also change and adapt to the seasons of your life to maintain your Christian growth. To do so means trusting in His grace to get you through hard times, letting go of your old life when the seasons again change, and trusting in His promise that springtime will come.

So reflect on the changes God has brought to your life and thank Him for the periods of growth that you have experienced as a result.

WILL YOU TELL THEM?

I am not ashamed of the gospel, for it is the power of God for salvation
to everyone who believes, to the Jew first and also to the Greek.

ROMANS 1:16 NASB

I f you had to move to a country where it was illegal to preach the Gospel, would it
change your life very much? It may seem like a hard truth to admit, but such a situation would not change many of our lives. Telling others about Jesus can at times be
intimidating because we live in a world where there is mounting pressure to subvert
the Gospel.

Immorality has become the standard, and the Gospel has somehow become sus-
pect. Lately, it seems that many people have become offended by the very name of Jesus.
But do not let your heart be troubled. There are some that come across your path every
day whom God wants to bring closer to himself. And He wants to use you to bring
them.

Did you know that you were chosen by God to shine as a light in this world? He
has given you His love, His power, and His Word not only to bless your life but also
to bless others. He has entrusted you with the honor of representing Him while you
live this life.

God desires that we all go forward and make disciples for Christ. He loves the
unbeliever just as much as He loves you. But He needs someone to accept the mission
of telling the world of His love. Will you tell them? Truly, there is a lot of love in your
heart to give. The reason is because the love of God lives inside of you. Try telling
someone of the love of Jesus today. It just might be the very thing that will bless their
day, or perhaps much more, their eternity.

GRACE FOR TODAY:

God loves the unbeliever just as much as He loves us.

RIGHT ON TIME

[Jesus said,] "Do not start worrying: 'Where will my food come from?
or my drink? or my clothes?' . . . Your Father in heaven knows
that you need all these things."

MATTHEW 6:31-32 GNB

Elmer Towns and his wife did not have much money, and they were attending college by faith. Elmer earned one dollar an hour for driving a school bus, which was just enough to pay for the couple's necessities, but there wasn't even a dime left over for a Coca-Cola. They prayed together daily for God to meet their needs—and He always did.

One evening, the only thing in the kitchen cabinet was a can of tuna, and so Elmer's wife cooked a tuna casserole. As they clasped their hands together to thank God for the food, Elmer prayed, "God, You know we are broke. You know it's still two days until payday. You know we are willing to fast until we get money, but we ask You to please take care of our needs."

As they finished praying, the laundry man came to the door. Elmer's wife met him to say, "No laundry today—we can't afford to have anything cleaned." But he had not come to pick up their cleaning.

The man explained, "A few months ago, your landlord asked me to pass along this twenty-dollar bill to you to pay for having thawed the pipes for him. I had forgotten about it until today."

Some people might have called that a coincidence, but Elmer and his wife knew that their prayer that day had reminded the laundry man to bring them the twenty dollars—right on time.

God knows what you need before you even ask Him, and as your loving heavenly Father, He is waiting to provide these things for you. All you need to do is ask!

GRACE FOR TODAY:

There are no coincidences with God. He is always
looking for ways to help us even before we ask.

THE FOLLY OF HUMAN WISDOM

In 1867, Russia was looking for a way to unload its unprofitable North American territories. Recognizing that the United States had the available cash, a Russian minister approached the Secretary of State, William Seward, with an offer to sell the land known as "Alaska." Seward responded eagerly and eventually convinced the Senate to approve the seven million-dollar deal.

Controversy immediately erupted when the American public learned of the purchase. Critics ridiculed the idea of paying millions for a remote and frozen piece of land, dubbing it "Seward's Folly" and America's "polar bear garden." Yet when gold was discovered thirty years later, people began to realize the value of this new American territory. Subsequent discoveries of oil and other natural resources in Alaska have further proven Seward's wisdom in negotiating the sale.

In a similar way, when you choose to follow God's wisdom, some may label your decisions as "folly." When you "turn the other cheek" instead of retaliating against someone who has wronged you, the world may say you are weak. When you refuse to cut corners to get ahead, you will be called close-minded and unassertive. When you decide to trust your life completely to the grace of God, you will be considered misguided.

At such moments, the cost of following God's wisdom may seem a high price to pay, but it is important to remember that human wisdom leads only to compounded problems, broken relationships, and uncertainty on how to proceed. However, God's wisdom will always provide you with the guidance you need to recognize the correct course of action in any situation. In the end, the investment you make in following God today will pay rich dividends later on in your life.

> GRACE FOR TODAY:
>
> **God's wisdom always leads to eternal good.**

The foolishness of God is wiser than man's wisdom, and the weakness of God is stronger than man's strength.

1 CORINTHIANS 1:25

GRACE-FILLED GIVING

By Warren W. Wiersbe

I f our giving is motivated by grace, we will give willingly, and not because we have been forced to give.

God sees the "heart gift" and not the "hand gift." If the heart wanted to give more, but was unable to do so, God sees it and records it accordingly. But if the hand gives more than the heart wants to give, God records what is in the heart, no matter how big the offering in the hand might be.

A friend of mine was leaving for a business trip, and his wife reminded him before church that she needed some extra money for household expenses. Just before offering, he slipped some money into her hand; and she, thinking it was their weekly offering, put it all in the plate. It was the expense money for the week.

"Well," said my friend, "we gave it to the Lord, and He keeps the records."

"How much did you intend to give?" asked their pastor, and my friend gave an amount. "Then that's what God recorded," said the pastor, "because He saw the intent of your heart!"

God sees not the portion, but the proportion. If we could have given more, and did not, God notes it. If we wanted to give more, and could not, God also notes that. When we give willingly, according to what we have, we are practicing grace giving.[46]

—m—

DEAR FATHER: I WANT TO FOLLOW YOUR EXAMPLE OF GRACIOUS GIVING— OFFERING MY GIFTS WILLINGLY AND FROM THE HEART. TAKE MY GIFTS AND MULTIPLY THEM TO BLESS OTHERS. AMEN.

You know the grace of our Lord Jesus Christ, that though He was rich, yet for your sakes He became poor, that you through His poverty might become rich.

2 CORINTHIANS 8:9 NKJV

THE CARPENTER IS BUILDING YOU

[Jesus said,] "In my Father's house are many mansions; if it were not so, I would have told you. I go to prepare a place for you."

JOHN 14:2 NKJV

Jesus' earthly father's name was Joseph. He was a carpenter by trade, and naturally, he trained Jesus to be a carpenter too. All through His childhood, Jesus worked with wood and nails. But His masterpiece was the work He fulfilled by laying His life down, being nailed to a wooden cross at Calvary.

That one work of grace changes our eternal outlook completely. Not only does it buy for us a second chance in this life, it also provides us with the hope of Heaven. Today, the carpenter's son is still building houses—mansions in Heaven for you and for me.

Jesus created the heavens and the earth in only six days. Can you imagine what He has in store for us? Probably not. Our simple minds could never dream up an image of our heavenly homes. But we know it will be quite wonderful.

GRACE FOR TODAY:

Our great Carpenter is not only building homes in Heaven for us, but a temple on earth as well.

Our great Carpenter is not only building homes in Heaven for us, but a temple on earth as well. You are that temple. Be sure to let Him place in you a firm foundation and furnish every room with love and joy, peace and patience. Let Him build you in His own special way, for His designs are perfect.

When the Carpenter is finished with you, you will feel right at home in your mansion in Heaven, the first day and every day for eternity.

HELPING HANDS

Each one should use whatever gift he has received to serve others, faithfully administering God's grace in its various forms.

1 PETER 4:10

God's grace flows through the spiritual gift of service.

When you are very young, the grace of your heavenly Father comes to you via your earthly parents. He sees to it that they meet your basic needs for food, shelter, and clothing—as well as such additional needs as toy assembly, bicycle repair, and kite retrieval. Your parents serve you daily, tying your shoes, washing your clothes, preparing your meals, cleaning up. They provide transportation services, education services, health care services, and more.

> **GRACE FOR TODAY:**
>
> God has not forgotten that we have practical needs. He meets those needs through the service of others.

The Lord doesn't abandon you once you fly out of the nest. God knows you still need help, and He continues to use others to assist you. This is especially true if you belong to a vibrant local church, a family of believers who faithfully obey God's command to "serve one another in love" (Galatians 5:13). In such a church will be some who are gifted in the area of service. These people are equipped and called by God to meet the practical needs of His children. They serve Him by lending others a hand.

God has likely touched your life through these people more times than you remember. Perhaps someone brought you a meal when you were indisposed. Maybe some guys from your church showed up when it was time to move out of that cramped apartment and into your first new house. Maybe your first new house wasn't so new, and they came back later to reroof it. Your Christian brothers and sisters may have helped you by running errands, helping with a garage sale, fixing the furnace, or babysitting so you could attend a Bible study.

Never take these loving acts of service for granted. They are drops of grace, proof that your heavenly Father cares deeply for you.

DIVINE HINDSIGHT

It is the Lord who gives wisdom;
from him come knowledge and understanding.

PROVERBS 2:6 GNB

L ike everyone, you probably have memories that haunt you.

Recollections of past failures, old wrongs, broken relationships, and lost opportunities lie fallow for a long while in the back of your mind, then leap into your consciousness unexpectedly, bringing guilt, causing pain, triggering sorrow. Time is supposed to heal them or make them go away, but time seldom does.

God, though, can heal these hurtful memories. He transforms them in a sense, not by changing them per se, but by shining the light of understanding into the dark places where they lurk, enabling you to see them differently and interpret them more accurately.

The Lord's perspective is far superior to ours! We think hindsight is twenty-twenty, but our perception of past events is nothing compared with God's infinite wisdom, knowledge, and understanding. He knows all the circumstances behind your disturbing memories, things you aren't aware of, like the history and motivations and intentions of every person involved in each painful incident. Most importantly, God alone can pinpoint the sin in each situation, making Him the only one qualified to pass righteous judgment and assign blame accurately. Thus He can also bring to light any sin on your part, if it exists, so you can acknowledge it, confess it, and receive forgiveness—often a significant step toward healing.

As God gives you the insight you need to better comprehend what happened and why, He raises you closer to His level of understanding, drawing you nearer as well to His level of love and compassion for everyone caught up in the matter. From this place, He hopes you will find it in your heart to forgive others—and yourself, if necessary. Then even more healing occurs.

And soon the whole thing is just a memory.

GRACE FOR TODAY:

God shines the light of understanding onto our painful memories, enabling us to see them differently and interpret them more accurately.

Love's True Colors

Love is patient and kind.
Love is not jealous or boastful or proud or rude.

1 CORINTHIANS 13:4-5 NLT

One of the most tender of God's mercies will touch your life when the Holy Spirit changes the hearts of those closest to you.

The home is where the rubber meets the road when it comes to living out the Christian faith. It's in the context of intimate family relationships that God's work in people's lives is most apparent. And it's within those day-to-day interactions that the impact of Christ's influence on His followers is most keenly felt.

The Bible says that God is love and the source of all love (1 John 4:7-8). When a family member experiences God's love and responds to it by allowing the Holy Spirit to begin molding his or her heart into the shape of God's, the rest of the family will reap tremendous benefits. As the Spirit uses passages of Scripture such as 1 Corinthians 13 to teach this family member about the true nature of love, what it is and what it isn't, the love of God starts to well up inside this person and flows out, and family dynamics are altered. A mother becomes less critical and more affirming, or a father less angry and more forgiving, or a son less rebellious and more obedient, or a daughter less selfish and more caring—and soon other members of the family are experiencing God's love.

If you desire this love for yourself and your family, ask God to make you the catalyst in the process. Draw nearer to Him through Bible study and prayer. Ask the Holy Spirit to produce God's love in your heart and to make His love evident to everyone close to you. Your family will respond, and all will be richly blessed, because when love's true colors are on display, the grace of God is revealed.

GRACE FOR TODAY:

God's grace reaches to the hearts of those closest to us.

TIMES OF REFRESHING

Which is more important, the two-week vacation or the half-hour lunch break?

Maybe you would argue for the former, but if you added up the amount of time each one allows you per year to escape from the pile of work on your desk, you might be surprised. A two-week vacation gives you 80 hours of time off annually, while a half-hour lunch break, five times a week for fifty weeks, provides 125 hours of rest. If you get an hour for lunch each day, you get twice that amount of time to rejuvenate!

God promises His children times of refreshing. These moments come in many shapes and sizes. Occasionally the Lord may bless you with a "mountaintop experience," an extended period of physical, mental, emotional, and spiritual restoration, such as a long stay in a woodland cabin or a lengthy visit to an oceanfront resort. Much more often,

GRACE FOR TODAY:

Each day God's grace comes to us through little times of refreshing.

however—in fact, on a daily basis—He will provide little times of refreshing, moments of reprieve from the grindstone, a few precious seconds when you can relax, refocus, and reenergize.

Think of how often each day God's grace comes to you through these little times of refreshing. Each time you glance up from the computer to rest your eyes and enjoy the sunshine outside your window. Every time you put down your tools, have a seat, and satisfy your thirst with a drink of cold water. A quick chat with a friend helps you feel connected and appreciated. A brisk walk through the park stretches your legs and clears your head. A few moments in God's Word puts everything in perspective and gives your life meaning.

God sustains you in countless little ways as you climb the mountain, so someday you can rest forever, enjoying the view from the highest peak.

[God says,] "I'll refresh tired bodies; I'll restore tired souls."
JEREMIAH 31:25 MSG

WE OWED A DEBT

By Warren W. Wiersbe

God's Word teaches that when we were unsaved, we owed God a debt we could not pay. Jesus makes this idea clear in His parable of the two debtors (Luke 7:36–50). Two men owed money to a creditor, the one owing ten times as much as the other. But neither was able to pay, so the creditor "graciously forgave them both" (literal translation). No matter how much morality a man may have, he still comes short of the glory of God. Even if his sin debt is one–tenth that of others, he stands unable to pay, bankrupt at the judgment bar of God. God in His grace, because of the work of Christ on the cross, is able to forgive sinners, no matter how large their debt may be.

Thus when we trust Christ, we become spiritually rich. We now share in the riches of God's grace (Ephesians 1:7), the riches of His glory (Ephesians 1:18; Philippians 4:19), the riches of His wisdom (Romans 11:33), and the "unsearchable riches of Christ" (Ephesians 3:8). In Christ we have "all the treasures of wisdom and knowledge" (Colossians 2:3), and we are "complete in Him" (Colossians 2:10). Once a person is "in Christ," he has all that he needs to live the kind of Christian life God wants him to live.[47]

—⁕—

PRECIOUS FATHER: THANK YOU FOR MAKING ME SPIRITUALLY RICH, FOR TAKING MY DEBT AND REPLACING IT WITH THE RICHES OF YOUR GRACE. TEACH ME TO WALK IN THOSE RICHES DAY BY DAY. AMEN.

The grace of God that brings salvation has appeared to all men. It teaches us to say "No" to ungodliness and worldly passions, and to live self–controlled, upright and godly lives in this present age.

TITUS 2:11–12

GOD'S TAPESTRY

The Lord is in his holy Temple; the Lord still rules from heaven. He
watches everything closely, examining everyone on earth.

PSALM 11:4 NLT

I f you've ever examined the pattern of a Persian rug or an intricately woven piece
of clothing, you might notice that the pattern looks rather chaotic up close. But
when you stand back and look at it again, everything changes—the individual strokes
take on depth and connectedness as part of the bigger design.

God has used a unique design to create each one of us. He sees and works with
every intricate detail, every twist and weave. Every inch was made under His super-
vision and care. But God also has the advantage of see-
ing us from a distance, standing back and looking at the
full picture. He sees the detail as well as how the design
works as a whole.

We often struggle with this part. We don't have
God's perspective. Instead, we are aware of being
twisted and shaped and arranged. We see every detail
and feel the pressure and discomfort as we are worked
and woven by the Great Designer. We obsess on our
trials and troubles because we aren't able to put them
into perspective.

For now, God asks us to simply trust Him—trust
that in the end our lives will be beautiful, unique tap-
estries. That takes faith and patience as we submit what
we see to the vision of the Creator. But one day, one glorious day, we will behold the
finished product; we will see the design from a new perspective.

Are you struggling with the details in your tapestry? Do they seem unordered and
chaotic? They aren't. God is at work, and one day you will see your life as He sees
it—perfect in every way.

> **GRACE FOR TODAY:**
>
> When God
> looks at us from
> a distance, He
> sees the beautiful
> tapestry that our
> lives will one
> day be.

HEADS, SHOULDERS, KNEES, AND TOES

The body is a unit, though it is made up of many parts; and though all its parts are many, they form one body. So it is with Christ.

1 CORINTHIANS 12:12

D ave is an intelligent, capable guy, a jack-of-all-trades. When the kitchen plumbing isn't working right, Dave can quickly find the problem and fix it. If the family car quits, Dave will analyze what's wrong and make the repairs. He built his own pole barn, he resided his own house, and when his wife decided that the backyard needed more sunshine, he got out some steel cables and a chain saw and took down a few tall trees.

But handyman that he is, Dave knows he is far from self-sufficient. He relies heavily on the tools, materials, and spare parts that others have designed and made. As he works at his job installing heating and cooling systems in homes and businesses, countless other able people are performing tasks essential to his well-being: teaching his children, policing his community, growing food for his family, providing energy and communication services to his neighborhood, delivering his mail, even monitoring the quality of the air he breathes.

God intended human society to reflect His design for the human body—a cohesive whole made up of many dissimilar parts that complement and support each other. Every day, the Lord blesses you through this ingenious structure of unified diversity. At the same time that you benefit from the talents of people around you, your life is given purpose as you put your skills to work for the good of others. This pattern is true of a city, it's true of a family, and it's particularly true of a local church. To varying degrees, God uses these institutions to meet your physical, relational, and spiritual needs, touching your life through the unique gifts of the wonderful menagerie of individuals He created.

> **GRACE FOR TODAY:**
>
> God blesses us each day through the diversity of the people around us.

TAKE CONTROL OF THE SHIP

Rash words are like sword thrusts,
but the tongue of the wise brings healing.

PROVERBS 12:18 NRSV

One of the greatest sailing ships built during the 1700s was a vessel known as the HMS Invincible. At over 200 feet in length and 50 feet in width, it was the largest ship of its time. Yet despite its great size, the HMS Invincible, like any other boat, depended upon a small wooden device known as a "rudder" to navigate its course.

In the morning of February 19, 1758, the crew was having difficulty raising the anchor. As they heaved and pulled at the rope to free the anchor, it suddenly shot up from the bottom and became lodged in the rudder. With no control over the steering, the ship tossed aimlessly on the waves, grounded onto the shore, and sank shortly thereafter.

In the letter of James, the author compares the "tongue" to the rudder of a ship. Though it is a small part of the body, the tongue has tremendous power to guide people through the situations that arise in their lives. If individuals have control over their tongues, others will respond favorably to their words and view them in positive ways. However, if people allow their anger to get the best of them and fail to control their words, others will be unfriendly towards them or just avoid them altogether.

Your speech is a reflection of your life in Christ. When you truly love others, the grace of God will flow from your heart to bless and encourage others. So strive to control your tongue and think before you speak out of frustration. For just as not having control over the rudder was disastrous for the HMS Invincible, not having control over your speech can be disastrous for you and your relationships.

GRACE FOR TODAY:

God has given us the privilege of using our speech to allow His grace to flow to others.

RAINBOW HUGS

[Jesus] took the children in his arms, placed his hands on each of them, and blessed them.

MARK 10:16 GNB

L ittle girls know what God's grace looks like. They can draw pictures of it.

A four-year-old lies on the floor by her daddy's desk and scribbles two stick people with a brown crayon, one taller than the other. Their body parts—heads, arms, legs, eyes, noses, and mouths—are distorted and out of proportion, but they're all there. And the mouths are both smiling.

She picks up a red crayon and sketches an arch that surrounds the figures, almost touching them, uniting them in the middle of the page. With a purple crayon she draws another arch outside the first one. Grabbing an orange crayon, then the brown one again, she traces two more arches. A green marker for the last arch adds an extra-special effect.

Finally, the little girl takes a blue marker and, under the smaller stick person, carefully writes her name. Four of the five letters are backwards, and the J looks like a U, but she knows her daddy will be able to read it.

Full of excitement, she interrupts his work. "Look, Daddy. It's a hug." Laughing, he takes the picture from her hand. "You're right, sweetie. It is a hug. It's a rainbow hug!" He stands up and stretches, then leans over and holds out his arms. "Why don't you give me one of your rainbow hugs right now?" The little girl leaps onto him, wrapping her arms and legs around him so tightly, it almost takes his breath away.

Soon he's down on the floor with her, wrestling, tickling, giving pony rides. The computer on his desk blinks, and the family budget is suddenly replaced with brightly moving shapes of purple, red, and green. Not that the little girl or her daddy have noticed. They are surrounded by colors all their own.

GRACE FOR TODAY:

The wonder of God's grace can be felt in
a child's embrace.

BUMBERSHOOTS

Soccer games are rarely called because of weather, so if your child is on the team, you'd better grab your bumbershoot—as Grandma used to say—before you head for the field on an overcast day. Take along an umbrella, and you'll enjoy the competition in relative comfort, staying dry and warm on the sidelines. Forget this important piece of equipment, and you might find yourself wet and cold, struggling to stay cheerful as you cheer on your young superstar.

Keeping the rain off at a sporting event is good. However, if you were to walk around holding up an umbrella all the time, you would constantly be under a shadow. And that's a good picture of the burden and the consequence of living under God's law rather than under His grace. God is omnipresent, and His grace shines down everywhere, like the rays of the sun. But if Jesus Christ has not relieved you of the requirements of God's law by fulfilling all of them on your behalf, that law separates you from God and prevents His grace from warming your shoulders.

> **GRACE FOR TODAY:**
>
> God's grace has changed His role in our lives from Judge to Father.

Prayerfully study the book of Romans to understand the difference between law and grace. Then give Jesus permission to take away your bumbershoot. He'll close it up and tuck it under His arm, its purpose finished—and suddenly you'll be basking in the light of God's glorious grace. From that point on, you'll see Him not as a Judge but as a Father. You'll see yourself not as a convicted sinner but as a child who is nurtured and guided and disciplined and protected, all the while surrounded by a deep, abiding love. And you'll relate to others not according to the old rules of retribution and revenge but according to the new guidelines of forgiveness and mercy.

You are not under law but under grace.

ROMANS 6:14 NKJV

MADE GREAT BY THE GRACE OF GOD

By John C. Maxwell

Let's look at the Apostle Paul. I think one of the key ingredients in his life was his vision. Not only did he see what he was, but he also saw what the grace of God could enable him to become. It was that vision that kept him steady throughout his ministry. In Acts 26:19, when he stood before King Agrippa, he said, "Consequently, King Agrippa, I did not prove disobedient to the heavenly vision." In spite of all the problems he had run into in his ministry, in spite of what was about to happen to him, he had been obedient to the dream God had given him.

What happened in Paul's life can happen in our lives. When we see ourselves properly, there are a couple of things that will happen. One, we'll see our position. We'll see where we are going. This can be discouraging because we may think, *I'm not accomplishing what I want to accomplish; I'm not being what I want to become.* But all people who have the potential for greatness first of all have to see themselves as they are, and usually that's discouraging.

When we have a vision from God and it stops us, not only do we see our position, but thankfully, we also see our potential. We see our possibilities. The good news is that God believes in you, and He will not allow you to see yourself and your problems without allowing you to see your potential. He's not going to frustrate us; He's going to encourage us and help us see what we can become.[48]

—∿—

LORD GOD: THANK YOU FOR THE DREAM YOU'VE PLACED IN MY HEART. BY YOUR GRACE I SEE MY POSITION, MY POTENTIAL, AND MY POSSIBILITIES. AMEN.

Paul [was] called to be an apostle of Christ Jesus by the will of God.

1 CORINTHIANS 1:1 NRSV

TIME TO UNWIND

Be at rest once more, O my soul, for the Lord has been good to you.

PSALM 116:7

Although Jack had a busy schedule, he had learned from experience the value of rest. Each morning, he would set aside some time before preparing for the day to read the Word of God and pray. Each evening, he would spend some time playing basketball or doing some other type of activity that he found enjoyable. Later at night, he would do things he found relaxing in order to "wind down" and be able to get to sleep.

Jack made it a point to truly leave his work behind when he left the office for the day and not let it affect his time of rest. As a result, he was less fatigued and had more energy throughout the day. His ability to rest allowed him to develop friendships and relationships outside of work and generally made him easier to deal with than those who were tired and stressed out.

Research has shown that the human body needs from six to nine hours of restful sleep each night. When this amount is shortened, the body is robbed of hormones that delay the effects of aging, enhance the immune system, lower cholesterol and blood pressure, rebuild bone and cartilage, elevate mood levels, and increase learning capacity.

More importantly, Jack understood the value of trusting his life to the grace of God. He consciously made it a point to let go of his worries and commit them to God's care. Because of this trust, he was able to step away from the pressures in his life and just relax, confident in the knowledge that God would always be by his side.

> **GRACE FOR TODAY:**
>
> God is able to change our worries to blessings when we entrust them to Him.

BEARINGS

[O God,] point out the road I must travel;
I'm all ears, all eyes before you.

PSALM 143:8 MSG

After the Apollo 13 spacecraft was damaged by an onboard explosion on its way to the moon, the three astronauts inside had to take unusual measures to get themselves safely back to earth. At one point they needed to adjust their trajectory to ensure that the ship hit the earth's atmosphere at precisely the right angle; if the angle was off by a few degrees one way or the other, disaster would result. The problem was, their navigational instruments were disabled. So they used the earth as a reference point, keeping it centered in the tiny window as they manually fired small rockets to put the ship back on course. By finding a way to keep their bearings, the astronauts made it home.

However, in many ways the world they returned to is in the same condition their spaceship was, and all humanity faces the same plight they did. Not long after its creation, our beautiful, peaceful planet was rocked as if by a huge blast when our ancestors rebelled against their Maker. Afterward, humankind was spinning crazily through space, off course, adrift in the cosmos. But God, in His great mercy and grace, provided us with a magnificent point of reference: His Son Jesus, the bright Morning Star.

GRACE FOR TODAY:

God has provided us with a way to find our bearings: His Son Jesus, the bright Morning Star.

We all experience humanity's dilemma personally. Before you were a Christian, the world may have seemed all right at times—but at other times, when you stared up at the stars and pondered the meaning of existence, suddenly everything seemed out of control. Even now, as a believer, you may struggle occasionally with questions about life. God has supplied an answer to this predicament, a way for you to get your bearings and find your way home. Simply fix your eyes on Jesus and keep them fixed on Him.

A PLACE AT THE TOP

God, being rich in mercy, because of His great love with which He loved us, even when we were dead in our transgressions, made us alive togeth-er with Christ (by grace you have been saved), and raised us up with Him, and seated us with Him in the heavenly places in Christ Jesus.

EPHESIANS 2:4–6 NASB

I t's a well-known fact that promotion often comes more quickly to those who have friends or family in high places. Who hasn't wished they had an uncle or brother or friend looking after them from the ranks of upper management?

You might be surprised to hear this, but you do have a friend and family member in high places. You can't get any higher than God—your heavenly Father—and He's also the best friend you could ever have. According to God's Word, He has already made a place for you at the top, paving the way for a future you could have never aspired to without Him. And here's where it gets really incredible. His influence on your behalf includes this earthly life and the life eternal that is yet to come.

As a benefit of God's grace, you have been given His favor, His love, His wis-dom, His strength. You have been granted instant access to His presence. You have been encouraged to go to Him with your needs—no request too great or too small.

God sits in the highest place of all. He is eternal and all-powerful. And He's been working on your behalf since the foundations of the earth. When you take His hand, receive His love, and avail yourself of His grace, you become one of the in-crowd. God is the greatest connection anyone could ever want or need.

GRACE FOR TODAY:

There is no relationship on this earth that can get you further in life than your relationship with God.

EXPOSÉ

Guide me in your truth and teach me, for you are God my Savior, and
my hope is in you all day long.

PSALM 25:5

"What is truth?"

Over two thousand years after he uttered it, Pontius Pilate's rhetorical question still hangs in the air.

In this world of universities teaching moral relativism, political parties spreading half-truths and doublespeak, and television networks broadcasting videotapes of people in contrived circumstances and calling it reality, it's no wonder many today shrug and repeat Pilate's words.

But long before the Roman governor posed his seemingly unanswerable question, God had resolved the issue once and for all. He simply divulged to Moses His name: "I am" (Exodus 3:14). The Lord expanded on this in His revelation to the apostle John: "I am the Alpha and the Omega, . . . who is, and who was, and who is to come, the Almighty" (Revelation 1:8). Jesus, being God incarnate, made an identical declaration: "I tell you the truth, . . . before Abraham was born, I am!" (John 8:58). He too added further clarification: "I am the way and the truth and the life" (John 14:6). Through these and other statements recorded for all time in the Bible, God lovingly shows us that His identity is synonymous with ultimate reality, so we don't have to go searching anywhere else for the truth.

Knowing this greatest, most basic fact about life frees you from the confusion and despair that so many people experience. It also serves as the foundation upon which all subsequent truths about life rest. By revealing to you that He is the Creator of, Sustainer of, and Reason for all existence, God opens your mind and your heart to receive the instruction, guidance, and wisdom His Word and Spirit offer. In this way the Lord enables you to discern all the important truths that spring from the one overarching fact of life, which is inherent in His name.

GRACE FOR TODAY:

God lovingly shows us that His identity is synonymous
with ultimate reality, so we don't have to go searching
anywhere else for the truth.

SPEAKING IN FINGERS

Have you ever been caught up in a worship song playing on your car radio but didn't quite know all the words? Your heart is full of love and praise for the Lord, but half the time—usually between the choruses—you are singing nonsensical syllables, like a scat singer in a jazz group. It doesn't matter, of course, because at that moment you are in intimate communion with God; both you and He know what you are communicating. The fellow in the next car may find your language odd if your windows are down, but perhaps in some small way, the experience can help you understand what the Bible means by speaking in tongues.

If you play a musical instrument—or paint or sculpt or make pottery or engage in similar artistic activities—you also have a sense of how God enables you to express your soul to Him through your fingers. If you dance, you know the wonderful feeling of being empowered by God to celebrate His grace through your body's graceful movements. In all these acts of worship, there is no language—yet there is. If such acts are committed in Christ and by the power of the Holy Spirit, your deepest thoughts and emotions are conveyed in a manner that surpasses words. And the God of Heaven understands. He receives such offerings of gratitude and praise, and He delights in them.

The Lord blessed you with fingers, hands, a body, a voice. Anything you do with these gifts can be done for God's glory (1 Corinthians 10:31). If you ask Him, He will teach you how to use the talents He gave you to honor Him and draw near to Him, and in so doing discover great satisfaction in His fellowship and presence.

> **GRACE FOR TODAY:**
>
> God delights in our expressions of love and praise.

Praise the Lord with melodies on the lyre;
make music for him on the ten-stringed harp.

PSALM 33:2 NLT

A Drop of Grace

By Johannes Tauler

A drop of grace is nobler than all angels and all souls, and all the natural things that God has made. Yet grace is given more richly by God to the soul than any earthly gift. It is given more richly than brooks of water, than the breath of the air, than the brightness of the sun; for spiritual things are far finer and nobler than earthly things. The whole Trinity, Father, Son, and Holy Ghost, give grace to the soul, and flow immediately into it. Even the highest angel, in spite of its great nobility, cannot do this.

Grace looses us from the snares of many temptations. It relieves us from the heavy burden of worldly anxieties and carries our spirit up to heaven, the land of spirits. It kills the worm of conscience, which makes sins alive. Grace is a very powerful thing. The person who receives even a tiny drop of grace is ruined for all else.

Grace makes, contrary to nature, all sorrows sweet, and brings it about that a person no longer feels any enjoyment for things that formerly gave great pleasure and delight. On the other hand, what formerly was found to be disgusting, now delights and is the desire of the heart—for instance, weakness, sorrow, inwardness, humility, self-abandonment, and detachment from others. All of this is very dear to a person, when this visitation of the Holy Ghost—grace—has in truth come to them.

—m—

DEAR LORD: HOW CAN I THANK YOU ENOUGH FOR EVERY DROP OF GRACE YOU'VE POURED OUT ON MY LIFE? IT MAKES ALL MY SORROWS SWEET AND BRINGS ME GREAT JOY. AMEN.

From the fullness of his grace we have all received one blessing after another.

JOHN 1:16

PITFALLS

I'm sitting in the dark right now, but God is my light. . . . He's on my side and is going to get me out of this.

MICAH 7:8-9 MSG

The road to life that Jesus spoke of (Matthew 7:13-14) is not only narrow, it is also steep at times and winds around dangerous hazards. But if you are walking closely with God, He will point out the pitfalls along the way.

These are traps that Satan sets beside the path to ensnare you. One of the blessings of God is that He provides you with perfectly reliable intelligence about the Enemy's plans and tactics. Through the Bible, God opens your eyes to the general methods Satan uses to entice people to sin. Through the Holy Spirit, God reveals the specific ways in which the Devil tempts you. The Lord shows you the territory in your life that is unsafe to tread upon, side roads that look appealing but diverge from the true path and quickly lead to disaster. Armed with this vital information, you are better able to anticipate Satan's traps and avoid falling headlong into them.

> **GRACE FOR TODAY:**
> When we walk closely with God, He is faithful to point out the pitfalls along our path.

Sometimes, however, your sinful human nature responds to the Enemy's lures, and despite God's forewarning you knowingly and willingly stray off the path of righteousness. It should come as no surprise when you suddenly find yourself in the bottom of a deep, dark pit, but it often does. And with this rude awakening comes the awful realization that not only have you wandered away from God and fallen into sin, you have stepped out of the realm of His favor and into the domain of His law, and therefore now lie under His wrath.

But praise God, He doesn't leave you there with no hope. The minute you cry out to Him in repentance, God shines a powerful rescue light into the pit, and Jesus reaches in, grabs you by the arm, and pulls you back up into God's grace.

NO REASON TO RUN

[Jesus said,] "The Son of Man came to seek out and to save the lost."

LUKE 19:10 NRSV

Living in the slums of London in 1888, Francis Thompson had undoubtedly witnessed bloodhounds tracking down criminals running from the law. He must have marveled how these creatures could relentlessly pursue their subjects for days at a time and over great distances, never giving up until they found what they were seeking. To Francis, God resembled these bloodhounds—relentlessly seeking out those who had strayed from His love in order to bring them back into relationship with himself.

In his most famous poem, "The Hound of Heaven," Francis recalled his own experience in running from the grace of God. Raised in a Christian household, he had encountered the love of God at an early age, but failure in life had left him feeling bitter and disappointed. Determining to live life on his own terms, he turned his back on God and fled to the streets of London to become a poet, where he soon found himself living in conditions of poverty, filth, and disease.

Yet even though Francis had rejected God, the Lord hadn't given up on pursuing a relationship with him. He brought a man named Wilfred Menell onto the scene, who rescued Francis from the slums, gave him food and clothes, and actively demonstrated the grace of God that Francis had so callously rejected.

No matter how far you may have wandered from the love of God, the Lord is always ready and willing to restore your relationship. With patient and steady determination, He seeks out those who have wandered from His straight and true path. For as the father welcomed home the prodigal son, the Lord is always ready to embrace you in His loving arms and shower you with His many blessings.

> **GRACE FOR TODAY:**
> No matter how far we have wandered from God, He is always waiting to restore us and shower us with blessings.

PENNIES FROM HEAVEN

God . . . will supply all your needs from his glorious riches, which have
been given to us in Christ Jesus.

PHILIPPIANS 4:19 NLT

At a recent exhibit of the Dead Sea Scrolls, visitors could see fragments of the ancient texts, as well as artifacts collected from the area where the scrolls were found. Among these items were coins that had been in use during Jesus' time on earth. They were round and silver, with people's faces, other images, and words stamped on them—strikingly similar to the coins you carry around today.

When Peter needed money to pay the temple tax, Jesus told him to go to the lake, throw out a line, and look in the mouth of the first fish he caught. There he would find a coin worth enough to cover the tax for both of them (Matthew 17:24–27). The Bible doesn't say how the coin got there. Perhaps God caused it to materialize suddenly in the mouth of the fish on Peter's hook. Or maybe Jesus somehow knew that some other fisherman out in a boat had a hole in his pocket, that a fish had tried to swallow his lost change as it sank to the bottom of the lake, and that Peter would just happen to catch this particular fish. Either way, the coin Peter discovered is a tangible example of God's gracious, sometimes miraculous, provision for His children.

Pull a coin out of your pocket and take a close look at it. Rub your thumb over its surface. Feel the weight of it in your hand. Coins really haven't changed much in over two thousand years. Neither has God. In fact, He hasn't changed one bit since time began! He's still ready, able, and willing to meet the needs of His loved ones—to meet your needs—even if it takes a supernatural act to do it.

GRACE FOR TODAY:

God works miracles if necessary to provide
for His children.

VITTLES

Everyone who thirsts, come to the waters;
and you who have no money, come, buy and eat.

ISAIAH 55:1 NKJV

Who put the cornflakes in your cereal bowl this morning?
Who made the earth with its rich, fertile soil? Who made the first corn plants to grow in that soil and produce the seeds which generations upon generations later, through a cyclical process that essentially hasn't changed since it was first begun, yielded our present—day crops? Who made the people who harvested those crops and delivered them to the factory? Who gave humankind the ingenuity, skill, and raw materials to design and build machines to transform corn into crunchy golden flakes?

God did it all, of course. By the way, He also made the milk you poured on your cereal, the blueberries you sprinkled on top, the orange juice in your glass, the toast and the butter and the jam.

One family has a little running joke about whether certain meals, such as those served in paper bags at fast—food restaurants, are "grace—worthy." They kid each other to gently remind themselves to stop, bow their heads, and thank the Lord for providing their food, because they recognize that every meal ultimately comes from God.

Because of the Fall, God ordained that you must work and pay for the food and drink your body needs each day. But the nourishment your soul needs—daily bread, meaning God's Word, and living water, meaning God's Spirit—the Lord offers to you free of charge. Jesus purchased them for you at tremendous cost to himself, dying on the cross so that by trusting in Him you would be made worthy of God's grace.

GRACE FOR TODAY:

God provides daily bread and living water for our
bodies—and also for our souls.

A REFLECTION OF GOD

Francis of Assisi was a man who appreciated the wonder of God's creation. The son of a wealthy Italian merchant, Francis had been raised in an environment of great wealth and opulence, but had forsaken it all in order to serve God and help the poor. Yet now, though he often lived without even a roof over his head, Francis considered himself truly blessed as he traveled across the countryside ministering to those in need.

Nature was more than just an expression of God's beauty to Francis—it was a reflection of the very nature of God and His handiwork. Francis viewed everything in nature that he encountered as a gift from God and an expression of His grace. Francis praised God for the joy that His creation brought to his life and sought to honor and protect all living things that were a part of it.

Do you stop and thank God when you see a beautiful sunset at dusk? Do you praise Him for His creation when you see the leaves of the trees change into their brilliant fall colors? Can you appreciate His creativity when you see the pattern on a seashell or the intricate design of a spider's web? Do you view nature as a gift of God's grace?

God has given you an incredible world that He wants you to explore and enjoy, so take time during the week to go on a short walk though the woods or the park. Open your eyes to the beauty around you and praise God for the works of His creation. Be thankful as Francis was that God cares so much for you that He wanted you to live in a world filled with beauty and wonder.

> **GRACE FOR TODAY:**
>
> God has given us an incredible world, yet our redeemed lives are His most treasured creation.

[Lord,] I think about what your fingers have created . . . about the moon and stars that you have set in place.

PSALM 8:3 NIRV

GRACE AND PEACE

By Martin Luther

The greeting of the apostle Paul when he says, "Grace and peace to you" is amazing to people of the world. Only those who belong to Christ comprehend the two words, grace and peace. Grace releases sin, and peace makes the conscience quiet.

The two fiends that torment us are sin and conscience. But Christ has defeated these two monsters and trodden them under His foot, both in this world and in the world to come. Therefore these two words contain the whole sum of Christianity in their meaning. Grace contains the remission of sins, and peace contains a quiet and joyful conscience.

But peace of conscience can never be had, unless sin is first forgiven. But sin is not forgiven by the fulfilling of the law; for no one is able to satisfy the law. But the law shows us sin, accuses and terrifies our conscience, declares the wrath of God, and drives one to desperation.

And one cannot take away sin through the works and creations of peo-ple, like strict rules, religious practices, vows, and pilgrimages. But there is no work that can take away sin; but instead works increase sin. For the perfection-ists and merit-mongers, the more they labor and sweat to bring themselves out of sin, the deeper they are plunged into it. For there is no means to take away sin, but through grace alone.

Therefore Paul, in all the greetings of his letters, sets grace and peace against sin and evil conscience. The words themselves are easy. But, it is hard to be persuaded in our hearts, that by grace alone—not by any other means either in heaven or in earth—we have remission of sins and peace with God.

HOLY FATHER: How can I thank You for Your grace and Your peace? They hold my world together, helping me through each day and ensuring my eternal future. Help me to walk in what You have given me. Amen.

Since we have been justified through faith, we have peace with God through our Lord Jesus Christ.

ROMANS 5:1

THE ULTIMATE TEST OF GREATNESS

This righteousness from God comes through faith in Jesus Christ to all who believe.

ROMANS 3:22

I n terms of power and accomplishments, one of the greatest kings of Israel after the time of David and Solomon was a man named Omri. During his reign, which historians believe lasted from 876–869 BC, Omri brought peace to the land and economic prosperity to the people. He ended almost 50 years of civil unrest and even established a dynasty for his descendants. He conducted widespread construction projects and established a new capital city in Samaria. So influential was Omri during his time that neighboring countries referred to Israel as "Omriland."

Yet you've probably never even heard of king Omri, for despite his greatness on earth he was considered unrighteous before God. In fact, his entire reign is summed up in a short section in 1 Kings 16:25,28, which concludes, "Omri did evil in the sight of the Lord . . . so Omri slept with his fathers and was buried in Samaria." Since Omri had failed the ultimate test of greatness—that of righteousness—the Old Testament authors felt little need to say anything else about his life.

In Romans 10:10 NASB, Paul states, "With the heart a person believes, resulting in righteousness, and with the mouth he confesses, resulting in salvation." When you accept the free gift of righteousness that the Lord offers to all who choose to accept His grace and follow His ways, you become "great" in His eyes.

Greatness on earth is fleeting, but God's gift of righteousness is eternal. When you focus on becoming "great" in the eyes of the Lord instead of the world, you allow God to change your attitude and your heart towards others. As you live according to the promises in His Word, you demonstrate to others the value of living a righteous life.

> **GRACE FOR TODAY:**
>
> God's gift of righteousness increases as we allow Him to change our attitudes toward others.

"NO FAIR!"

He always loves those who keep his covenant . . . [and] does what is right
for those who remember to obey his commands.

PSALM 103:18 NIRV

Philip looked with apprehension as the sun began to slowly set in the west. He had enjoyed playing ball with his friends in the park all afternoon, but now that it was getting dark, he knew that he would soon have to go home. His parents had specifically told him to be home before dark, and Philip knew that he had to obey.

Of course, this didn't mean he was happy about it. "No fair!" he said to his mom and dad when he got home. "The other parents let their kids stay at the park after dark. Why can't I? You don't want me to have any fun with my friends."

"No, Philip," said his mom. "We asked you to leave the park before dark because it's dangerous to be out so late at night. We love you and want you to be safe."

"Besides, tonight is a school night," said his father, "and if you stay out late you'll be too tired tomorrow. You can play with your friends tomorrow."

Sometimes, you may find yourself wondering why God asks you to obey. His commands may seem unfair at times or make you feel He is taking away your "fun" by not allowing you to do the things you want to do. Yet it is important to remember that God imposes rules only because He loves you and wants to keep you from harm. He wants to guide and direct you along the course that will bring you the greatest joy, fulfillment, and peace in your life.

> GRACE FOR TODAY:
>
> God's rules are designed to protect, guide, and bring joy, fulfillment, and peace to our lives.

Trust in God's guidance and submit to His will. For when you do, He will bless your life and cover you with His grace.

PLEASANT PLACES!

The lines have fallen to me in pleasant places;
indeed, my heritage is beautiful to me.

PSALM 16:6 NASB

A prominent psychiatrist once said, "The next time you sit down to a simple supper, crawl into a cozy bed, have a warm chat with a friend, imagine that you are at the end of the rainbow, that this is life, and it's wonderful."

It's easy to lose sight of the blessings in life. So many little things that we have are unique to our time and culture: hot water, electricity, indoor plumbing. Because we are rarely without these things, we often forget what life would be like without them.

In *The Manhood of the Master* (1913), Harry Emerson Fosdick wrote:

Jesus made the best out of one of the most un–ideal situations that ever faced a great soul. He did not demand a different farm to labor on; he went to work on the farm that he had, and grew harvests on that, which have been feeding the world ever since. His life sounds a courageous call to all of us: Stop whining; stop pitying yourself; see what you can do, by the help of God, with your un–ideal situation, for God never would have given it to you without some fine possibilities in it.

No matter how "un–ideal" you feel your life may be, you still have received many amazing gifts from God, the greatest of which is salvation through His Son, Jesus Christ. The lines have fallen for you in pleasant places!

GRACE FOR TODAY:

God can transform your "un–ideal" situations with
His ideal possibilities.

COUNT YOUR BLESSINGS

Give thanks to the Lord for his unfailing love and
his wonderful deeds for men.

PSALM 107:8

The pilgrims who left England for the New World on September 6, 1620, had little idea of the hardships that awaited them. During the initial voyage, they were
rocked by stormy weather that lasted nine weeks. The first New England winter they
encountered in the new land was unusually harsh, and they were completely unaccustomed to such extended periods of cold weather. In addition, the supply ships from
England often did not arrive as scheduled, leaving the pilgrims with little food and other
provisions.

Spring finally arrived in 1621, and the pilgrims were able to plant their crops. The
harvest that fall was bountiful, and the governor of the colony recognized that they had
much to be thankful for. Calling the pilgrims together, he issued a proclamation calling
for a public day of giving thanks to God for their survival. Thus, the first "thanksgiving" feast consisting of turkey, cornbread, squash, and pumpkin was held to honor God
for His provision.

The important lesson to be learned from the pilgrims is that even though they
endured tremendous hardships, they had the ability to recognize the blessings the Lord
had bestowed upon them. Rather than blame God for their former bad fortunes, the pilgrims were able to focus on the positive aspects of their current condition and give
thanks to God for His incredible grace.

No matter what life throws at you, always remember that God is with you.
Though you will have to persevere through difficult times, He will always extend His
grace to you in times of need. So let your life be a reflection of God's grace, and let
others see that you bless and honor God in all things.

GRACE FOR TODAY:

Hardships cause us to recognize God's grace in our lives.

THE JOY OF CREATION

Few individuals in the history of Japanese art have matched the creativity of the man known as "Hokusai." Born in the village of Edo in the year 1760, Hokusai began his career as an artist at the age of fifteen. By the age of eighteen, he had already been accepted as an apprentice to the famous Japanese art school under the master Shunsho.

Hokusai was a man who loved his work and the simple act of creation. As he finished one drawing, he would often toss it to the floor and immediately begin sketching another. When the papers piled up and his house became too disorderly, he simply moved to another residence—something he did ninety-three times during his life. A prolific artist, Hokusai produced over 30,000 drawings by the time of his death in 1849.

Hokusai was not afraid to use his talents and express himself through creativity. In the same way, you should never be afraid to use the creative abilities that God has placed inside you. Worrying that your skills are not "good enough," that you have nothing new to offer the world, or that others will laugh at your attempts only deny the power that God has to inspire and direct your efforts and rob you of the joy of creation.

You will be amazed at the lives you will touch as you allow God to nurture and develop your innate creativity. Your words will motivate others, your ideas will encourage their hearts, and your actions will inspire them to achieve greatness. Through your creativity, you will truly bless others and fill their lives with God's grace.

> GRACE FOR TODAY:
>
> God motivates others through the creative abilities He has placed in our lives.

[God says,] "I have filled him with divine spirit, with ability, intelligence, and knowledge in every kind of craft, to devise artistic designs, to work in gold, silver, and bronze, in cutting stones for settings, and in carving wood, in every kind of craft."

EXODUS 31:3-5 NRSV

FULL OF GRACE

By Augustine of Hippo

Why should there be such great glory in one of human nature? This is undoubtedly an act of grace. No obvious merit comes from having Christ in the form of a human except that those who consider such a question faithfully and soberly would have here a clear demonstration of God's great grace. Then they might understand how they themselves are justified from their sins by the same grace, which made it so that the human Christ had no power to sin.

Therefore the angel hailed His mother when announcing to her the future birth: "Hail," he said, "full of grace." And he said shortly after, "You have found favor with God." And it was said of her, that she was full of grace, since she was to be mother of her Lord, indeed the Lord of all.

Yet, concerning Christ himself, when the Evangelist John said, "And the Word became flesh and dwelt among us," he added, "and we beheld His glory, the glory as of the only begotten of the Father, full of grace and truth" (John 1:14 NKJV). When he said, "The Word became flesh," this means "full of grace." And when he said, "The glory of the only begotten of the Father," this means "full of truth."

Indeed it was Truth himself, God's only begotten Son—and, again, this not by grace but by nature—who, by grace, assumed human nature into such a personal unity that He himself became the Son of Man as well.

—⁓—

FATHER GOD: THANK YOU FOR SENDING YOUR ONLY BEGOTTEN SON TO LIVE IN A HUMAN BODY THAT I MIGHT KNOW THE REALITY OF YOUR GRACE. AMEN.

So the Word became human and lived here on earth among us. He was full of unfailing love and faithfulness. And we have seen his glory, the glory of the only Son of the Father.

JOHN 1:14 NLT

VAYA CON DIOS

[God] guards you when you leave and when you return, he guards you
now, he guards you always.

PSALM 121:8 MSG

Good-bye means much more than "So long"; it's an alteration of the phrase "God be with you" (Merriam Webster's Collegiate Dictionary, tenth edition). Every time you wave to a friend and shout, "Bye!" you're offering a prayer for the Lord's protection. Each time you hug your child and whisper, "Bye-bye," you're committing your young one to God's care.

GRACE FOR TODAY:

God gives us the grace to entrust our friends and loved ones to His watchful care.

What a blessing it is every day to be able to release loved ones into His keeping, so that in this uncertain world you don't have to worry about them during those times when you must be apart. This wonderful gift of God's grace allows those who have placed their faith in the Lord peace of mind and freedom to focus on their tasks for the day as they go about fulfilling His purposes for them.

Christians trust and rely on God's promises of safety and protection. Yet we also recognize that God's sovereign will is a mystery to humankind, and therefore we cannot predict the things He will allow to happen, or when He will allow them to occur. We are at a loss to explain why He allows bad things to happen at all; we can only bow before Him and acknowledge that He is God and cling to the knowledge that He is good and that someday all will be explained. In the meantime we tell our loved ones good-bye, place them in the Lord's arms, and at the deepest level know that no matter what happens, they will ever be safe there.

Of course, this raises the issue of friends and family members who are not believers—loved ones for whom there is no such guarantee. For them, perhaps our good-byes should become prayers not only that God will stay close to them but that His grace will open their hearts to Him.

GET BACK IN THE GAME

There is therefore now no condemnation for those who
are in Christ Jesus.

ROMANS 8:1 NRSV

Roy Riegels sat in the locker room with a blanket around his shoulders and his face in his hands. It was halftime at the Rose Bowl and he had just committed one of the most embarrassing mistakes in the history of the game.

Near the end of the second quarter, a player from the opposing team had lost control of the ball. Riegels had scooped it up and taken off down the field—but in the wrong direction. He nearly scored for the other team before one of his own teammates tackled him at the one-yard line. Now, with halftime drawing to a close, Riegels refused to go back on the field.

"I've ruined you," he told his coach. "I couldn't face the crowd in that stadium to save my life." But his coach would hear nothing of it, saying, "Roy, get up and go back. The game is only half over."

When you make a mistake, it is important to admit your error, ask for forgiveness, accept the grace of God, and move forward. Dwelling upon past mistakes (which you can do nothing about) only leaves you feeling guilty and depressed. The memory of your failings can keep you tied down and unable to free yourself from the burden you have placed upon your own life.

GRACE FOR TODAY:

God's forgiveness allows us to give up our guilt and shame and put the past behind us.

God wants you to lift up your head and take the field. He desires for you to give up your guilt and shame to Him so that you can let go of the past. For only when you accept the grace of God in your life can you begin to learn from your mistakes and receive His strength to persevere for the times ahead.

ASSURANCE

God has said, "I will never fail you. I will never forsake you."
That is why we can say with confidence, "The Lord is my helper,
so I will not be afraid."

HEBREWS 13:5-6 NLT

God's grace provides you with the confidence you need for every step of life's journey, from the little ones to the big ones. His promise to walk with you gives you the courage to go everywhere He leads you to go in this world. It emboldens you to walk onstage at a business conference and speak to a large audience or walk across the street to a neighbor's house to share your faith. It empowers you to walk into an office building for an employment interview or walk away from a steady job to start a new business. It enables you to walk down the aisle to make your wedding vows or walk into the hospital to experience the birth of your first child.

The sworn presence of the Lord gives you an assurance that comes, not from faith in yourself, but from faith in someone whose wisdom and power is infinitely greater than yours. It also comes from the deep knowledge that even if God allows you to stumble at this step in your journey, He will be with you forever, and that's all that really matters. The things of this world may be shaken, but that which cannot be shaken—God and His kingdom—will remain forever. And nothing can ever separate you from God's everlasting love.

The Lord has given you many great and wonderful promises, and He has revealed in His Word and proven throughout history that He is able to keep every one. God will walk with you through this life, beside you every step of the way, if you're willing to let go of whatever self-confidence you possess and put your trust completely in Him. Every journey begins with a single step, and in this case it's a step of faith.

GRACE FOR TODAY:

We are blessed in our earthly walk by God's great and
wonderful promises.

SOMETHING WORTH FIGHTING FOR

Pursue righteousness, godliness, faith, love, patience, gentleness.
Fight the good fight of faith.

1 TIMOTHY 6:11-12 NKJV

When Adam and Eve rebelled against God, He could have abandoned the human race to its own devices. The Lord could have said, "Very well, you have chosen your path. I grieve for you because I know what will happen next. You'll go off and attempt to fend for yourselves the best you can. You'll try to scratch out an existence somehow on this planet I've created, and you'll fight each other over all the material things in it. You'll search for happiness and peace in this world, but you won't ever find it, because I'm leaving you now to rule your own lives, as you wished." And human history would have begun a long downward spiral into chaos and oblivion.

But our gracious, compassionate, forgiving God wouldn't allow that to happen. Instead He sent His Son Jesus to the cross on our behalf, giving each of us a second chance, another opportunity to choose. We can reject Jesus' sacrifice and continue in our rebellion, or we can be reconciled with God through Christ's blood and begin striving—with the Holy Spirit's help—to live righteously. God's grace offers us a better way of life than the one our ancestors chose for us, a noble cause to pursue, something worth fighting for. Rather than ignobly battling each other for land, natural resources, precious metals, and other worldly goods, we can fight honorably for righteousness, godliness, and all the fruit of the Spirit.

God chose not to walk away from His creation after the Fall. Instead He stayed in the picture, ensuring that we would also have a choice, that we could determine a better destiny for ourselves, resolve to live with purpose and hope, and contend for the worthiest of goals: to know the Lord and walk in His ways.

GRACE FOR TODAY:

God's grace offers us a better way of life than the one our ancestors chose for us. It's one worth fighting for.

BURIED TREASURE

There was nothing especially interesting about Andreas Gaitatzis' farm in Greece. It was a plain-looking plot of land that resembled most of the other fields in the area that were planted with various types of crops. Yet there was something different about Andreas' field, for one day as he sifted through the earth on his land, he discovered a two thousand-year-old solid gold wreath—only the third of its kind ever found in Greece.

Lured by the unusual find, archeologists raced to the scene and began to uncover more artifacts on Andreas' land. Within a short time, they discovered an entire ancient city known as "Apollonia" beneath Andreas' simple-looking farmland. The insights gained from this discovery have since proved invaluable to historians seeking knowledge on ancient life in Greece.

Sometimes, you may view your life as bland and meaningless. It is easy to buy into the world's idea that value is based on such things as social status, appearance, youth, and success. With such messages surrounding you each day, it is tempting to believe that you are less valuable if you do not have these things. Yet God sees you for who you are and considers your life to be incredibly valuable.

Like the farmer in the field, God is just waiting to uncover the beauty in your life and show you all the treasures that lie just beneath the surface. He wants to show you how much He loves and cares for you as an individual part of His creation. So allow Him to lift you up and bless you with His grace, so that you can use the talents He has given you and let your life shine for His glory.

> GRACE FOR TODAY:
>
> We are God's treasure. He cherishes us and reveals our inner beauty and talents to others for His glory.

We are what he has made us, created in Christ Jesus for good works, which God prepared beforehand to be our way of life.

EPHESIANS 2:10 NRSV

THE LIGHT OF GRACE

By Meister Eckhart

What God makes in the simple light of the soul is more beautiful and more delightful than all the other things He creates. Through that light comes grace.

Grace never comes in the intelligence or in the will. If it could come in the intelligence or in the will, the intelligence and the will would have to rise above themselves. The true union between God and the soul takes place in the little spark, which is called the spirit of the soul. Grace doesn't take any work to unite. It is an indwelling and a living together of the soul in God.

Every gift of God makes the soul ready to receive a new gift, greater than itself.

God has never given any gift, so people might rest in the possession of the gift, but gives every gift that He has given in Heaven and on earth, in order that He might be able to give one main gift, which is himself. So with this gift of grace, and with all His gifts, He will make us ready for the one gift, which is himself.

No one is so coarse or stupid or awkward that they cannot, by God's grace, unite their will wholly and entirely with God's will. And nothing more is necessary than that they should say with earnest longing: O Lord, show me Your dearest will, and strengthen me to do it.

And God does it, as sure as He lives, and gives them grace in ever richer fullness, until they come to perfection.

—⁓—

GRACIOUS FATHER: I CALL UPON YOUR GRACE AND SUBMIT MY WILL COMPLETELY TO YOURS. MAKE ME READY TO RECEIVE YOUR GREATEST GIFT—THE GIFT OF YOURSELF. AMEN.

If, by the trespass of the one man, death reigned through that one man, how much more will those who receive God's abundant provision of grace and of the gift of righteousness reign in life through the one man, Jesus Christ.

ROMANS 5:17

SELF-KNOWLEDGE

We have different gifts, according to the grace given us.

ROMANS 12:6

A t what point in life does a person discover who he or she is? When does a kid swinging at fastballs in a coin-operated batting cage realize that he's training for his career in the major leagues? When does the boy in the next cage recognize that in spite of all his dreams of baseball glory, his calling in life is to do medical research?

Everybody wrestles with the question, "Who am I?" You could consult any number of sources for the answer—your parents, your friends, your teachers, your employers, your spouse. You could do a lot of soul-searching as well. But who better to turn to than God? James 1:5 promises that if you ask the Lord for wisdom, He will graciously give it to you. And God knows you better than anybody does, including yourself. He masterfully formed you in your mother's womb, endowing you with certain physical attributes and a distinct personality type; and ever since your birth He has continued to skillfully mold you through your upbringing, education, and experiences.

You may already think you know who you are and where you fit into this world. You may have no clue. Or you may be disappointed because you don't seem to be developing into the person you'd hoped to be. If you look to God for wisdom, He will either affirm your sense of identity or reveal to you the person He designed you to be. He may show you His plan for your life immediately or unveil it little by little over time. In any case, remember that the story doesn't end with self-knowledge. It's important to nurture your relationship with your Creator, because He's still creating you, and you're going to need His help to achieve all the purposes He has for you.

THE UNEARNED GIFT

[God] saved us, not because of righteous things we had done, but because
of his mercy. He saved us through the washing of rebirth and renewal by
the Holy Spirit.

TITUS 3:5

Most of us recall the excitement we felt as children when our birthdays came
around. Some of us would even start counting down the days as much as a
month in advance. We wanted to get our hands on the gifts we knew would be waiting for us on our special day—unearned gifts, simply
celebrations of the fact of our births. When the day
finally arrives, we are surrounded by friends and family, all eager to join in our happiness.

GRACE FOR TODAY:

Did you know that we also have spiritual birthdays? These are celebrations of the day we were
born—for the second time. Born to newness of life in
vital relationship with God through His Son, Jesus
Christ. The Bible says that at such times the angels celebrate with us, rejoicing that we have been born into
the kingdom.

The gift of
grace is
unearned. We
receive it when
we are born
into the
Kingdom of
God.

And on the basis of our second birth, God has
given us a gift—again unearned and undeserved. That
gift is grace. And what a gift it is. It opens up Heaven
and gives us access to all the goodness of God—forgiveness, atonement, eternal life, spiritual gifts and call-
ings, a heavenly home, and most of all, entrance into the presence of God himself.

Do you have a reason to celebrate today? If you have ever sinned, your answer
should be a resounding "yes!" Because of the gift of grace, you have been given the
opportunity to start life with a clean slate. Let the party begin!

IS THE TRUTH REALLY TRUE?

Therefore do not throw away your confidence, which has a great reward.

HEBREWS 10:35 RSV

Did you know that the Bible contains not just 1, not just 100, not just 1,000 but more than 1,200 promises? There are promises that show that God is with us no matter where we are and what we are going through. There are promises of love and forgiveness, healing and provision, wisdom and understanding. Promises of eternal life and heavenly delights. Promises of sanctification and reconciliation with God. In fact there are promises in the Bible that have an impact upon every area of our lives.

But a promise is only as good as the person who makes it. And that's exactly why the promises in the Bible are so amazing. They were made by Almighty God himself, backed up by the Creator of the universe. And that's where His credentials begin. All that He is will never be known to us—our human minds simply couldn't contain it.

So what makes us hesitate to claim God's promises? Are we afraid we wouldn't qualify? Given the consistency of our failings, that would seem to be true. But it absolutely isn't. God promises even to make us eligible to receive His promises by pouring out His unmerited favor on us. When we weren't right, He made us right by paying our debt with the life of His pure and sinless Son.

In our society, we are inundated with promises. Brighter clothes, better sleep, cleaner teeth. But only God's promises have been proven and tested. Only God's promises are worthy of our trust. So what are you waiting for? Open up the Bible and take God at His Word!

GRACE FOR TODAY:

God's promises are relevant, powerful, and eternal. They do not disappoint.

Thou Art Mine!

Thus saith the Lord that created thee, O Jacob, and he that formed thee, O Israel, Fear not: for I have redeemed thee, I have called thee by thy name; thou art mine.

Isaiah 43:1 KJV

Have you ever seen children engaged in name-calling? Perhaps when you were a child, you did the same thing. Or maybe you were the target of such painful words.

It might surprise you to know that God is a big name-caller. He starts by calling us His children. And when He does, He's just warming up. He goes on to call us forgiven, redeemed, justified by faith. He calls us Beloved, Chosen Ones, and Friends. He calls us blameless, holy, and Heaven-bound. He calls us wise, worthy, and filled with hope. He calls us confident, courageous, and content. He calls us righteous, worthy, and victorious. He calls us strong, successful, and rich. He calls us these names and more, not because we live up to the names, but because He has covered us with His love and grace.

God also calls himself names: The Beginning and the End. Comforter, Counselor, Creator. Deliverer, Day Star, Door. Faithful, Father, Friend. Helper, High Priest, Horn of Salvation. The Way, The Truth, and The Life. Here, too, His grace gives us the right to call Him by these names without fear of rejection.

Isn't it time for you to become a name-caller? Time for you to understand and walk in the reality of who you are to God and who He is in your life? Perhaps you need Him to be the Wonderful Counselor and the Prince of Peace in your life—only you and God know what you need. He's listening and waiting for you to call Him by name.

Grace for Today:

God has given us His name to assure us that we can call on Him to meet our every need.

EAT WHAT IS GOOD FOR YOU

During special times of the year like holidays and birthdays, families get together to celebrate over a feast. Usually, those feasts feature delicacies that are good for us. However, the fact that the food is good for us is not necessarily indicative of the taste. There are usually other less nutritious foods at the table that are much more fun to eat. For example, the banana-nut bread is always more fun to eat than the spinach salad. In most instances, junk food tastes much better than health food.

Did you know that God has provided for us food that will nourish the spirit? His food contains sustenance for every area of life, and He has invited us to treat ourselves generously to the best spiritual food anyone could ever have— the Word of God. From start to finish, everything in the Bible is good for you.

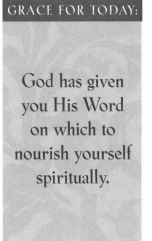

GRACE FOR TODAY:

God has given you His Word on which to nourish yourself spiritually.

But in a life where we have delicacies such as movies, DVDs, the Internet, and cable television, God's Word is admittedly much more nutritious, but not always the best-tasting dish at the table.

Clearly, we cannot live off of banana-nut bread. If we tried, we would find ourselves malnourished. In the same way, we cannot expect to survive spiritually if we fill ourselves with spiritual junk food. Today, treat yourself to what is good for you. Read your Bible consistently, and you will grow stronger day by day. Then, in the day that you find yourself in need of spiritual strength, you will realize that you've grown to be a strong and healthy Christian.

Jesus answered him, saying, "It is written, 'Man shall not live by bread alone, but by every word of God.'"

LUKE 4:4 NKJV

THE NATURE OF GRACE

By Thomas Watson

It is the nature of grace to change the heart and make it peaceable. By nature we are of a fierce cruel disposition. When God cursed the ground for man's sake, the curse was that it should bring forth "thorns and thistles" (Genesis 3:18 NASB). The heart of man naturally lies under this curse. It brings forth nothing but the thistles of strife and contention.

But when grace comes into the heart it makes it peaceable. It infuses a sweet, loving disposition. It smoothes and polishes the most knotty piece. It files off the ruggedness in men's spirits.

Grace turns the vulture into a dove, the briar into a myrtle tree, the lion-like fierceness into a lamb-like gentleness. (See Isaiah 55:13.) "And the wolf will dwell with the lamb, and the leopard will lie down with the young goat," (Isaiah 11:6 NASB). It is spoken of as the power that the gospel shall have upon men's hearts; it shall make such a metamorphosis that those who before were full of rage and antipathy shall now be made peaceable and gentle.

Peace shows us the character of a true saint. A saint is given to peace. They are the keepers of peace. The saint is "an heir of peace."

—⁂—

PEACEFUL FATHER: YOU HAVE POURED OUT YOUR PEACE ON ME AS A GIFT OF YOUR AMAZING GRACE. YOU HAVE STILLED THE STORM IN MY HEART AND MADE THE TROUBLED WATERS CALM. YOU HAVE ERASED MY ANGER AND BITTERNESS AND GIVEN ME LOVE AND RECONCILIATION. THANK YOU FOR MAKING ME AN HEIR OF YOUR PEACE. AMEN.

I will listen to what God the Lord will say; he promises peace to his people, his saints.

PSALM 85:8

RUSH TO FORGIVE

As far as the east is from the west, so far hath he removed
our transgressions from us.

PSALM 103:12 KJV

We all sin. We all do things wrong. We all fail ourselves and those we love. We all fail God who created us for a wonderful, eternal purpose. But despite all that, God has done something wonderful, something unspeakably gracious. Not only did He arrange for someone else to pay the price for our sin, our wrongs, our failings, He has also provided a way for us to walk free of new transgressions. He says 'just ask' and we will be forgiven. We serve a God who rushes to forgive.

> **GRACE FOR TODAY:**
>
> We serve a God who rushes to forgive.

You may think that you are just a hopeless case. Not only do you have a past that seems unforgivable, but the future doesn't seem too bright either. Even right now today, you find yourself making terrible choices. It seems like you are caught in a vicious cycle of wrong living and wrong thinking.

The God who rushes to forgive has not given up on you even if you have given up on yourself. He longs for all—even the worst of the worst—to receive salvation through His grace and be reconciled to Him. (See 1 Timothy 2:5.) And He's ready and waiting to lift you up, wash you off, and make you His own child. In Psalm 40:2, the psalmist tells us what God did for him: "[God] lifted me out of the slimy pit, out of the mud and mire; he set my feet on a rock and gave me a firm place to stand."

Don't stay in the mud. Call out to God.

FAITHFUL AND TRUE

I saw heaven standing open and there before me was a white horse,
whose rider is called Faithful and True.

REVELATION 19:11

Before you were born, before you drew your first breath, God had a plan for your life. Not a plan that would restrict and confine you, but a plan that would draw out all the richness of the gifts and talents placed in you, all the nuances of character, all the unique aspects of your one-of-a-kind personality. Pursuing and fulfilling that plan is the most glorious thing you can do in your life.

That is not to say that it will be easy. His plan includes discipline to refine your character and develop your gifts. God will allow storms and trials to stimulate and encourage your faith. And you will be asked to run for the prize—pressing, reaching, totally committed for a lifetime.

There are probably very few people on earth who wouldn't say they want to reach their full potential. We all talk about having a plan and making it work. The problem is that many people forego God's plan, thinking that their own would be better. They go after a career or pour their energies into family. They learn a craft or pursue a talent. But they don't ask God to show them the "real" plan—the one designed to touch every part of who they are, the one designed to bring them peace with God and deep fulfillment. When their own plans fail, they sometimes even blame God.

What plan are you following today? Have you asked your Creator to reveal His will for your life? Don't settle for anything less than the very best—God's plan and purpose.

> GRACE FOR TODAY:
>
> God has a wonderful plan for our lives, and He's eager to tell us all about it.

PARDONED!

[Christ] was wounded for our transgressions, he was bruised for our iniquities: the chastisement of our peace was upon him; and with his stripes we are healed.

ISAIAH 53:5 KJV

The prisoner walked the hallway to his final destination, accompanied by his minister, two prison guards, and the prison warden. The taste of his final meal was still on his lips, and bits and pieces of his crimes were flashing across his mind. He couldn't help but think also of those who loved him, those he would never see again, all because he had been unable to control his actions. Oh, he was guilty all right! Guilty of selfishness, hatred, violence, murder, and now he would be paying the wages for his sins—death!

But then something amazing happened. News came that he had been pardoned. His life would be spared, and he would be set free to live again. How would he live this time, he wondered. Would he return to his crimes, or would he walk out of that prison ready to live in a new way?

You may not know it, but your crimes (your sins) were leading you to a death chamber—the death of your soul. But like the guilty man in the story, you have been unexpectedly pardoned. You deserved punishment, but instead you've been offered freedom from the prison of your own making.

In your case, the pardon isn't shrouded in mystery or hooked to a technicality. Simply put, someone else—someone completely guilt-free—died in your place. He literally took the guilt of your sins on himself and paid the penalty with His own body. Now you are free to walk from death into newness of life. What will you do?

GRACE FOR TODAY:

By His grace, God sent His Son to pay the price for our sins.

Your Divine Life

We have this treasure in jars of clay to show that this all-surpassing
power is from God and not from us.

2 Corinthians 4:7

For thousands of years, people have been creating vessels for common use—cups,
jars, vases, urns. Archeologists carefully unearth these treasures from ancient
sites and study them to learn more about the people who made them.

The Bible says we are vessels created by God for His use. What use is that? As
amazing as it might sound, God has created us to carry His all-surpassing power. That
power is the Holy Spirit. We are simple clay vessels, unworthy dwelling places for
God's Spirit; yet, by His grace, He has seen fit to fill us with unimaginable treasure.
Those who meet us and study our lives will soon learn a great deal about our
Creator—that He has truly made our lives divine.

The next time you are tempted to view your life as anything less than divine,
remind yourself that God designed you with a divine purpose in mind. You are the
vessel that carries His Spirit in this world. You are the one who will take Him to those
who are suffering with guilt and loneliness. You are the one who will reach out to the
sick and weary with His touch. You are the one who will carry the divine message of
redemption and reconciliation to those who have not heard.

God has created you with a divine purpose in mind. You are His vessel—a vessel fit for a king.

Grace for Today:

By His grace, God has made us vessels worthy to
carry His divine presence.

WHAT GOD HAS PREPARED

Fancy cars, fine houses, luxurious yachts—there is no end to the "things" a person can purchase if he or she has enough money. But God has prepared something for you that is so great, money could never buy it. Even the wealthiest billionaire who ever lived could not purchase it. Your brain could never even imagine it. This great thing He has prepared for you is the glory of Heaven.

One day, our eyes will see mansions that will be greater than any house on earth. And one of them will be ours. Also, when we look at the landscape of the world to come, it will contain unspeakable brilliance that will always be new. And what makes all of this so wonderful is, it won't cost us a dime. We have a kingdom that has been set up for us, and only one thing qualifies us for it—that we be God's beloved children. We are destined for a kingdom that was purchased for us by God's own dear Son. It is a kingdom of grace.

Today, as you face your current circumstances, remember that there is a world beyond the one you see now—a world that has been prepared just for you. And whether you are rich or poor, you will someday live in this wonderful place that God has prepared for you.

> **GRACE FOR TODAY:**
>
> As we face our current circumstances, we must remember that there is a world beyond the one we see now.

No one's ever seen or heard anything like this, Never so much as imagined anything quite like it—What God has arranged for those who love him.

1 CORINTHIANS 2:9 MSG

PONDERING OR PRAYING?

By Evelyn Christenson

Much of what we think is prayer actually is only pondering. Even when we are on our knees in our prayer closets, it is easy just to roll our own thoughts and our own answers around in our minds, not really including God at all. This is not a prayer; it is only pondering.

My dictionary defines ponder like this: "to consider something deeply and thoroughly; to meditate over or upon, to weigh carefully in mind; to consider thoughtfully; to reflect, cogitate, deliberate, ruminate." This is a healthy process as it helps us sort out whys, unravel perplexing puzzles, come to conclusions, and even put to rest hurtful events. But people frequently think they have prayed when they have spent time pondering. Pondering is not prayer. Only when we involve God in this process does it turn into prayer.

In the supernatural battle for our families, pondering is inadequate. It is powerless to change the family problem that we are deliberating.

But when we include God, our pondering suddenly involves the omniscient, all-wise God of the universe. The God who never makes a mistake. The God who knows all the whys, all the outcomes, all the perfect He intends through everything that happens to our families. When God becomes personally involved in our pondering, there are accurate conclusions and correct attitudes in and for our families—supplied by a loving, caring, all-knowing God.[49]

—∞—

DEAR FATHER IN HEAVEN: THANK YOU FOR PROMISING TO HEAR ME EVERY TIME I PRAY. I CALL ON YOUR GRACE CONCERNING THE ADVERSE CIRCUMSTANCES IN MY LIFE AND ASK YOU TO TAKE CHARGE, DOING FOR ME WHAT YOU THINK BEST. IN JESUS' NAME. AMEN.

Draw near to God and he will draw near to you.

JAMES 4:8 NRSV

HELP THAT WILL NOT FAIL

I lift up my eyes to the hills—from where will my help come? My help comes from the Lord, who made heaven and earth.

PSALM 121:1-2 NRSV

D o you remember when you were in elementary school and the teacher asked who wanted to be her "helper" for the day? It was always a great thing to be the teacher's helper—erasing the boards, taking attendance, picking up the papers, whatever she needed during the day. That doesn't sound like an assignment for Almighty God, does it?

GRACE FOR TODAY:

God's help is never in the way, and it's always on time.

Yet, that's one of the ways the Bible describes God. Hebrews 13:6 says He is a "helper." Now this doesn't mean that God runs around doing our bidding like the child in the classroom. But it does mean that He wants to be a resource for us—Someone who can help us accomplish His purpose for our lives. Someone who can offer solutions when we run up against obstacles. Someone who can keep us moving in the right direction.

We will always face times in our lives when only the help of God will do. And during those times, we can depend upon God to give us a hand. He is the healer when sickness arrives. He is your provider and your peace in the midst of the stormy days of life. He can provide wisdom and counsel as you make tough decisions. In fact, there isn't one single thing that you could possibly need that He cannot help you with.

God wants to be your helper today. No matter what you're struggling with, He's waiting, ready to help as soon as you ask.

WHAT IT REALLY MEANS TO LOVE

When he saw the crowds, he had compassion for them, because they
were harassed and helpless, like sheep without a shepherd.

MATTHEW 9:36 RSV

D o you remember these words from a well-known song: "What the world needs now is love, sweet love?" That's very true today, and it was true when Jesus walked the earth. No wonder people have been drawn to Him in every time and every generation. He teaches us what it means to love.

Jesus was a walking example of love. He showed love by healing the sick and reaching out to the outcasts of society. He showed love by feeding the hungry and nourishing their souls. He showed love by giving an honest answer to tendered questions—regardless of whether the question came from one of His followers or one of His enemies. He showed love by meeting people where they were and showing them the way to truth and forgiveness. God's love was and is manifest in Jesus.

Now that Jesus has taught us what it means to love, He wants us to teach others. That will mean doing more than telling them. Just as Jesus showed us, we will have to show others.

Do you know of someone in your neighborhood who is lonely? Reach out with friendship. Is someone struggling with illness? Make some soup and offer to pray. If you're looking, you will see that there are needs all around you. And each time you respond, you are showing the world what it means to love. Let God's love be manifest in you just as it is in Jesus.

> **GRACE FOR TODAY:**
>
> God's love was and is manifest in Jesus, and He wants us to demonstrate it to the world on His behalf.

GOD WILL NOT LEAVE

[God] Himself has said, "I will not in any way fail you nor give you up
nor leave you without support. [I will] not, [I will] not, [I will] not
in any degree leave you helpless nor forsake nor let [you] down
(relax My hold on you)! [Assuredly not!]"

HEBREWS 13:5 AMP

H ave you ever felt that God was far away, unaware or unconcerned about the troubles you are facing? We all feel like that at times. Human beings are used to counting on their feelings. Just because you can't feel Him doesn't mean He isn't there, however. God says that He will never leave us, never forsake us; and that's something we must understand and know by faith in His character rather than faith in our feelings.

God is always close by, watching you, ready to help. If you're a parent, you may remember how you crouched just beyond your child's reach and allowed him or her to take those first few tentative steps on his own. Your child couldn't touch you, but he felt confident that you were only a few steps away. God has not left you—He simply wants to see you take a few steps of faith. Once you do, He will be right there, enfolding you in His arms and celebrating your effort.

Whether you are experiencing resounding joy or tears of sorrow, God is there, sharing that moment with you. And even during those times when it seems like He is not there, He is as close as He will ever be. You are not alone, and you never will be. He is committed to blessing your life immensely. He wants to be the source of your strength and your faithful companion in adversity. From this day forward, remember that you will always have someone to help.

GRACE FOR TODAY:

God is never more than a few steps of faith away.

A FIRM RESOLVE

Do not cast away your confidence, which has great reward. For you have need of endurance, so that after you have done the will of God, you may receive the promise.

HEBREWS 10:35-36 NKJV

Did you know that as a Christian, you are running a race? The name of the race is called life. In this race of life, there is a finish line that awaits the arrival of those who endure. This finish line is Heaven—where there are rewards that this earth can never provide.

In the race of life, there will be many opportunities to give up. Fear, doubts, and overwhelming challenges often serve as obstacles that can hinder your course if you lose heart. To finish well, you will need a firm resolve. That means placing your confidence in God's ability rather than your own. Don't worry—He knows you won't be able to do it on your own. He wants you to lean on Him. He expects it.

When you trust in God, His strength takes over where your weakness begins. And as long as you keep yourself focused on Him, His strength will not go away. At times, it may even seem as though He is carrying you. Even the most difficult situations of life will not rattle you the way they used to. You will have the power to overcome every barrier that stands in your way. By trusting in God constantly, you will surely endure. And at the end of this life, when you reach the finish line, your reward will be greater than anything you could ever have imagined.

GRACE FOR TODAY:

God gives us the strength we need in order to endure this race.

WOULD YOU LIVE FOR GOD?

Have you ever wondered how to truly live for God? The thought of doing so often brings the idea that we have to become missionaries to Africa or quit our jobs and enter the ministry. While this is true for some people, it is not necessarily true for you. But even though you may not be a preacher or a missionary, God still expects you to live for Him. The good news is that you can do so and still be just who you are. In fact, you may not have to change much about your lifestyle. But if you are going to commit yourself to live for Him, your focus may have to change dramatically.

No matter what your vocation, to live for God means to be dedicated to His desire. This means everything you do should be done to bring glory and honor to Him. God requires this commitment not for His own sake, but for ours. When we are living for Him, we are obedient children on whom He feels free to pour out His blessings and meet every need.

Could you, from this day forward, live for God? Certainly, you can. Your life can be so enveloped in His desire that you will literally live as an offering of praise to Him. But to live such a life is a choice you have to make—a choice you will never regret. In the end, you will live a life of blessing and favor. You will live a life of victory. You will live the life you truly desire.

> **GRACE FOR TODAY:**
>
> When we live in right relationship with God, He is able to pour out all His blessings on us and meet all our needs.

When Christ, who is our life, shall appear,
then shall ye also appear with him in glory.

COLOSSIANS 3:4 KJV

THE HAPPIEST PEOPLE

By John C. Maxwell

Who are the happiest people in the world? Are they young people? Are they healthy people? Are they wealthy people? The happiest people in the world are those who are living out their dreams. In giving themselves to something bigger than they are, they're giving themselves the impetus to rise above their problems. If you want to know real happiness, dream a dream that is bigger than you are; find something you can lose your life in. Jesus said if you keep your life you will lose it, and if you lose your life you will keep it (Luke 9:24). Isn't there something better than watching "As the World Turns" every afternoon?

Think of the great men and women who continued to pursue their dream even into old age. Think of people like Moses, who at 80 years of age led 3.5 million people out of captivity. Or Caleb, who at 85 years of age said, "Give me that mountain." Or Colonel Sanders, who at 70 years of age discovered "fin-ger–lickin' good" chicken. Or Ray Kroc, who after 70 introduced a Big Mac to the world. Then there's Casey Stengel, who at 75 became the manager of the Yankees baseball team. And there's Picasso, still painting at 88, and George Washington Carver, who at 81 became head of the Agriculture Department. There's Thomas Edison, who at 85 invented the mimeograph machine, and John Wesley, who was still traveling on horseback and preaching at age 88.

It's the dream that keeps us young; it's the vision that keeps us going.[50]

—⁓—

DEAR LORD: THANK YOU FOR GIVING ME A DREAM THAT WILL LAST THROUGHOUT MY LIFE. I WILL NEED YOUR GRACE IN ABUNDANCE AS I WALK EACH DAY IN ACCORDANCE WITH YOUR PLAN AND PURPOSE. I'M GRATEFUL THAT YOUR GRACE IS ALWAYS MORE THAN ENOUGH FOR ME. AMEN.

To the one who pleases him God gives wisdom and knowledge and joy.

ECCLESIASTES 2:26 NRSV

ONE FINE DAY

The Lord will perfect that which concerneth me: thy mercy, O Lord,
endureth for ever: forsake not the works of thine own hands.

PSALM 138:8 KJV

One day, everything will be clear. We will see the truth in all its glory, and the darkness we have been so accustomed to will fade away for all eternity. On that day, we will see the One our souls long for—our Savior, Jesus Christ.

Sure, it's tough here. As citizens of the world, we struggle with illness, poverty, disappointment, doubt, depression, fear. Wars rage around us, and we are betrayed and harassed on every side. We work hard to overcome sin in our own lives and protect ourselves and our children from sin in the lives of others. We read in 2 Corinthians 4:8–10 NKJV: "We are hard pressed on every side, yet not crushed; we are perplexed, but not in despair; persecuted, but not forsaken; struck down, but not destroyed—always carrying about in the body the dying of the Lord Jesus, that the life of Jesus also may be manifested in our body."

That's what makes the glory of that "one fine day" so exceedingly wonderful in our hearts and minds. It encapsulates our hope in a better life that awaits us, our faith in the grace poured out on us through God's Son, our trust in a God who has promised that we will be well rewarded if we endure to the end. Knowing we will see Him face to face—that makes it all worthwhile.

> **GRACE FOR TODAY:**
>
> God has planned a glorious day of reward for those who place their trust in Him.

NOT JUST A SET OF RULES

Keep my message in plain view at all times. Concentrate! Learn it by heart! Those who discover these words live, really live; body and soul, they're bursting with health.

PROVERBS 4:21-22 MSG

D oes Christianity seem as though it is nothing more than a long list of rules, designed to keep you from enjoying life? Sometimes it can feel that way. But God's desire was never to sit in Heaven, waiting for us to break one of His rules so that He could punish us. His intention is to make our lives better, not worse.

Could you imagine a life where stealing, lying, and pagan worship were permissible? Or, could you imagine the chaos that would come about if killing was not a sin? Clearly, mankind has the potential to commit unthinkable evils. We see and hear of these things every day. In a very real sense, it is the moral values outlined in the Bible that serve as the foundation for our laws and keep the flood of evil from overwhelming all of our lives.

And that's not all the Bible does. In the scriptures, you will learn of all the great things that God has placed inside of you. You will clearly see how greatly He loves you and how much grace He has placed upon your life. You will also learn of His promises, which He is committed to keeping—promises that cover every area of your life.

GRACE FOR TODAY:

God has given us His commandments —to instruct us, encourage us, convict us of sin, and help us avoid a lifetime of painful mistakes.

Reading God's Word brings life, saves lives, and makes life better. It is more than just a set of rules. It is more than a book full of decrees and commandments. It is a book that contains the words that bring life. Today, find time to be thankful for the fact that God has given us His Word, the Bible.

A ROLLER-COASTER RIDE

Yet what we suffer now is nothing compared to the glory
he will give us later.

ROMANS 8:18 NLT

D o you remember your first roller coaster? Looking up at the tracks hundreds
of feet above your head would be intimidating for anyone. You feel it in the pit
of your stomach—knotting, unknotting—a mixture of excitement and fear. The long line
gets closer to the entrance, and you take a deep breath, anticipating the thrill. Once
inside, you feel the strap being pulled across the seat so tightly that you can barely
move. As the car starts to move, you grab the rail and hold on tight.

For many, there is no time on a roller coaster that is scarier than the long trip to
the top. As the slow progression continues, the people on the ground become smaller
and smaller. Then, in the blink of an eye, you flash through a series of dips, climbs, and
loops. By this time, the fear is subsiding. You've fully committed to the ride and put
your trust and confidence in its ability to take you safely back to where you started.

Does it seem as though you are about to face a huge roller-coaster ride? Are you
in a place right now where you are uncertain of what the future holds? God has given
you the assurance of security. But hold on tight, anyway. The only way to remain stable and secure in this wild ride of life is to cling to the One carrying you through. Once
you're used to trusting Him, once you are fully committed, you'll begin to enjoy yourself, knowing that you can depend on Him to get you where you need to be.

GRACE FOR TODAY:

The only way to remain stable and secure in this wild
ride of life is to cling onto the One who is
carrying us through.

YOUR UNSTOPPABLE PURPOSE

Let us be bold, then, and say, "The Lord is my helper, I will not be afraid. What can anyone do to me?"

HEBREWS 13:6 GNB

The Bible says that Satan is our "adversary" (1 Peter 5:8 KJV). That means that he is set against us in all we try to do for God. Our adversary has many weapons he uses against us, but the greatest one is fear.

Left unchallenged, fear shatters our confidence and robs us of the ability to fulfill God's plan for us here on earth. But God has not left us defenseless. By His grace, He has given us a weapon far greater than fear. That weapon is faith. The kind of faith that stands up by the power of the Holy Spirit and says, "My God is able." The kind of faith that focuses on the vision God has placed in your heart and refuses to be moved from the path. The kind of faith that is sure of the One who has promised to see you through every circumstance and around every obstacle.

We read in Hebrews 11:1 that faith is the "substance" of things unseen. It has breadth and depth and height. But fear? Fear is nothing more than smoke and mirrors, a sorcerer's trick to intimidate and deceive. It has no power over us—no power at all! Stand up tall in God's grace and by faith declare your intention to do all that God has called you to do. Make good on God's promise. His grace is there to sustain you as you go in faith.

GRACE FOR TODAY:

God's grace allows us to overrule fear and take hold of something more substantial—faith.

PILLOW TALK WITH GOD

Secrets can sometimes be hard to hold inside. We often go through things in life that can bring guilt and shame to us, and they force us to hide a part of our lives from everyone. Everyone, that is, but God.

Our conversations with God are the most intimate conversations we will ever have. No one knows us more deeply. God knows every secret of our lives, yet He still loves us with an everlasting love. He patiently waits for us with a motive to quickly forgive. His gentle hand remains upon our lives, even when we have sinned. All He desires is for us to repent.

The word "repent" often brings about the thought of an angry God, listening to our plea for forgiveness. But actually, to repent means to have a change of heart. This change includes those deepest secrets that only you and God know of. There is no need to hide from Him. He knows everything about you, and He wants pillow talk. He wants conversation so intimate that it can be spoken of only in private.

God holds you dear in His heart and wants to be the confidante who will have mercy upon you, rather than judging you. Would you like to have a friend this close, this intimate? Get alone and talk with Him. He is waiting to hear from you so He can bring resolution to every problem you have. Release every burden and every secret of your life today, and He will take care of you.

> **GRACE FOR TODAY:**
>
> God holds us dear in His heart and wants to pour out His grace on us.

[Jesus said,] "When you pray, go away by yourself, shut the door behind you, and pray to your Father secretly. Then your Father, who knows all secrets, will reward you."

MATTHEW 6:6 NLT

WHO DO YOU SAY I AM?

By John MacArthur Jr.

Jesus was talking to His disciples and asked, "Who do men say that I am?"

They answered, "Oh, some people think You are Jeremiah; some people think You are Elijah; some people think You are one of the prophets."

He said, "Who do you think I am?"

Peter responded, "Thou art the Christ, the Son of the living God" (Matthew 16:16). Then, I feel sure, he wondered, Where did that come from?

Jesus said, "Flesh and blood did not reveal this to you, Peter, but My Father in heaven did" (Matthew 16:17).

Peter probably said, "I thought so. I surely didn't know that." You see, when Peter was near Jesus, not only did he do the miraculous, he said the miraculous. Is it any wonder he wanted to be near Jesus?

When he was near Christ, Peter had miraculous courage. He was in the Garden of Gethsemane when a whole band of soldiers—as many as 500—came to arrest Jesus. They came marching in with all their regalia. In front of them came the chief priests, and before the chief priests came the servants of the priests. Peter was standing with the Lord. Maybe his thoughts went something like this: "They think they are going to take Jesus away. No, they won't."

Since Peter did not ever want to be removed from the presence of Jesus, he took out a sword. He started with the first guy in line, who happened to be Malchus, the servant of the high priest. The Bible says Peter cut off Malchus' ear, but if I know Peter, he was going for his head. Peter was ready to take on the whole Roman army. You see, when he was with Jesus, he had miraculous courage.[51]

—⁂—

PRECIOUS FATHER: I WANT TO KNOW YOU THE WAY PETER DID—INTIMATELY, MIRACULOUSLY, COURAGEOUSLY, WALKING DAILY IN THE FLOW OF GRACE THAT COMES FROM YOUR PRESENCE. AMEN.

It is God who arms me with strength and makes my way perfect.

PSALM 18:32

Topical Index

Achievement 228
Adversity 231
Appearances 105
Atonement 78
Attitude 15, 234
Balance 141
Bible 102, 247, 313
Blessings 193, 211
Change 29, 253
Children 181
Choices 96
Christ's Return 242
Christian Growth 66, 74
Christian Life 89
Christlikeness 148
Church 112, 201, 223, 265
Comfort 107, 140, 152
Commitment 220
Communion with God 57, 67, 103
Compassion 238
Confidence 143, 290, 309
Conscience 221
Contentment 191, 205
Courage 236, 317
Creation 156, 183, 280, 303
Creativity 90, 187, 286
Daily Walk 179
Desires 139
Despair 113
Disappointment 56
Discernment 229
Discipleship 175, 298
Discipline 33, 49, 83, 91, 164, 244
Encouragement 136, 163, 188
Eternal Life 26, 245
Eternal Rewards 133
Failure 109, 138
Faith 11, 21, 129, 147, 182, 200, 214, 215, 315
Family 38, 202, 261
Fellowship 153
Forgiveness 28, 37, 64, 82, 92, 149, 150, 162, 289
Freedom 85, 251
Friendship 70, 199, 210
Giving 25, 130, 252, 257
God 62, 135, 145
God's Armor 44
God's Authority 76, 94, 121
God's Care 6, 7, 122, 144, 165, 308
God's Character 297
God's Faithfulness 203, 243, 264
God's Grace 17, 34, 41, 95, 101, 119, 137, 169, 239, 263, 267, 268, 272, 275, 281, 287, 293
God's Love 12, 168, 177
God's Power 35
God's Presence 39
God's Promises 296
God's Protection 160, 237, 249, 276, 288
God's Provision 255, 278, 279
God's Timing 55, 68, 98, 170
God's Will 132, 197, 302
God's Word 8
Grace 295, 300, 316
Gratitude 198
Grief 32, 171
Guidance 271
Healing 260
Heaven 43, 258, 304
Help 190, 306
Holiness 227
Holy Spirit 50, 97
Honesty 20
Hope 19, 22, 79, 208, 246
Humility 104, 154
Identity 54, 217, 240, 292
Inspiration 226
Integrity 212
Jesus 69, 126, 219
Joy 18, 51, 84, 194
Judgment 65, 180, 192
Justice 172
Laughter 88
Leadership 218
Listening 106
Loneliness 111
Love 31, 42, 100, 110, 117, 142, 186, 277, 307
Marriage 178
Mercy 63
Music 87
Needs 59
New Life 14, 23, 71
Obedience 283
Openness 241
Patience 81, 93, 115
Peace 40, 46, 60, 77, 232, 299
Persecution 225
Perseverance 13, 127, 189, 195, 206
Plans 36, 301
Praise 61
Prayer 16, 58, 73, 80, 134, 155, 161, 167, 173, 184, 185, 305
Priorities 24, 45
Purpose 294
Renewal 151
Respect 75
Rest 86, 118, 262, 270
Righteousness 282, 291
Salvation 9, 146, 166, 176, 222, 302, 310, 312
Security 314
Service 99, 116, 207, 248, 259
Sincerity 209
Speech 266
Spiritual Growth 204, 224
Strength 125
Success 10, 108
Surrender 72
Thankfulness 124, 233, 284, 285
Trials 120, 131
Trust 157, 230, 250, 273
Unity 128
Victory 174, 196
Vision 269, 311
Wealth 27
Wisdom 213, 256
Witness 30, 52, 123, 159, 216, 254
Worry 47, 48, 53, 235
Worship 114, 158, 274

Author Index

Augustine of Hippo 287
Evelyn Christenson 125, 131, 305
Meister Eckhart 293
Gene Getz 11, 29, 137, 245
Martin Luther 281
John MacArthur Jr. 47, 53, 77, 101, 191, 215, 233, 317
John C. Maxwell 35, 143, 149, 269, 311
Luis Palau 59, 89, 107, 113, 179, 197, 203, 209, 221, 227
Dr. Charles Stanley 155, 161, 167, 173, 185
Johannes Tauler 275
Thomas Watson 299
John Wesley 95
Warren W. Wiersbe 17, 23, 41, 65, 71, 83, 119, 239, 251, 257, 263

Endnotes

1. *Encouraging One Another* by Gene Getz. Copyright 1981, 1997, 2002 by Gene Getz. Published by Cook Communications Ministries. All Rights reserved. Pages 120–121.
2. *Be Encouraged* by Warren W. Wiersbe. Copyright 2004 by Cook Communications Ministries. Published by Cook Communications Ministries. All Rights reserved. Pages 36–37.
3. *Be Encouraged.* Pages 38–39.
4. *Encouraging One Another.* Pages 129–130.
5. *Be All You Can Be* by John C. Maxwell. Copyright 2002 by Cook Communications Ministries. All rights reserved. Pages 13–14.
6. *What's So Amazing About Grace?* by Philip Yancey. Copyright 2002 by Zondervan Publishing Company. All rights reserved. Page 71.
7. *My Utmost for His Highest Devotional Bible*, "The Shadow of an Agony," by Oswald Chambers, page 122.
8. *Be Free* by Warren W. Wiersbe. Copyright 1975 by SP Publications, Inc. Published by Cook Communications Ministries. All rights reserved. Pages 16–18, 22.
9. *Anxiety Attacked* by John MacArthur, Jr. Copyright 1995 by John MacArthur, Jr. Published by Cook Communications Ministries. All rights reserved. Pages 15–16.
10. *Anxiety Attacked.* Pages 28–29.
11. *Stop Pretending* by Luis Palau. Copyright 1985, 2003 by Luis Palau. Published by Cook Communications Ministries. All rights reserved. Page 7–8.
12. *When All Else Fails . . . Read the Instructions* by James W. Moore.
13. *Be Encouraged.* Pages 60–61.
14. *Be Encouraged.* Page 64.
15. *Anxiety Attacked.* Pages 86–87.
16. *Be Free.* Pages 113–114.
17. *Stop Pretending.* Pages 63–65.
18. *Merriam Webster's Collegiate Dictionary*, tenth edition.
19. Taken from a 1740 sermon by John Wesley.
20. *Anxiety Attacked.* Pages 92–93.
21. *Stop Pretending.* Pages 9–10.
22. *Stop Pretending.* Pages 18–20.
23. *Be Encouraged.* Pages 138–140.
24. *A Journey into Spiritual Growth.* Copyright 1999 by Evelyn Christenson. Published by Chariot Victor Publishing, a division of Cook Communications. All rights reserved. Pages 113–114.
25. *A Journey into Spiritual Growth.* Pages 115–116.
26. *Encouraging One Another.* Pages 121–122.
27. *Be a People Person* by John C. Maxwell. Copyright 2004, 1994, 1989 by Cook Communications Ministries Inc. All rights reserved. Pages 38–39.
28. *Be a People Person.* Pages 18–19.
29. *Handle with Prayer* by Charles Stanley. Copyright 1982, 1992 by SP Publications, Inc. Published by Cook Communications Ministries. All rights reserved. Page 56.
30. *Handle with Prayer.* Page 53.
31. *Handle with Prayer.* Pages 11–12.
32. *Handle with Prayer.* Page 30
33. *Stop Pretending.* Pages 45–46.
34. *Handle with Prayer.* Pages 57–58.
35. *Anxiety Attacked.* Pages 112–113.
36. *Stop Pretending.* Pages 27–28.
37. *Stop Pretending.* Pages 39–41.
38. *Stop Pretending.* Pages 33–34.
39. *Anxiety Attacked.* Pages 53–54.
40. *Stop Pretending.* Pages 29–31.
41. *Stop Pretending.* Pages 31–32.
42. *Anxiety Attacked.* Pages 32–33.
43. *Be Free.* Page 121.
44. *Encouraging One Another.* Pages 157–158.
45. *Be Free.* Pages 115–116.
46. *Be Encouraged.* Pages 87–88.
47. *Be Free.* Page 117.
48. *Be All You Can Be.* Pages 52–53.
49. *A Journey into Spiritual Growth.* Pages 207–208.
50. *Be All You Can Be.* Pages 60–62.
51. *Found: God's Will* by John MacArthur, Jr. Copyright 1973 SP Publications, Inc. Published by Cook Communications Ministries. All rights reserved. Pages 23–24.

Additional copies of this and other Honor Books products
are available from your local bookseller.

The following titles are also available in this series:

Daily Grace for Teachers
Daily Grace for Teens
Daily Grace for Women

If you have enjoyed this book,
or if it has impacted your life,
we would like to hear from you.

Please contact us at:

Honor Books, Dept. 201
An Imprint of Cook Communications Ministries
4050 Lee Vance View
Colorado Springs, CO 80918
Or visit our Web site:
www.cookministries.com

Inspiration and Motivation for the Seasons of Life